Dialects in Schools and Communities

Dialects in Schools and Communities

Second Edition

Carolyn Temple Adger
Center for Applied Linguistics

Walt Wolfram
North Carolina State University

Donna Christian
Center for Applied Linguistics

Routledge
Taylor & Francis Group
New York   London

Copyright © 2007 by Lawrence Erlbaum Associates, Inc.
All rights reserved. No part of this book may be reproduced in any
form, by photostat, microform, retrieval system, or any other means,
without prior written permission of the publisher.

First published by Lawrence Erlbaum Associates, Inc., Publishers
10 Industrial Avenue
Mahwah, New Jersey 07430
www.erlbaum.com

This edition published 2013 by Routledge

Taylor & Francis Group
711 Third Avenue
New York, NY 10017

Taylor & Francis Group
2 Park Square
Milton Park, Abingdon
Oxon OX14 4RN

Cover design by Kathryn Houghtaling

Library of Congress Cataloging-in-Publication Data

Adger, Carolyn Temple.
Dialects in schools and communities / by Carolyn Temple Adger,
Walt Wolfram, Donna Christian. — 2nd ed.
    p. cm.
Includes bibliographical references and index.
Wolfram's name appears on first edition.
ISBN 978-0-8058-4315-9 — 0-8058-4315-9 (cloth)
ISBN 978-0-8058-4316-7 — 0-8058-4316-7(pbk.)
1. English language—Dialects—United States. 2. Language and educa-
tion—United States. 3. Community and school—United States. 4.
Students—United States—Language. 5. Children—United States—
Language. 6. Language arts—United States. I. Wolfram, Walt, 1941. II.
Christian, Donna. III. Title.
PE2841.W654 2007
427'.973—dc22   2006030182
                                                                          CIP

Contents

Preface   ix

1   Language Variation in America   1
    Issues and Definitions   1
        Popular Meanings of Dialect   2
        Accent and Dialect   3
        Levels of Language Differences   4
    Sources of Dialect Difference: Region and Social Class   5
    Language Standards   7
        Language, Logic, and Language Complexity   11
        Standard English   13
    Dialects and Understanding   15
    Deficit Versus Difference   17
        Cultural Differences   20
    Multiple Dialects in Schools   21
    Language Attitudes in Society   22
    Dialect Change in the United States   27
    Further Study   28

2   Exploring Dialects   30
    Dialect Study   30
    Considering Social Factors   31
        Examining Particular Patterns   33
    Variation in Linguistic Systems   36
        Pronunciation Differences   37
        Regional Dialects   38
        Social Dialects   39
    Grammar Differences   43
        Suffixes   43
        Other Differences in the Verb System   46

> *Other Grammatical Differences*   48
> *Illustrative Dialect Samples*   49
> *Appalachian Ghost Story*   49
> *Wild Life*   50
> *Notes on Transcripts*   52
> *Vocabulary Differences*   55
> *Vocabulary Matters Across Dialects*   56
> African American English   58
> *The Origins of African American English*   59
> *The Changing State of African American English*   60
> *Dialect or Language?*   61
> Further Study   62

3   **Social Interaction**   63
> Conversational Politeness   64
> Making Meaning   66
> *Cooperation in Communicating*   67
> *The Role of Context in Making Meaning*   67
> *Figurative Language in Context*   69
> Language Rituals   70
> Conversational Misadventures   71
> Cultural Styles in the Classroom   73
> *Understanding Students' Language Behavior*   77
> Researching Classroom Interaction   78
> *Data Collection*   78
> *Data Analysis*   79
> Living With Language Behavior Differences   81
> Classroom Rules   81
> Further Study   84

4   **Interpreting Language Difference**   86
> Perceptions of Language Standards   87
> Are Students' Language Skills Declining?   89
> Diversity and Test Scores   89
> Differences and Disorders   90
> *Language at Home and at School*   92
> *Early Literacy*   93
> Dialect Differences and Curriculum Content   94
> Further Study   97

5   **Oral Language Instruction**   98
> Standard English and Social Reality   98
> Group Reference and Dialect Learning   99
> Positions on Dialects and Dialect Education   100
> Policy Development   103

Curriculum Development 104
Methods of Teaching Spoken Standard English 108
Promoting Language Development 110
Further Study 111

6 Dialects and Writing 113
Oral and Written Language 113
Vernacular Dialect and Writing 115
Vernacular Influence in Writing 115
Difference and Error in Written Language 116
Teaching Writing 117
Editing 119
Approaches to Editing 119
Peer Editing 120
Writing in the Vernacular Dialect 120
Choosing the Vernacular 121
Dialogue Journals 121
Assessment of Writing Ability 122
Further Reading 124

7 Language Variation and Reading 125
Written Language and Spoken Language 126
What Do Teachers Need to Know About Dialects 127
to Teach Reading?
Language Form 127
Beyond Language Form 129
Teaching Children to Relate Sound and Print 130
Effects of Dialect Differences on Reading Aloud 131
Dialects and Meaning-Based Reading Instruction 132
Teaching Children to Comprehend Text 133
Vocabulary 134
Comprehension Strategies 134
Background Knowledge and Comprehension 135
Reading Materials and Dialect Differences 136
Matching Materials and Dialects 136
Dialect Readers 136
Language Experience 138
Vernacular Dialect for Rhetorical Purpose 139
Reading and the Acquisition of Standard English 139
The Social Context of Reading 140
Reading Tests and Dialect Differences 141
Pronunciation, Grammar, and Vocabulary Differences 142
Background Knowledge 143
Other Fairness Factors 148
Further Reading 150

8   Dialect Awareness for Students   151
         Resources for Learning About Dialects   153
         Working With Data   154
         Dialect Awareness   156
             Introduction to Language Diversity   156
             Levels of Dialect   157
             The Patterning of Dialect   166
             Language Change   179
         Implementing Dialect Awareness Curricula   181
         Further Study   186

Appendix: An Inventory of Distinguishing Dialect Features   187
         Phonological Features   188
             Consonants   188
             Vowels   191
         Grammatical Features   195
             Adverbs   201
             Negation   203
             Nouns and Pronouns   205
             Other Grammatical Structures   208

References   209

Author Index   217

Subject Index   221

Preface

Curiosity about language variation and the role that dialects play in society is natural. In education, concern with this topic has always been high, rising cyclically to extraordinary levels. The current awareness that America's students represent a rich array of linguistic and cultural resources highlights this topic, with many of the related issues from the past still unresolved. In *Dialects in Schools and Communities*, we have addressed this natural interest and educational concern about dialects by considering some of the major issues that confront educational practitioners. This work is rooted in questions that have arisen in workshops, surveys, classes, discussion groups, and conversations with practitioners and teacher educators. Thus, the work is intended to address important needs in a range of educational and related service fields. No background in linguistics or sociolinguistics is assumed on the part of the reader.

Although the discussion in this volume has an empirical research base, we do not give detailed documentation in the text. Instead, we synthesize current understandings and provide key references to our own work and that of others. In a sense, this is a kind of translation and interpretation work in which we attempt to bring together the practical concerns of educators and the vantage point of sociolinguistics.

The first edition of this book (Wolfram, Adger, & Christian, 1999) was inspired by the response we received to our earlier work, *Dialects and Education: Issues and Answers*, by Walt Wolfram and Donna Christian, published by Prentice-Hall, Inc. (1989). In this second edition of *Dialects in Schools and Communities,* we have reconsidered and expanded our discussion of many of the issues addressed in those earlier works, taking into account especially the research on dialects and publications for audiences beyond linguistics that have appeared since the first edition.

In chapter 1, "Language Variation in America," we note popular concerns with the nature of language variation, and in chapter 2, "Exploring

Dialects," we consider more specific, technical issues about the characteristic structures of different dialects. In chapter 3, "Social Interaction," attention turns to various interactive patterns characteristic of social groups. Chapter 4, "Interpreting Language Difference," looks at perceptions of declining standards for language and education and at some of the ways in which language differences can be construed as problems. The school impacts of dialect differences in speaking, writing, and reading are considered in chapters 5 through 7. Chapter 5, "Oral Language Instruction," takes up questions about teaching Standard English—whether to do it and how it might be done more effectively. Chapter 6 moves on to dialects and writing, and chapter 7 addresses issues of dialect and reading. The final chapter, "Dialect Awareness for Students," points to the value of dialect education in schools so that students will come to understand dialects as natural and normal language phenomena. This chapter describes concrete strategies for addressing the misunderstandings about dialects that contribute to inequity at school and elsewhere in the society. Each chapter concludes with some suggestions for further reading. The volume ends with a catalogue of vernacular structures described in more technical terms. It is not a complete inventory of any dialect or all vernacular features, but it organizes and expands on the structural descriptions discussed in the chapters.

This volume is intended for use by teacher interns and practicing teachers in elementary and secondary schools; early childhood specialists; specialists in reading and writing; speech/language pathologists; special education teachers; and students in various language specialties. Most of these fields now consider information about language variation to be an important part of professional preparation. This discussion also illuminates the language issues that arise in other content areas as increasing emphasis is placed on oral and written language in learning. Finally, the treatment of social and cultural dimensions of language use is relevant to the teaching of social studies.

Obviously, this re-examination of dialects in schools and communities cannot answer all of the questions that practitioners raise about dialect variation and education. We have attempted to respond to practitioners' concerns as far as possible and to admit where the research findings are limited or ambiguous. We offer the book as an updated, still-interim report on the state of language variation and education in the United States. We hope that we have represented faithfully the kinds of concerns that practitioners have brought to us in the past few decades, and we dedicate this work to those who have raised them. In the process of examining the issues concerning dialects in schools and communities, we have learned that there are few easy answers to the questions about language variation raised by practitioners.

Many colleagues and friends have commented on portions of this text after reading our earlier work or drafts of this one. We thank each one heartily: John Barnitz, John Baugh, David Bloome, Ken Goodman, Yetta Goodman, Susan Hoyle, Joy Kreeft Peyton, Jeffrey Reaser, John Rickford, Peg Steffenson, and Rose Marie Weber. Thanks especially to those with enough faith in us to experiment with parts of the text with their students. We deeply appreciate the gifts of those who have helped in these and other ways, including Lupe Hernández-Silva and Marge Wolfram.

—Carolyn Temple Adger
Washington, DC

—Walt Wolfram
Raleigh, North Carolina

—Donna Christian
Washington, DC

1

Language Variation in America

ISSUES AND DEFINITIONS

Every language differs to some degree from place to place and from group to group. We use the term *language variation* to refer to the fact that a language is not uniform. Instead, it varies according to social characteristics of groups of people, such as their cultural background, geographical location, social class, gender, or age. Language variation may also refer to differences in the way that language is used in different settings, such as in the home, the community, and the school, and on different occasions, such as telling a friend about a trip or planning a trip with a travel agent.

People who share important cultural, social, and regional characteristics typically speak similarly, and people who differ in such characteristics usually differ in language or dialect as well. The term *dialect* is generally used to refer to a variety of a language associated with a regionally or socially defined group of people. This definition of *dialect* is not a rigorous one, but it carries an important implication. Technically (as linguists use the term), the relative status of a dialect with respect to other dialects (its social standing) is only a matter of language difference. Linguistically, no dialect is more valuable, interesting, or worthy of study than another. The term *dialect* used this way is neutral—no evaluation is implied, either positive or negative.

Consider this example of a dialect difference: The patterns or *rules* of some dialects require that *anymore* be used only in negative sentences (those with *not* or some other negative), such as *I don't go there anymore*, or in questions such as *Do you go there anymore*? In other dialects, *anymore* can occur in affirmative sentences as well as negative, such as *Houses in this neighborhood are expensive anymore*. This dialect difference usually corresponds to regional characteristics: All speakers of English use the structure in nega-

1

tive contexts; those who also use it in affirmative (called *positive anymore*) are generally located in midland areas, running through Pennsylvania, Ohio, and westward. The important point is that neither use of *anymore* is linguistically right or wrong. They are merely different: The pattern of some dialects includes a restriction on *anymore* that others do not have. According to the technical meaning of *dialect*, one pattern is not better than another.

A person cannot speak a language without speaking a dialect of that language. Everyone is part of some group that can be distinguished from other groups in part by how group members talk. If a person speaks the English language, that person necessarily speaks some dialect of the English language.

This chapter raises some basic issues for education and society that grow out of the contrast between differing perspectives on dialect: Research shows that dialects are all complete linguistic systems and thus have structural integrity, but social evaluation gives some dialects higher status than others. That is, views of the relative merit of a language variety are based on social, not linguistic, grounds.

Popular Meanings of Dialect

The term *dialect* is often used in ways that contrast with the neutral technical meaning just presented. A common use of the term carries a negative connotation. *Dialect* is sometimes used to refer to a social or geographical variety of English that is not the preferred—or standard—one. For example, native Midwesterners hearing the speech of an African American from the deep South or a European American from rural Appalachia might say that that person speaks a dialect (and believe that they themselves do not). Such use of the term *dialect* assumes that only certain groups of people speak a dialect. These assumptions are unwarranted, however, because everyone speaks some variety—or dialect—of their language. Some dialects may be more noticeable than others because of the social and political positions of different groups and the salience of their distinguishing linguistic traits, but this does not mean that only some people use dialects.

Dialect is also sometimes used popularly as a synonym for *language*. For example, people sometimes refer to the languages of Africa as African dialects or Native American languages as American Indian dialects. In reality, many separate languages are spoken by Africans and Native Americans, as well as by Europeans and Asians. Equating dialect with language may occur in situations where the languages are far removed from the life of the observer.

Language specialists avoid the term *dialect* because of the different possible interpretations it can have and because of the negative sense it may carry. Instead, they use the terms *language variety, language difference, lan-*

guage variation, and *linguistic diversity* to avoid the negative connotations sometimes associated with *dialect*.

The question of terminology becomes especially difficult when we want to refer to the speech of people who do not speak a standard variety. The most common labels have been *nonstandard dialect, nonmainstream dialect*, and *vernacular dialect*. Although these terms can be used synonymously and all are in common use, we use the designation *vernacular dialect* here. We prefer that term because it highlights the dimension of the indigenous communities associated with language varieties that differ from the standard. This term also seems more neutral than the term *nonstandard* and leads to somewhat less confusion than the label *nonmainstream*, which has been used to refer to a range of groups considered outside of mainstream society for one reason or another.

Accent and Dialect

When it comes to language differences, the term *accent* is popularly used to refer to how people pronounce words. So, if a person pronounces *car* without the final *r*, as in "cah," or *creek* something like "crick," these pronunciations might be considered characteristic of a particular accent. References to accent may include differences other than pronunciation, but the focus is usually on pronunciation.

Situations in which someone might use the term *accent* can provide a basis for comparing what is commonly meant by *accent* with what may be meant by *dialect*.

1. A French waiter asks some diners what they would like to order. His question is English, but the pronunciation sounds as if he were using French rather than English sounds. The patron might remark, "That waiter has a very heavy accent."
2. Someone who grew up in northeastern New England visits Chicago. A native Chicagoan might observe, "You can tell where she's from the minute she opens her mouth—she really has a strong New England accent."
3. Someone originally from Chicago visits northeastern New England. A New Englander might remark, "That person must be from Chicago. She says some words with a real accent."

The restaurant situation involves someone who most likely learned English as a second language and whose speech still shows influence from the native language. This is the classic foreign accent that might be more specifically labeled as a French accent, a Swedish accent, and so forth. The other two situations contain references to variation within a single language. Here the meaning of *accent* is closer to the technical meaning of *dialect*. Of course, *ac-*

cent is more restricted because it refers primarily to pronunciation, and there are differences other than pronunciation among dialects. The term *accent* often carries some negative connotations similar to those for the popular use of *dialect*, although they are typically less severe. Despite the fact that each variety of English includes its own pronunciation pattern, it is often assumed that only other people have accents. Thus, the native Chicagoan meeting someone from New England may think that it is only the New Englander who speaks with an accent, whereas the native New Englander may think that only the Chicagoan speaks with an accent. Of course, both of them have an accent, just as everyone speaks a dialect. Some accents (and dialects) are the subject of wider comment than others, including, for example, what people call a Southern accent, a Boston accent, a New York accent, and a British accent, all of which have stereotyped features that others recognize quite readily. Although negative connotations are sometimes associated with having an accent, there can be positive evaluations as well. For instance, many North Americans hold a British accent in high regard.

Levels of Language Differences

Pronunciation is one level at which dialects may differ from each other. There are other levels. One fairly obvious one is vocabulary: For example, in some regions of New England, *tonic* refers to what in other regions of the United States is called *pop*, *soda pop*, or simply *soda*. The retention of the term *icebox* by members of older generations where younger speakers say *refrigerator* also reflects this level of difference, as do the British forms *jumper*, *chemist*, and *boot* for American *sweater*, *drugstore*, and (car) *trunk*, respectively.

Dialects also contrast with each other in terms of the way words are composed and the way that words are combined in sentences—the grammatical patterns of the language system. For example, in some rural areas of the South (reflecting an affinity with dialects of the British Isles), the plural *-s* may be left off of nouns of measurement, as in *four mile down the road* or *sixteen pound of fish*. Other dialect areas would use the plural *-s* in these phrases. With respect to the combinations of words in sentences, an indirect question may be expressed as *He asked me could he go to the movies* or as *He asked me if he could go to the movies*, and negative patterns may be expressed as *He didn't do anything* or *He didn't do nothing*. In some dialects, both of these alternatives are used; in others, only one. Similarly, a grammatical difference between British and American English reveals itself in responses to the question *Have you read that book?* A British speaker might say, *No, but I should have done*, and an American speaker might say, *No, but I should have*.

Beyond differences in levels of pronunciation, vocabulary, and grammatical structure, there is also variation in how members of groups use particular language forms in social interaction. A Northerner and a Southerner may both use the terms of respect *sir* and *ma'am*, but in contrasting ways that reflect different sociocultural conventions governing respect and familiarity. One social group may feel that it is appropriate to ask people what they do for a living, whereas another group may consider that question rude or invasive. Some of these rules are explicitly discussed in socializing children, but many are part of our unconscious knowledge as a member of our speech community about how to get along in the world through talking. Patterned differences in language use related to social and cultural group differences may be hard to pinpoint, but they can readily lead to cross-cultural communication conflict because they often represent highly sensitive areas.

Groups of people who share basic expectations about language use—speech communities (Hymes, 1974)—also differ in the ways that they carry on conversation. For example, in some speech communities, speakers overlap each other's talk enthusiastically in a good, satisfying conversation, whereas in others, a speaker is likely to stop talking when another one starts. Even what makes for a good conversational contribution can vary from group to group (Tannen, 2005). Garrison Keillor often refers humorously to what a good Minnesotan or a good Lutheran would say. One of his stories includes a conversation in which a new boat owner responds to compliments by talking about the expense and time involved in maintaining the boat—as a good Minnesotan should, says Keillor—rather than saying how much fun it is (National Public Radio broadcast, July 1986). Speakers of English from other backgrounds might find such a response to a compliment to be inappropriate and even insulting.

SOURCES OF DIALECT DIFFERENCE: REGION AND SOCIAL CLASS

Language differences on all levels ultimately reflect basic, patterned behavior differences among groups of people. There may be diverse reasons underlying differences in language, but they all derive from this basic principle. When groups are physically or socially separated in some way, language differences can be expected as groups of people follow different paths of language change. These differences are an important source of language change, and languages are always changing.

Many of the regional differences in U.S. English can be traced to combinations of history and physical factors in the country's geography. Some patterns can be explained by looking at settlement history, which suggests the language patterns of the early settlers. The movement of the population, historically and currently, also has a bearing on the language of regions because people take their language practices with them when they move. Finally, characteristics of physical geography affect language change. Natural barriers such as mountains and rivers that have cut people off from each other historically have created a natural basis for dialect differences to emerge and be maintained. The terrain serves to set people apart so that communication networks cannot be formed.

Social and cultural factors are also responsible for diversity in ways of speaking. Social status and ethnic distinctions in our society are often reflected in language differences, along with age and gender distinctions. Typically, the greater the social distance between groups, the greater the language differences. This principle does not always work exactly, but it is a reasonably accurate predictor of how language differences reflect group behavior differences.

Social status and regional differences interact. Thus, it can be expected that a lawyer from Arkansas will speak differently from a Northern automobile factory worker, or a White Appalachian farmer in an isolated mountain area will speak differently from a Black California business executive, or a Native American artist in New Mexico will speak differently from an Italian American police officer in New York. These characterizations include geographical, social, and cultural factors, all of which have been prominent in distinguishing groups of individuals from each other in American society. The same distinctions are important in understanding language differences.

Studies of various dialect groups generally indicate that regional dialects tend to be distinguished by pronunciation and vocabulary features, whereas social dialects show variation in these areas as well as in grammatical usage. We might guess that someone is from Eastern Massachusetts if he or she pronounces the word *idea* with an *r* sound at the end ("idear") in a phrase like *the idear of it* and drops the *r* sound on a word like *star* ("stah"), *saw a falling star last night*. But many pronunciation differences concern the vowel sounds in words. For instance, many Southern regional dialects vary from those in other parts of the country according to the way that speakers pronounce words with vowel glides, such as *line* or *ride*. (A glide is a vowel quality that is attached to a main vowel. The vowel in *line* or *ride* consists of a main vowel, *a*, that flows into a vowel with the quality of *ee* or *y* [e.g., "layn" or "rayd"].) People from Southern areas of the United States are likely to say something like "lahn" or "rahd," without the glide, whereas people from Northern areas would pronounce these words with the glide, as in "layn" or "rayd." Other pronunciation variants involve particular words, rather than sets of words with particular sounds. For some people, *route* rhymes with *boot*; for others, with *bout*. Similarly, *creek* is pronounced as "crick" in some Northern areas, but as "creek" elsewhere. These pronunciation differences are popularly referred to as *accent*.

Regional dialects also differ in vocabulary. Depending on what part of the country you were in, for instance, you would need to order a *sub* (or *submarine*), *hoagie*, *grinder*, *hero*, and so forth to get a particular type of sandwich. Water might flow through a *faucet*, *tap*, or *spigot*; and children would *favor* or *resemble* one of their parents. Such alternative vocabulary items are readily noticed and commented on when speakers from different regions meet.

There have been a number of attempts to delineate dialect groups of English in the United States by region (e.g., Carver, 1987; Kurath, 1949; Labov, Ash, & Boberg, 2006). Linguistic geographers generally recognize several major dialect areas in the United States and a number of subareas within them. Many cautions are given about the impossibility of identifying discrete boundaries and the relative importance of different lines, but the map of dialects shown in Figure 1.1 represents a fairly common agreement among dialectologists (i.e., linguists who study dialects) on how dialect boundaries can be roughly delineated. This map, from Carver (1987), gives only a regional distribution, however, and it is based on vocabulary differences alone. In Figure 1.2, a map based on pronunciation from Labov, Ash, and Boberg (2006) is superimposed on the map based on vocabulary in Figure 1.1. Despite the difference in the level of language and a time lapse of a half century in terms of the date collection for the maps, there is an amazing parallel in the regional dialect configuration. Within and across areas, there are, of course, social, cultural, age, and gender considerations as well, which complicate the picture immensely.

Social dialects show variation in vocabulary items and pronunciation features, but they also have differences in grammatical structure. Some members of rural, working-class communities might say, *You was right* and *I done it*, whereas a middle-class office worker in a city might use *You were right* and *I did it* to mean the same thing. Variations in the verb are typical of grammatical differences between dialects. They affect the systems for relating subjects to verbs (i.e., agreement patterns) and for choosing a form of the verb for a particular tense. Chapter 2 gives more information about the language features that vary across the regional and social dialects of English.

LANGUAGE STANDARDS

People sometimes ask how many dialects of English there are. Somewhat surprisingly, there is no agreed-on answer to this question, even after decades of research on differences in American English. Linguists study the many differences in the speech patterns of different groups of people, but deciding where one dialect ends and another begins and then counting how many there are is a different matter. Dialects do not come in neat packages; and many factors of varying degrees of importance must be considered in distinguishing them.

It is safe to say, however, that the English language is made up of numerous dialects. The first section of this chapter primarily concerned English in the United States. Imagine the range of variation if we include England, Australia, Jamaica, and other countries where English is spoken! Yet there

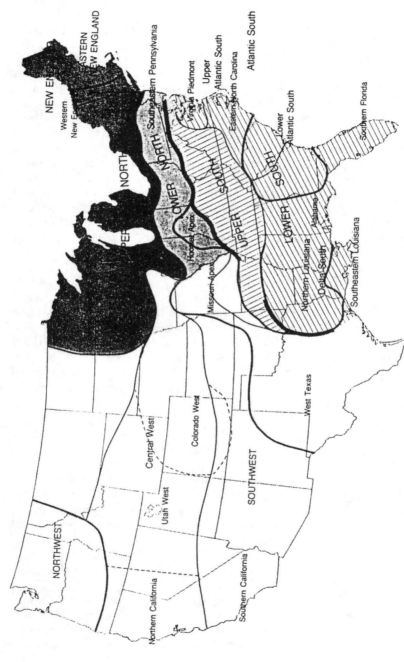

Figure 1.1. Dialect map of the United States. (From *American Regional Dialects* [1987] by Craig M. Carver.) Copyright © 1987 by University of Michigan Press. Reprinted with permission.

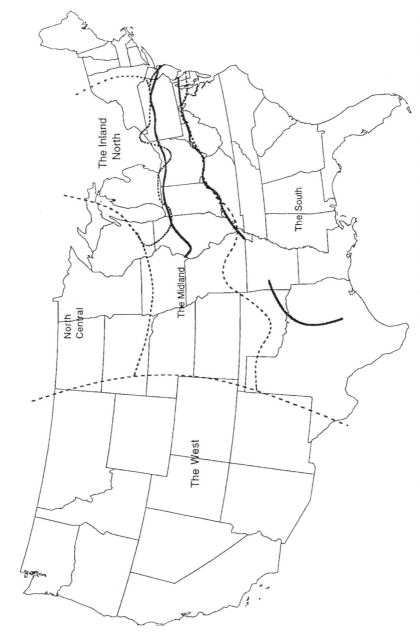

Figure 1.2. Comparison of the major dialect boundaries of Carver (1987) and the boundaries of an overall view of North American Dialects from the Atlas of North American English (Labov, Ash, & Boberg, 2006). Used with permission.

9

is no one correct way to speak English, in the sense that one set of language patterns is inherently better than all the others. Certain language patterns are preferred over others, according to social norms (which may vary as well) and power relations among groups. Preferred patterns are often referred to as the correct use of English, but in this case correctness involves decisions based on social acceptability, not linguistic value. Judgments of correctness in other areas are typically based on some objective set of information. For example, the result of an addition problem, such as 7 plus 3, has one correct solution (10), and all others are incorrect (11, 9, etc.). To compare correctness in arithmetic and language use, we must look for a set of facts against which we might judge whether something in language is correct or incorrect.

One relevant set of facts is the one that underlies the ability of proficient English speakers to decide what can and cannot count as English. So, for example, when we hear a sentence like *They will arrive tomorrow*, we can observe that it is English and therefore correct in that sense. However, we know that *Arrive will tomorrow they* or *Ils arriveront demain* are both incorrect as English sentences in that same sense, although the latter would qualify as correct for another language. Similarly, we would judge *pencil* to be a correct form in English, but *tloshg* would not be accepted. In each case, we seem to be identifying what speakers of English might say, as opposed to what they would not say, based on our knowledge of the language. Here is one set of objective facts that English speakers share.

When it comes to ways of speaking that are not shared by all speakers of English, however, the notion of correctness becomes much more elusive and, at the same time, quite controversial. Consider two English sentences that may be used by native speakers of English: *I done it wrong* and *I can't see nothing*. It is clear that these are both possible sentences of English: When someone says a sentence like this, we would not want to claim that they aren't speaking English. In this sense, then, these are both English sentences, in contrast with non-English. However, if you ask someone about them, you may be told that they aren't good, proper, or correct English. In this case, correctness is determined by social acceptability, rather than accuracy or intrinsic worth. There is no single basis, in terms of objective facts, for determining whether *I did it wrong* or *I done it wrong* is a better way to convey information.

It is not possible, then, to identify just one way of speaking English as the correct way. The socially unacceptable forms, like *I done it*, are often termed *nonstandard*, to contrast them with *standard* forms or those that conform to social norms. These norms are based on judgments of social acceptability, rather than technical assessments of linguistic patterning.

The value placed on a certain way of saying something is closely associated with the cultural identity or social status of the people who say it that way. This valuing is not an individual decision: It is the society's evaluation of different groups, including their ways of speaking. As children are so-cialized, they learn these attitudes—sometimes unconsciously, sometimes through expressed regulations and rules—just as they learn eating behavior. They learn to eat peas with a fork instead of with a spoon or their fingers. The nutritional content of peas is the same regardless of how they eat them, and all three ways succeed in getting the peas into their mouths; but society socializes us into viewing one way as proper or correct and the other ways as unacceptable. In a similar way, the communicative effectiveness of *I done it* or *I did it* is identical, but we have been socialized into considering only one alternative as correct or proper and the other as incorrect or bad. In terms of social evaluation, then, correctness does not involve intrinsic linguistic value or assessment by any objective standard. What is acceptable according to the standards of the dominant group in society is considered correct; what is not acceptable to them is looked on as incorrect.

Beliefs about language correctness are shared by most members of society. Speakers from groups whose dialects are not regarded highly generally feel that their language is not as good as other people's. Those from groups who speak the favored dialects are likely to feel that their way of speaking is obviously preferable and to be aware of only some of the differences between their language variety and other varieties.

The U.S. situation is in no way unique. General acceptance of a standard language variety accompanied by negative attitudes toward the other language varieties is an unavoidable product of the interaction of language and society (Preston, 1996).

Language, Logic, and Language Complexity

Like the notion of correct language, the idea that some dialects are more logical than others results from the broader social attitudes that surround language. Believing that standard forms of English are inherently better than others, some people maintain that certain linguistic structures are more logical than others, more systematic, and even more advantageous for cognitive development. There is no evidence, however, to support the contention that any language variety will interfere with the development of reasoning ability or the ability to express logical concepts. All dialects and all languages provide adequately for conceptualizing and expressing logical propositions, but the manner of doing so may differ.

The use of so-called double negatives—two negative forms in a single sentence—is often cited as evidence that a particular language variety is illogical. According to this argument, two negatives in a sentence such as *They can't go nowhere* should cancel each other so that the meaning becomes positive (*They can go somewhere*). Because sentences like this are intended to have a negative interpretation, the claim is made that the structure is illogical. (According to this position, *Nobody can't go nowhere*, with three negatives, would have to be accepted as a negative sentence.) However, the natural logic of language users is not identical to formal mathematic logic, where for some operations (e.g., multiplication), two negatives do yield a positive. Natural logic allows both *They can't go anywhere* and *They can't go nowhere* to have a negative interpretation, depending on the language use conventions of the particular dialect community. Both are expressions of the logical concept of negation, but the singly negated form is socially acceptable, whereas the doubly negated form is not.

It is interesting to note that multiple negation was an acceptable structure for English in the past. During the Old English (approximately 500–1100 AD) and Middle English (approximately 1100–1500 AD) periods, the only way certain negative sentences could be formed was through the use of double negatives (e.g., "There was no man nowhere so virtuous" [from Chaucer's *Canterbury Tales*, cited in Pyles & Algeo, 1982]). Favoring the use of a single negative in sentences like *They can't do anything* is a relatively recent development. (Many other modern languages have extensive use of double negatives as part of their standard grammar. In French, the use of two negative words [ne … *rien*] is the current standard for making a negative utterance, as in *Je ne sais rien, I don't know nothing*. Similarly, in Spanish *no* and *nada*, as in *No hace nada, She or he isn't doing nothing*, is the standard form for making a negative utterance.)

Another interpretation of vernacular features is that they reflect incomplete learning of the standard dialect. Common terms for certain language features reveal and reinforce this notion, such as *leaving off the endings of words* or *not using complete sentences*. In some cases, the English speakers who are said to leave off the endings of words are really applying a pronunciation pattern that all English speakers use to a limited degree. For example, in casual speech, all speakers of English sometimes pronounce a word like *fast* as "fas'," leaving off the final *t* sound, as in "fas' break." If you listen carefully to the speech of those around you, you will probably notice this process in use to varying degrees. It is one of the pronunciation rules of English that applies more often in casual speech.

But this pronunciation rule applies somewhat differently in certain dialects, and it is often noticed by speakers of other dialects. One difference is that the rule is applied more often in some dialects, and this higher frequency makes it noticeable. Another difference is in where the pronunciation rule applies. If *fast* is pronounced "fas'" in a phrase like *fas' or slow*, speakers of other dialects are more likely to notice the absence of the *t* sound before the vowel at the beginning of the next word than they would its absence before a consonant, as in *fas' break*. So leaving off endings of words is really a case of an English language rule of pronunciation that is used with minor, but noticeable, differences by different groups, but this practice is not restricted to any one group.

The differences between dialects do not show that dialects are simpler or more complex versions of the same language. These differences show only that dialects are related versions of a language. Some differences may involve extensions or retractions of shared structures; others reveal unique language forms that mark subtle but important meaning differences. Verb forms in sentences such as *I liketa died, I done took out the garbage,* and *I be doing my homework* encode meaning differences that are unique to vernacular dialects. Standard varieties of English would have to use alternative phrasing to capture the precise meaning of the nonstandard forms. For example, to capture the exact meaning of *I be doing my homework* in Standard English, one would have to frame the sentence as *I always do my homework*; or to capture the specific meaning of *I done took out the garbage,* one would have to say something like *I have already finished taking out the garbage.* The relationship between standard and vernacular forms in English obviously cannot be reduced to a matter of faulty logic, incomplete learning, or language simplification.

Standard English

There is really no single dialect of English that corresponds to a standard English, although many believe that such a dialect exists in the speech of those who use so-called good English. This belief is actually close to the social reality: The speech of a certain social group of people does define what is considered standard in English. However, the norms for Standard English are not identical in all communities. Furthermore, there are two sets of norms in any community: the informal standard and the formal standard.

The norms of language usage that members of a society consider to be acceptable constitute their informal language standard. This set of norms correlates with the way certain people actually speak and allows variation between speech communities within the society. It is fairly flexible and regionalized so that there is an informal Standard American English for the South, the Northeast, and so forth. These norms are also subjective: Different people may evaluate standards somewhat differently based on their background.

Formal Standard English, in contrast, includes the norms prescribed in grammar books. This set of norms is most typically reflected in the written language. For example, the formal standard dictates that distinctions should be made in the use of *lie* and *lay*, one should avoid ending a sentence with a preposition, and so on. However, acceptable spoken language usage does not necessarily conform to these norms. Informal Standard English would allow sentences such as *They're the ones you should depend on* with no stigma attached, despite the final preposition. In fact, an utterance like *They are the ones on whom you should depend* is probably less acceptable in everyday social interaction because of its formality. Formal Standard English patterns that differ from the informal standard ones are often taught in English language arts classes.

If the formal standard is used as a reference point, it is unlikely that anyone speaks the standard language consistently. The formal standard is generally limited to the written language of educated people, and it is heard only in the most formal speaking style of highly educated members of society. The informal standard is spoken, however, by those whose language usage sets the guidelines for what is acceptable in each community.

Two further observations need to be made about the informal standard. First, because all speakers use a range of styles, depending on the situation of speaking, someone who is considered a speaker of Standard English may at times use certain language patterns that are clearly not standard. For example, in an appropriate situation, a standard speaker might use double negatives or *ain't*. In fact, a U.S. president once said in a nationally televised address that "Washington ain't seen nothin' yet!" This usage did not indicate that the president had suddenly become a speaker of a vernacular dialect. Presumably, this nonstandard form was used to evoke a sense of toughness and resiliency, characteristic connotations of vernacular dialect forms. Nonstandard uses of language may fill an important communicative function even among the highest authorities in our country.

Second, a number of different varieties qualify as informal Standard English. For example, a standard speaker from Maine and a standard speaker from Tennessee would have quite different pronunciation patterns and probably certain other differences as well at other levels of language. They would both be accepted as Standard English speakers in their own communities, however, and in most others as well, despite the fact that their accent might be noticed outside their home region. Although the informal standard for American English includes a range of language patterns, particularly in the area of pronunciation, there is a unified notion of what is not acceptable (unless used for effect as in the earlier example).

In every society, there are people whose position or social status makes their judgments about language use more influential than those of others, including, for example, teachers and employers. These people decide who will get what placement in school and who will be hired. Their judgments about what is acceptable and unacceptable in language enter into evaluations made ostensibly on other bases, such as people's experience and achievement. Such judgments have more weight and consequence than casual remarks about others' language in the course of daily life. These influential people are often looked up to by other members of their community whose opinions about matters like language are also typically respected. The speech habits of this social core are often admired, and thus serve as a model of acceptability.

Standard American English, then, is a composite of the real spoken language of this group, generally professionals, the educated middle class. Because members of this group in Chicago might sound quite different from their counterparts in Atlanta, it is important to recognize the existence of a number of dialects of Standard American English. For the most part, there is more shared structure in the grammar of Standard English speakers across communities than in pronunciation, but there are still some regional grammar differences that keep us from concluding that a single set of standard grammatical features exists. Different communities may have slightly different norms, and this informal set of norms is the one that really counts in terms of social acceptance. It is important, for this reason, to carefully distinguish between those norms that make up the formal standard and the informal, yet highly influential, norms of social acceptability that govern most everyday, interactional evaluations of standardness.

The situation becomes quite a bit more complicated when we consider World Englishes—the varieties of English spoken in other countries. Just as in the United States, there are standard and vernacular English language varieties in countries that were colonized by English speakers, where English has become the mother tongue of most people (e.g., New Zealand) or a second language spoken by nearly everyone for certain purposes, such as business and higher education (e.g., Nigeria). English is used for special purposes in many other countries as well, and local standards have developed. When English speakers travel abroad, they may find that speech considered standard in their own country is difficult to understand, odd, even nonstandard according to the standards of the host country. Here again Standard English is relative to the particular norms of the speech community. Standard Singapore English is very different from any version of Standard American English. Thus, it is more accurate to speak of Standard Englishes than of just one Standard English.

We use the term *Standard English* as a proper noun with a capital *s* on standard, but we intend it as a collective noun. Standard English is a collection of the socially preferred dialects from various parts of the United States and other English-speaking countries.

DIALECTS AND UNDERSTANDING

Given the differences among English dialects, it stands to reason that communication among speakers of different dialects might be flawed occasionally. Although problems in comprehension and interpretation can arise, the severity of these problems and their precise source are not always clear.

Certainly, there are Standard English speakers who claim not to understand vernacular speakers. To put this in perspective, however, we have to realize that we may also hear this claim from a person traveling through another region, such as a Northerner in the South or a person from the mainland visiting a historically isolated island area in the Chesapeake Bay or the Outer Banks off the coast of North Carolina. In most cases, such reports are exaggerated based on a few items that may legitimately prove troublesome for an outsider to comprehend. An outsider in Appalachia for the first time may have difficulty comprehending certain *ire* words such as *fire* (pronounced much like *far*) or *buyer* (pronounced much like *bar*), or a vocabulary item such as *garret* for *attic* or *vittles* for *food*, unless there is sufficient context to interpret these items. Such isolated problems would not usually result in a breakdown of conversation. Adjustments might have to be made to comprehend certain pronunciations, grammatical patterns, and distinct vocabulary uses, but most speakers of Standard English seem able to do this with ease. Certainly, most people who interact with speakers of another dialect on a regular basis do not encounter severe comprehension problems.

One of the factors that makes objective assessment of comprehension difficult relates to language attitudes. If speakers of a dominant dialect feel that a vernacular version of the language is simply an unworthy approximation of what they perceive as the real language, then problems in comprehension are attributed primarily to vernacular speakers' inability to make themselves understood. Studies of comprehension and social relations in other language contact settings have shown that the relative status of groups can play a prominent role in the comprehension of language varieties (Fasold, 1984). Typically, the higher status group claims comprehension difficulties with the lower status groups, not the converse. In fact, the relative social status of groups may be a more important factor determining intelligibility than the actual language differences. Speakers of the mainstream variety may be unwilling to make the usual kind of language adjustments that enhance comprehension across dialects.

Vernacular speakers generally indicate less overall comprehension difficulty with standard varieties of English than Standard English speakers do with vernacular varieties (Lippi-Green, 1997). Vernacular speakers are typically exposed to Standard English varieties through educational and official institutions and the media, whereas Standard English speakers usually do not have comparable exposure to vernacular dialects. As pointed out earlier, society simply expects and assumes that vernacular speakers will comprehend standard varieties, whereas the converse does not hold. Questions about comprehensibility have not been laid to rest, however, and additional research in this area would be helpful to educators.

The conclusion that vernacular speakers seem to comprehend standard varieties better than standard dialect speakers comprehend the vernacular does not, however, mean that comprehension of the standard dialect can be assumed to be equivalent for all speakers of English regardless of their dialect background. In fact, people of different dialect and cultural backgrounds may comprehend particular constructions differently. For instance, there may be differences in literal or nonliteral interpretations of sentences: *See you later* may be interpreted simply as a ritualistic way of taking leave or as a commitment to return. Different inferences may be drawn from particular sentence constructions or word choices: Instructions in a testing situation to "repeat what I say" may be interpreted by students from some backgrounds as a request to paraphrase the test-giver's words and by those from other backgrounds as a request to repeat the utterance verbatim.

Subtle types of miscomprehension of standard language conventions by vernacular speakers can have an effect just as significant as more transparent cases of vocabulary comprehension difficulty. For example, standardized educational tests assume that all students understand the Standard English directions for the task in exactly the same way. If this is not the case, however, then the scoring of differential responses given by different groups of students as correct or incorrect may be called into question. Only painstaking, detailed analysis of extended sequences of interaction can uncover meaning loss, but these cases are extremely important in understanding the full range of potential miscomprehension across dialects.

DEFICIT VERSUS DIFFERENCE

We have repeatedly observed that no variety of a language is inherently better than another in terms of how languages are organized. No speakers have a diminished ability to function cognitively and expressively as a result of the variety of the language that they acquire. Notwithstanding this linguistic truth, the realities of social attitudes about language cannot be denied, and these attitudes strongly influence how language variation is interpreted.

Two schools of thought concerning groups that contrast linguistically and culturally with mainstream society have been identified: the *deficit position* and the *difference position*. In terms of language, proponents of the deficit position believe that speakers of dialects with vernacular forms have a handicap—socially and cognitively—because the dialects are illogical, sloppy, or just bad grammar. Intelligence test scores and results of standardized language measures may be cited as evidence for this position (Hernnstein & Murray, 1993). In this assessment, issues of test bias may be overlooked. On the basis of test scores, recommendations may be made for remedial language and other educational services. To a large extent, the concept of compensatory programs evolved from this position. Educational programs were designed to fill in the gaps in language and other skills caused by what was called *linguistic and environmental disadvantage*. Members of the more powerful groups often believe that members of the stigmatized groups must change in order to be accepted. Success in school for children from these disenfranchised groups, for example, may depend on changing aspects of their language and language use and adapting to school norms, which are generally more like the norms of the powerful groups than those of the stigmatized groups. For members of a mainstream, powerful group, no change or adaptation is necessary. In this sense, children from some groups may be at risk for school failure, although they are not intrinsically disadvantaged. The contrasting perspective, and the one advocated here, is the difference position that views groups of speakers simply in terms of the differences among their language systems. Because no one linguistic system can be shown to be inherently better, there is no reason to assume that using a particular dialect is associated with an inherent deficit or advantage. The difference position calls into question the evidence from test scores and school performance that is used to prescribe remediation. If educators assume that a particular dialect is best, if they formally accept and encourage only that dialect, and if they test ability and achievement only through the medium of that dialect, then it should not be surprising that students who enter school already speaking it fare better than those who use a different dialect. An understanding of the social attitudes and values concerning dialects and their speakers is thus essential for dealing with language differences.

From time to time, these contrasting positions, which have been discussed for decades now, produce acrimonious debate in the public arena. For example, in December 1996, the Unified School Board of Oakland, California, adopted a resolution that recognized Ebonics, or African American English, as a language system to be taken into account in teaching school children Standard English. The resolution provoked wide comment, much of it scathing denunciation of vernacular dialect and the school system's acceptance of what was thought of as deficient language. Everyone had something to say—prominent persons in government, civil rights, entertainment, and education; ordinary citizens; national organizations concerned with linguistic research and language teaching (see Box 1.1); and

---

Box 1.1

The Linguistic Society of America Resolution on the Oakland Ebonics Issue (Retrieved from http://www.lsadc.org/info/lsa-res-ebonics.cfm, April 15, 2006)

Although there has been a great deal of discussion in the media and among the American public about the December 18, 1996, decision of the Oakland School Board to recognize the language variety spoken by many African American students and to take it into account in teaching Standard English, the Linguistic Society of America, as a society of scholars engaged in the scientific study of language, hereby resolves to make it known that:

a. The variety known as "Ebonics," "African American Vernacular English" (AAVE), and "Vernacular Black English" and by other names is systematic and rule-governed like all natural speech varieties. In fact, all human linguistic systems—spoken, signed, and written—are fundamentally regular. The systematic and expressive nature of the grammar and pronunciation patterns of the African

(Box 1.1 continued)

American vernacular has been established by numerous scientific studies over the past 30 years. Characterizations of Ebonics as "slang," "mutant," "lazy," "defective," "ungrammatical," or "broken English" are incorrect and demeaning.

b. The distinction between *languages* and *dialects* is usually made more on social and political grounds than on purely linguistic ones. For example, different varieties of Chinese are popularly regarded as dialects, although their speakers cannot understand each other, but speakers of Swedish and Norwegian, which are regarded as separate languages, generally understand each other. What is important from a linguistic and educational point of view is not whether AAVE is called a language or a dialect, but rather that its systematicity be recognized.

c. As affirmed in the LSA Statement of Language Rights (June 1996), there are individual and group benefits to maintaining vernacular speech varieties, and there are scientific and human advantages to linguistic diversity. For those living in the United States, there are also benefits in acquiring Standard English, and resources should be made available to all who aspire to master Standard English. The Oakland School Board's commitment to helping students master Standard English is commendable.

d. There is evidence from Sweden, the United States, and other countries that speakers of other varieties can be aided in their learning of the standard variety by pedagogical approaches that recognize the legitimacy of the other varieties of a language. From this perspective, the Oakland School Board's decision to recognize the vernacular of African American students in teaching them Standard English is linguistically and pedagogically sound.

Chicago, Illinois
January 1997
LSA position statement on Ebonics

many, many reporters and editorial writers. In fact, the debate even extended to a Senate subcommittee hearing on the topic. At the heart of the Ebonics controversy was the long-standing conflict between the deficit and the difference positions.

Taking the view that Ebonics, the language spoken by many of their African American students, is a legitimate linguistic system, different from the Standard English system, Oakland schools use students' knowledge of Ebonics in teaching Standard English. In this way, the schools respect and exploit students' linguistic competence as a resource for language development rather than a deficit. Their intention is neither to eradicate Ebonics nor to teach it, as some thought, but to help students add another language system.

Most educators are generally aware that dialect differences can interfere in education, but the Ebonics debate shows that the deficit position is still widely held and that there is no consensus on how dialect differences should be accommodated.

Cultural Differences

Linguistic differences between groups are just one element of a larger set of cultural differences. Groups are identified by their own members and by others according to the set of linguistic and cultural characteristics that they share. *Culture* is used here in just this sense: patterns of behavior, including language behavior, shared by members of a group. Not only ways of speaking, but also values, attitudes toward education, conceptions of politeness, and virtually all socially determined constructs can vary from one group to the next. Mainstream groups—roughly corresponding to the middle and upper middle class—are generally considered to exhibit acceptable behavior, both linguistically and culturally. As with language, their norms for behavior define a standard because they control access to attractive educational and work opportunities. Other groups' norms tend to diverge to some extent from the mainstream norms on both counts—language and culture.

The classroom consequences of cultural differences are similar to those caused by linguistic differences; in fact, there is considerable overlap because cultural norms constrain how language is appropriately used. Cultural attitudes affect the interactions of students with teachers and fellow students. Research reports have noted numerous instances in which behaviors have been misinterpreted because of a cultural difference between teacher and student. For example, studies show that Native American children in the Southwest have been labeled as passive or nonverbal and have had their level of intelligence misjudged because they seem unresponsive in the classroom to Anglo teachers (Erickson & Mohatt, 1982; Philips, 1993). According to the rules of their own culture, however, they are behaving appropriately; active participation would be impertinent. Other researchers report culture clash and misunderstanding in ethnically mixed classrooms. African American children sometimes get reprimanded for calling out an answer before being nominated by the teacher or humming and making other sounds while working independently (Delpit, 1995). Although these actions may reflect cultural patterns that are expected and valued in the children's community, a teacher from a different cultural background may see them as disrespectful and disobedient.

Shirley Brice Heath has looked carefully at the language and culture patterns that children bring to school from their home community. In a classic study of three communities—working-class White, working-class African American, and middle-class townspeople—Heath (1983) traced difficulties faced by both sets of working-class children in the middle-class-oriented schools. The ultimate explanation, she found, was due to differences between the school and home communities. Although structural dialect patterns were involved, the differences extended to discourse. For example, the conception of what story and storytelling mean, a crucial notion in language arts instruction, turned out to vary from one community to another. For one group, the term was used in a narrow and negative sense of an untrue account intended to deceive; in the other group, a story could include departures from fact, but with no intention to mislead the audience. Another revealing area of difference concerned how and when reading and writing events occurred. For adults in both working-class communities, reading and writing were used in restricted ways in the home and community (primarily in church-related activities) and played little or no role on the job. The perspective that children from these communities developed on the uses and usefulness of reading and writing skills influenced their approach to school tasks. Heath's studies point out that broad patterns of language and cultural beliefs and behavior, and subtle differences among groups, are relevant to children's success in the educational context.

All too often in the education arena, people have avoided discussing differences between home and institutional expectations frankly because these matters are considered too political. However, being realistic about differences is important: Ignoring the practical consequences of these differences, or pretending they do not exist, certainly is not in the best interests of children. The specific course of action taken in response to variation should depend on the beliefs and goals of the school and the community, and it is likely that disagreements will arise. Whatever decision is reached about policy and programs, the people involved should understand the facts of the language and culture situation, as opposed to popular mythology, in order to make informed choices. This includes examining and acknowledging one's own and others' attitudes toward different varieties of English and culturally based discourse styles.

MULTIPLE DIALECTS IN SCHOOLS

Three basic alternatives exist for dealing with multiple dialects in schools:

- accommodate all dialects
- require that a dialect of Standard English be learned and used, or
- identify a position somewhere between these two.

The first alternative, accommodating all dialects, derives from the fact that all dialects are inherently equal and the assumption that no one should be penalized because of his or her dialect. This alternative could mean making a conscious effort to allow full use of a student's native dialect of English as the base on which learning will build. Special programs might be implemented to lessen any interference from the native dialect in the acquisition of skills and concepts in the school setting.

The other extreme position is to formally establish that a dialect of Standard English must be acquired to replace the vernacular dialect. Support for this position comes from the belief that a standard variety is needed for success in education and access to society. Following this philosophy, special programs might specifically teach forms of Standard English, but other programs would not need to be changed. This position basically calls for the eradication of the vernacular dialect in schools in favor of Standard English.

The third alternative falls between these two extremes. It is undoubtedly the direction most often followed, usually implicitly, in schools. The native dialect is accepted for certain uses, and a dialect of Standard English is encouraged or demanded for other uses. In terms of mastering certain skills, a plan like the following might be formulated. In recognition of the fact that most written language uses a standard variety, a student would be expected to develop the capability to read and write a Standard English dialect, but would not be required to eliminate the native dialect in classroom talk. Teachers would help students work toward competence with the standard written forms of the language, both in reading and in writing. The student would thus be using two (or more) dialects of English for different purposes, much as people naturally use different styles of speaking for different situations.

This is one example of the type of compromise that can be reached between the accommodation and the eradication positions on vernacular dialect. An advantage to such an arrangement is that the oral dialect in which children are expert when they come to school can be overtly valued rather than merely tolerated. An advantage to following an explicit policy concerning dialects is that children will encounter similar language expectations from classroom to classroom.

LANGUAGE ATTITUDES IN SOCIETY

The issues arising over language variation in education are just one reflection of dialect issues in the broader social context. The most pervasive issue concerns attitudes about language. Research studies focusing on language attitudes show that speakers of vernacular dialects are generally held in low esteem (Lippi-Green, 1997; Preston,1996; Shuy & Fasold, 1973). This view typically extends well beyond their language to other personal attributes, including their morality, integrity, and competence. Attitudes about language can trigger a whole set of stereotypes and prejudices based on underlying social and ethnic differences. In research on discriminatory practices in housing, John Baugh discovered that when callers to rental agents sounded Anglo, they were more likely to be shown a house or apartment than were callers who sounded African American or Chicano. Baugh (2003) calls this practice *linguistic profiling* after the practice of racial profiling in other realms of social conduct, such as identifying motor vehicle violations, felons, or terrorists.

An interesting aspect of language attitude studies is the evidence about the young age at which such attitudes may be acquired. In fact, one study showed that children as young as 3 to 5 years of age were quite accurate in recognizing differences in language and made associations with other types of behavior on the basis of language differences (Rosenthal, 1977). Such findings are in line with research about the socialization of prejudice, which begins early in life and manifests itself in many different details of behavior.

Of course some dialect differences are observed without prejudice in American society. Many regional vocabulary differences are considered matters of curiosity alone, such as the different words for a paper container (*bag, sack,* and *poke*), or the variant terms for submarine sandwiches noted earlier. Americans typically would not think a person uneducable, incompetent, or immoral simply because the person called a soft drink *pop, soda,* or *cola*. At the same time, the dialects spoken by members of particular class and ethnic groups are, in fact, subject to equally unjustified stereotypes related to intellectual capability and morality.

There are two possible ways of dealing with these inequities regarding the social dialects of English. One would be to eliminate the differences between dialects; the other would be to change the negative attitudes toward some dialects that are the source of the inequities.

Complete elimination of dialect differences is not a practical solution because variation is an inherent characteristic of language. The dynamic nature of language leads to continual processes of differentiation in language forms and use by different groups of speakers. Leveling in American English dialects may be happening in a limited way for certain language features, but most differences appear resistant to leveling forces. New differences are emerging. Research has shown that certain vowel sounds are differentiating the populations of northern U.S. cities such as Buffalo, Cleveland, Chicago, Detroit, and other large northern metropolitan areas (Labov, 1994) from other regions of the United States. Among other changes, the vowels of *lock* and *flock* are likely to sound more like the vowels of *lack* and *flack*, and the vowels of *bag* and *lag* are likely to sound more like the vowels of *beg* and *leg*. The existence of variation is a basic fact about language, and the use of variable features in oral language by members of different social groups is a basic fact about society. These principles are not likely to yield easily to efforts to change them.

The other possibility, eliminating the misconceptions about the significance of dialect differences, involves working on people's language attitudes. The set of attitudes about what is good and what is bad in language usage that children acquire with their native language develops into a set of opinions used to judge people by the way they speak. Language attitudes are generally shared by the members of a speech community, leading to a common evaluation of certain language patterns and the people who use them. Box 1.2 illustrates a common attitude toward vernacular and Standard English expressed in the response to an article on dialects.

Box 1.2

Speaking of Prejudice
The job interview was going smoothly. And then the applicant wrapped a double negative around a regularized verb in the sentence, *Nobody never growed nothing like that in this area*. The interview essentially ended at that point, the rejection of the candidate irretractably stamped. Was this a case of legitimate disapproval based on language or an instance of dialect discrimination?

No one can deny the cosmetic role of language in self-presentation, along with other aspects of public demeanor. But the sweeping assumption that the use of a nonstandard or vernacular dialect is related to general intelligence and specific job performance is an unwarranted instance of language stereotyping.

More than two decades of research on language variation and language attitudes in American society have led me to conclude that dialect prejudice remains one of the most resistant and insidious of all prejudices in our society. Public discrimination on the grounds of ethnicity, religion, and social class differences is no longer acceptable; yet discrimination on the basis of dialect is still quite tolerable, although many of the differences that serve as the basis for exclusion correlate with regional, class, and ethnic variables. People who speak stigmatized dialects such as African American Vernacular English or Southern vernacular English continue to be rejected on the basis of their speech even when their dialects have nothing to do with their performance of job-related tasks and general competence.

Debate over language standards is hardly novel, but several studies and media reports during the past year have once again piqued interest in the role of language differences in multicultural education. I

---

[1]Wolfram, W. (1993, March–April). Speaking of prejudice. *The Alumni Magazine of North Carolina State University, 65*(3), 44.

(Box 1.2 continued)

always find the treatment of language in such reports fascinating, but often because of what is left out rather than what is included. *A Time for Understanding and Action: Preparing Teachers for Cultural Diversity*, a report prepared by the NC Professional Practices Commission (September 1992), is fairly typical in its approach to language in multicultural education. The report urges teachers to learn another language. I applaud that. Nevertheless, the report is conspicuously silent in its acknowledgment of English dialects such as Southern, Appalachian, and African American Vernacular English.

Dialect differences represent one of the most commonly misunderstood and misinterpreted symbols of cultural diversity in American society. Popular myths view vernacular dialects as conceptually impoverished, linguistically unworthy approximations of Standard English that have no rightful place in English. In reality, vernacular dialects of English are intricately patterned linguistic systems, possessing a distinctive array of linguistic rules framed within a unique sociohistorical background. For example, unconjugated *be* in *Sometimes they be playing* and *done* in *They done finished the job* are more than stigmatized icons of English; *be* uniquely indicates a habitually occurring activity, and *done* marks a completed or intensive action in the verb system of vernacular dialects. The despised "illogical" double negative was prominent in an earlier period of English that extended from Chaucer to Shakespeare, to say nothing of its use in the majority of the world's major languages.

If multicultural education is to be truly multicultural, it cannot simply ignore or minimize dialect differences. Nor should it treat dialects as mere obstacles to be overcome in learning Standard English. Instead, dialect variation should be studied as a genuine resource that provides an essential and intriguing window into how language works, how it develops, and how it reflects cultural traditions. Teachers, students, and the general public all have much to gain from a perspective that views dialects as an authentic sociocultural resource, not as an unjustified emblem of one's intelligence, competence, and morality.

A Reader's Response[2]

It was with some disappointment … that I read the comments of Walt Wolfram …. To tell a student [who] speaks bad English that he is

---

[2]Fulghum, J. S., Jr. (1993, June). Letter to the editor. *The Alumni Magazine of North Carolina State University* 65(4, June 1993), 43.

(continued on next page)

(Box 1.2 continued)

merely suffering from dialect discrimination is so disingenuous and unfair as to be cruel. Initially, I thought the piece was some type of satire or parody, but it was so neat and concise in its silliness that I knew the author must actually be taking this seriously. To not know the forms of proper English usage is ignorance; to know them and then still not use them because of your desire to be "culturally diverse" is attempted murder upon the English language. Both conditions are apparently applauded by the author but seem to be strange "icons" in a center of learning [i.e., the university], which I had hoped was off-limits to such sophistry.

Language prejudices seem more resistant to change than other kinds of prejudice. Members of the majority culture, the most powerful group, who would be quite willing to accept and champion equality in other social and educational domains, may continue to reject the legitimacy of a dialect other than their own. It is safe to say that dialect prejudice is one of the last prejudices to go. For example, in contemporary American society, the rejection of an applicant for a job based on gender or ethnicity could result in litigation. But rarely is rejection on the basis of being speech-challenged; and when it is, the challenge may be deemed frivolous. Dominant culture members are not the only ones who show language prejudice against vernacular dialects. Vernacular dialect speakers themselves may hold vernacular dialects in low esteem, at least with respect to occupational and social competence in mainstream society. It is not unusual to find a spokesperson for a minority group who decries prejudice in other spheres of behavior, but who exhibits the same kind of prejudice against the vernacular dialect as mainstream authorities do. This attitude may make dialect prejudice seem more acceptable. The high level of dialect prejudice found toward vernacular dialects by both mainstream and vernacular speakers is a fact that must be confronted honestly and openly by those involved in education about language and dialects.

The key to attitudinal changes lies in developing a genuine respect for the integrity of the diverse varieties of English. Knowledge about dialects can reduce misconceptions about language in general and the accompanying negative attitudes about some dialects. Informal attitude surveys before and after the presentation of information about dialects demonstrate that such attitudinal change does occur (Reaser, 2006). Because the educational implications of language attitudes are so great, developing a knowledge base about dialects in schools is especially important.

Change can begin through examining language myths. Collecting comments about dialects expressed in casual conversation or in the media can make clear just how vehement people can be about other people's talk. A close look at this evidence may suggest the nature of underlying language attitudes not only about language, but also about other attributes of individuals who use certain language varieties.

Another productive approach to combating unwarranted language beliefs is teaching students to study language variation in their own communities. Chapter 8 includes sample lessons from units on language variation that have been taught in English language arts and social studies classes. Students in both elementary and secondary classrooms find dialect study fascinating partly because they can contribute their own knowledge to it. These lessons provide a model for developing further units on language variation, as well as interdisciplinary units on human variation.

DIALECT CHANGE IN THE UNITED STATES

One of the questions we are frequently asked about dialects concerns the effect of the media on their development. Most people simply assume that common exposure to the media is making us all talk more like each other. The precise effect of the mass media on dialect differences is difficult to determine, but a couple of points need to be made to counter this common assumption. For the most part, individuals are not prone to use media language, such as that of national newscasters or journalists, as a model for their own speech. People may recognize media language as different, and even as representing a prestige variety, but not as a model to emulate. This lack of influence by the media on audience speech is partly due to the fact that people are not in direct social contact with the writers for the print media and the speakers in the broadcast media. Generally, people talk like those they identify with and whose approval they seek (Bell, 2001). There is little point in adjusting your speech to match that of TV newscasters if they will never know you did it. This lack of direct social contact makes the mass media much less influential than peer group members with whom a speaker interacts frequently. The evidence suggests that, on the whole, the influence of the media on language leveling has been exaggerated.

Yet media language reveals the usefulness of dialect differences and may even reinforce them. Some personalities project a regional and/or ethnic dialect, or conversational style, as a positive attribute. When they are reported on in print or in the broadcast media, the dialect they use receives favorable attention. In local programming, the use of regional and ethnic dialects may be planned to appeal to a local population.

One of the most frequent questions we are asked by journalists and lay people is whether people in different areas of the country are talking more similarly now than they were 50 years ago. The examination of dialect differences across different generations does show some leveling across dialects over time (Wolfram & Ward, 2006). Older speakers of different social, regional, and ethnic varieties tend to differ more in their speech than members of the younger generation. The exact cause of this age contrast is hard to determine, although increased education, increased accessibility to formerly isolated geographical areas, and expanded occupational opportunities have all played some role. Probably a combination of factors, rather than one primary reason, accounts for this leveling.

The fact that some dialect differences have lessened should not be taken to predict the extinction of English dialects in the United States. There is every reason to believe that different dialects will continue to be maintained and even enhanced in some instances. For example, recent research studies about language variation in the western United States show advancing dialects in regions of California (Eckert & Mendoza-Denton, 2006), Utah (Bowie & Morkel, 2006), and Portland, Oregon (Conn, 2006). In the long run, these differences are a tribute to the dynamic traditions and heritages that combine to make up the fabric of American life.

This chapter has raised important issues regarding dialects in schools and communities. In those that follow, these issues are addressed in more detail.

FURTHER STUDY

Alvarez, L., & Kolker, A. (Producers). (1987). *American tongues*. New York: Center for New American Media.
This award-winning video (available in a 56-minute full-length version and a 40-minute secondary school version) is an invaluable supplement to any presentation of American English dialects. In a highly entertaining way, it presents a basic introduction to the nature of dialects and dialect prejudice. It can be used with a wide range of audiences representing quite different backgrounds (e.g., students in Grades 4 on up, civic groups, professional development for educators, human relations seminars), and it can be counted on to provoke a lively postviewing discussion. Although it is somewhat dated, it still dramatically exposes the extremes in language attitudes in American society.

American Speech. A publication of the American Dialect Society. Durham, NC: Duke University Press.
This quarterly journal publishes articles on American dialects of all types, balancing more technical treatments with shorter, nontechnical observations.

Battistella, E. L. (2005). *Bad language: Are some words better than others?* New York: Oxford University Press.
Language correctness is the focus of this book—correctness in writing, grammar, vocabulary, and pronunciation. Although the author does not focus on the classroom, his discussion of language standards may interest teachers.

Carver, C. M. (1987). *American regional dialects: A word geography*. Ann Arbor, MI: University of Michigan Press.
This work offers the most complete discussion available of all major regional dialects of the United States based on vocabulary differences and includes summary maps of each region. Criteria for distinguishing regional varieties of English are also discussed. It is intended for dialectologists, but can be read by serious students in other fields as well.

Cassidy, F. G. (Chief Ed.). (1985, 1991, 1996). *Dictionary of American regional English* (Vols. I–III): Hall, J. (2002).Vol. IV. Cambridge, MA: Belknap Press of Harvard University Press.

Four volumes of this massive dictionary of American regionalisms are now available: Volume I, covering entries from A to C (Cassidy, 1985); Volume II, covering entries from D to H (Cassidy & Hall, 1991); Volume III, covering entries from I to O (Cassidy & Hall, 1996); and Volume IV, covering entries from P to Sk (Hall, 2002). The front matter in the first volume presents important background information about American dialects that is well worth reading for its own sake.

Finegan, E., & Rickford, J. R. (2004). *Language in the USA: Themes for the twenty-first century*. New York: Cambridge University Press.

This anthology covers a broad range of issues relating to English and other languages in the United States. It is divided into sections on American English, other language varieties, and the sociolinguistic situation.

Lippi-Green, R. (1997). *English with an accent: Language, ideology and discrimination in the United States*. London/New York: Routledge.

Social attitudes toward accents are institutionalized in courts and perpetuated in the media and at work, so that people whose accents are not considered prestigious may suffer discrimination and job loss.

McKay, S. L., & Hornberger, N. H. (Eds.). (1996). *Sociolinguistics and language teaching*. Cambridge, UK: Cambridge.

Teachers in culturally diverse schools will find important background information in this collection of chapters on Language and Society, Language and Variation, Language and Interaction, and Language and Culture.

Napoli, D. J. (2003). *Language matters: A guide to everyday thinking about language*. New York: Oxford University Press.

This small volume gives straightforward answers to a range of frequently asked questions about language: How do we acquire language? Why is it hard to learn a second language? Does language equal thought? The section on language in society addresses dialects and creoles, gender differences in language use, spelling reform, and the status of English in the United States.

Nero, S. J. (Ed.). (2005). *Dialects, Englishes, creoles, and education*. Mahwah, NJ: Lawrence Erlbaum Associates.

Contributors to this volume focus on a number of varieties of English and creole languages in educational perspective, including Caribbean Creole English, Hawaii Creole English, Hispanized English, West African English and creoles, Indian English, and Philippine English. They explore issues of language attitudes, language policy, and educational programming for speakers of these varieties.

Wolfram, W., & Ward, B. (Eds.). (2006). *American voices: How dialects differ from coast to coast*. Malden: Blackwell.

This collection presents short, readable essays by well-known linguists about both familiar and little-known dialects thriving in North America and beyond. The sections are divided into the South, the North, the Midwest, the West, Islands, and Sociocultural Dialects. It is the most complete discussion of particular dialects currently available.

2

Exploring Dialects

Because language plays such a central role in teaching and learning, educators often want to know more about the language patterns of the community from which their students come. Unfortunately, there are few resources that make careful descriptions of dialects accessible to those not specializing in linguistics, and the resources that exist do not fully apply to every community within a broader dialect group. But teachers and practitioners have direct access to dialect data. They can learn about the local dialect norms by looking in detail at the actual speech of their students in the classroom, in the hallways, and on the playground.

This chapter provides direction for practitioners who recognize the importance of knowing their students' language systems. Steps that sociolinguists follow in describing dialects are laid out. Then some contrasting patterns in pronunciation, grammar, and vocabulary are presented as examples of what teacher-researchers might notice in dialect research.

DIALECT STUDY

Certainly, investigating students' language patterns has not been a common task for teachers, and it is not easy. Not only does it take time, but it also calls for some knowledge about language structure that has not been part of a traditional teacher preparation. In addition, the scope of the task can be broad. Practitioners may need to look at language patterns in more than one speech community because fewer and fewer schools serve linguistically homogeneous populations.

Although dialect description is challenging, it is not beyond the reach of practitioners. We worked with a team of speech/language pathologists in Baltimore City Public Schools who conducted field work to describe the local vernacular dialects. Using an inventory of vernacular features drawn from research, team members checked to see which features occurred in their students' speech. They also identified some previously undescribed vernacular features. As a result of their work, Baltimore's speech/language assessment procedures take into account the local language norms so that vernacular dialect speakers are not inappropriately labeled *language disordered* based on language variation (Wolfram & Adger, 1993; see also Adger & Schilling-Estes, 2003).

Dialect study can be integrated into teachers' work in other ways. They can involve their students in scientific inquiry into language variation in their communities, as suggested in the dialect awareness lessons outlined in chapter 8. At the school district level, the curriculum and instruction department might integrate dialect description projects into multidisciplinary curricula for students, ongoing professional development for teachers, speech/language assessment updating, and so on. Dialect description projects also fit well into standards implementation and curriculum revision efforts because various national and state standards (typically language arts and social studies) specify that students should understand dialect variation. Such projects offer teachers, administrators, and school districts a way to channel their concern for linguistic diversity into concrete, knowledge-building projects. Involving many educators and students lightens the work, creates a cadre of language resources, and signals that diversity is acknowledged and addressed.

Anyone can begin to explore dialects simply by listening more closely to speech in everyday life. In fact, most people are already good observers of language in a selective way. They readily notice features in others' speech. But what they notice and how they interpret their observations are filtered through their attitudes and assumptions. For example, adults who notice that a child does what is called dropping the *g*'s at the ends of words like *going* or *running* may fail to realize that they sometimes do the same thing in informal situations. Because it is hard to monitor your own casual speech, you may assume that your speech reflects what you feel is good (or bad) about language usage and be unaware of what actually happens. To understand the precise nature of language patterning, it is essential to document both social and linguistic factors.

CONSIDERING SOCIAL FACTORS

Formal studies of language differences have found significant variation among groups defined by age, socioeconomic status (SES), gender, ethnic group membership, and geographical region (Labov, 1972; Wolfram & Schilling-Estes, 2006). For instance, speakers aged 30 to 50 may use certain language patterns that are different from those of teenagers and the elderly. Sometimes this contrast occurs because teenagers adopt some language patterns that are characteristic of their age level and their use of these patterns diminishes as they get older. This pattern is referred to as *age grading*.

Slang words are a good example of this transitory state in an individual's language development, but there are age-graded pronunciation and grammar features as well.

In other cases, the differences between age groups stem from language patterns that individuals acquired early and have maintained more or less throughout life. These represent generational differences that signal language changes over time. In certain parts of the South, for example, members of the older age group were found to pronounce words like *water* and *war* without an *r* sound at the end of the word. Younger speakers, in contrast, consistently used an *r* after a vowel. Similarly, in rural Appalachia, older speakers use an *a-* form as in *He went a-hunting and a-fishing,* whereas younger speakers and adolescents are much less likely to do so (Wolfram & Christian, 1976). Such age group differences point to changing language patterns in the community: The older group maintains the speech patterns they acquired as children, and the younger ones use the pattern that is being acquired currently. Age can be an important factor to consider when examining the language patterns of a community because differences typically do exist between age groups. This means that characteristics of children's language in a community should not be inferred from the speech of the adults. A balanced picture of a dialect must be based on listening carefully to the speech of members of different age groups.

Other social factors—SES, gender, ethnicity—can operate in similar ways within a community. As with age, these social differences often correlate with linguistic differences. Region as a social factor usually applies to communities in different geographical areas. Its relevance to studying language in a single community is in differentiating individuals who are native to the area from those who moved there from some other area and in accounting for subregions within a community.

In addition to social attributes of speakers, aspects of the context of speaking have significant influence on speaking. These factors, which are discussed further in chapter 3, must be considered in studying language behavior. Speakers have a range of options in their linguistic repertoires, and they make unconscious choices from this range depending on such factors as how formal they feel the situation is, their relationship with others in the situation, and what others have just said. With a close friend, someone might say something like *Watcha feel like doin'?* in a conversation about going out; and with a casual acquaintance it might be *What d' ya wanna do?* In a more formal context, it might be more like *What would you like to do?* Although these are not precise reflections of how the sentences would sound, we can see that pronunciation, word choice, and grammar can all change according to the circumstances of speaking.

So in observing language patterns, it is important to keep in mind the social factors that link with differences in language forms. Although it is instructive to sample a range of styles if that is possible, the natural language patterns of a community are clearest in the casual style. In a casual setting, people tend to use their language rules in the most natural way, avoiding overcorrection or irregular fluctuation of language items.

Examining Particular Patterns

The most reasonable approach to investigating dialect differences is a systematic, organized study of particular language structures. As a rule, it is most effective to single out one or two features at a time for scrutiny because it is difficult to keep track of multiple structures. The common technique used by linguists is to select a structure, investigate it in detail, and then move on to another structure. Although this approach does not produce an overall description of a language variety, it increases the potential for an accurate description of particular features.

The first steps in studying different language items are quite simple. Although linguists have had specialized training for investigating language structures and writing formulas to describe them, anyone can make significant observations about language patterns by following scientific principles concerning careful observation. The procedure begins with noticing an item in someone's speech (including our own). For example, in a Southern or Northern urban school setting, we may hear some children using forms like *He home today* or *You out*. We know that other speakers might use *He's home today* or *You're out* in these same contexts, and so we decide to investigate this structure further. We start listening to other children as they talk at lunch time in order to get a casual style of speech. Basically, we can listen for these structures anywhere that language is used in the community in an unself-conscious way. We go to the grocery store; we stand in line at the movie theater, the drugstore, the athletic event, and we can't avoid overhearing conversations. Data gathered informally suggest that the forms that originally drew our attention are not just a slip of the tongue because they occur in the speech of many community members. This indicates that we are dealing with a language pattern that deserves a closer look. We start by filing (on 3 x 5 cards we carry around, in data management systems, etc.) our examples of the natural use of language. It is particularly important to catalogue examples rather than rely on memory so that we can look back at the data to get some ideas concerning the organization of specific patterns.

When we collect examples from real language use, we are likely to make two general observations. First, different people use the structure in different ways. Second, the same speaker may use the structure at some times, but not at others. These observations are basic to analyses of language variation. Investigation of language variation asks (a) what alternative forms occur in different language varieties? and (b) when and where does the form under study occur? With this in mind, we return to our examples, *He home today* and *You out*. With reference to alternatives in other dialects, we observe that the dialect in question does not use a verb form where Standard English uses *is* or *are*:

Vernacular English   Standard English
He home today   He's home today
You out   You're out

For this structure, our first study question is answered fairly simply: The difference between dialects lies in the presence of certain forms of the verb *be*, as opposed to their absence. (In other cases, the alternatives are distinct items or sets of items, rather than a relationship of presence or absence.)

The second study question is a little more difficult because it requires looking at the language context surrounding this form. The question about the context for this dialect structure is this: Where can a speaker manifest the absence of *be*? As a starting point, we assume that patterns of language structure govern where a form is permissible and where it is not. In this case, there is a pattern for where the *be* can be absent and where it must be present. It is this pattern that we are looking for. We then turn to our examples and start figuring out exactly where the absence of *be* would not occur. Along the way, we make certain hypotheses that we check with the data. This involves coming up with ideas about how a pattern works, testing the ideas against the data, and revising them if necessary. Our own intuition can help if we use the pattern in our dialect, but only to a limited extent as discussed earlier, because we may not be totally aware of what we actually do in our casual speech. We can see how this analytic process works by looking at some data that might be found on our observation cards.

Absence of be

He in the army now	He at school
They messing around	They not here
We in trouble today	She taking medicine
She not home now	Y'all messing around now
You nice today	We in school—don't mess around
We playing around now	He gonna do it—I know he is

Our first impression from listening to the speaker(s) might have been that the verb *be* can be absent in their dialect wherever it is present in Standard English. However, when we start looking at the examples more closely, we find that the pattern is less extensive than that. Taking into account all of the different forms that *be* can take, we may initially notice that absence occurs only where *be* would take a conjugated form in Standard English. That is, the examples include no cases where *be* is absent in a sentence like *He wants to be home* (i.e., no examples such as **He wants to home*) or *He should be here now* (i.e., no examples like **He should here now*), and there are many cases where *be* is present as nonfinite forms like *to be, should be,* and so forth. (The asterisk indicates that the sentence is ungrammatical according to the patterns of the dialect.) From looking at the examples, we conclude that the pattern is limited to certain constructions: the conjugated forms of *be* (*is, are,* etc.). That conclusion provides a working hypothesis that we will target in more data collection and analysis until we are reasonably satisfied that the pattern holds.

Continuing to search for further restrictions, we notice that there are no examples of *be* absence where Standard English would use *was* or *were*. We have plenty of examples of past tense, and all of them use *was* or *were*; meanwhile, we find no past-tense sentences such as **We there yesterday*. We look at our data closely, checking out this hypothesis. This restriction turns out to be supported by the data. The absence of *be* thus appears to be limited to present-tense, conjugated forms.

We look further. Are there more restrictions? We consider the subjects of the sentences. An examination of the data shows no cases of *be* absence with the pronoun *I* as subject. Is this just an accident or is this a real pattern governing the *be* absence rule? From our data, it appears that it might be a genuine pattern because we have no examples of *be* absence with *I*. To verify that this is a pattern and not a matter of missing data, we need to get examples with *I*. We start listening again, taking down examples with *I*, such as *I'm first, I'm taking it home*, looking for sentences where a form of *be* is absent. The fact that the verb form always appears when the subject is *I* leads us to conclude that absence of *be* can correspond to *is* or *are*, but not *am*.

This case demonstrates an important point about observing forms:

> When looking for a pattern in language variation, you can't look only at those cases that contrast with another dialect; you must look at similarities as well.

We found that *be* absence with *I* was impossible in both dialects. We had to look at all kinds of cases with *be* in order to find the pattern of *be* absence.

We could continue the investigation to find some more details of conjugated *be* absence. But the point here is to demonstrate the data analysis process. We proceeded systematically, making a hypothesis and checking it with the data. One by one, we varied grammatical features in the linguistic context—conjugated versus bare form of the verb, tense, pronoun person and number. The rule emerged from actual data—dialect items as used in a natural discourse context—rather than from our first impression. Invariably in dialect study, questions come up that weren't anticipated in the original observations. For that reason, linguists often tape-record speech. When we have extensive recordings, we can simply go back and note certain things we hadn't looked at previously. Without tape recording, we may need to collect more data when new questions arise. In our example with *be*, we needed to go back and look for cases with the pronoun *I* very closely to see if any absence of *am* occurred.

One way of getting additional data is to ask leading questions—questions that would raise the potential for certain structures to occur. For example, if we were trying to increase the potential for *I* to occur with a form of *be*, we might ask some personal questions that would probably be answered in the first person (e.g., "Tell me about your science project"). This strategy does not guarantee the use of certain structures, but it increases their probability and has been used successfully in a number of studies.

It is also possible to elicit certain forms quite directly. Word games have been created for this purpose. The idea is to set up a probe so that the response should contain one of the forms in question. For example, if we wanted to see what happens to *be* verbs when the subject is *I*, we might set up a simple task of changing a stimulus sentence with a nonfirst-person subject to a response sentence with a first-person subject. Speakers from the community can be oriented to the task with sample items unrelated to the forms you are interested in (e.g., "Here are some sentences that I want you to change: I will give a sentence like *He went to the store* and you say, *I went to the store, too*"). After they have learned the pattern, they are given stimulus sentences with the form being studied (e.g., Stimulus: *They going to the game*; Response: *I'm going to the game, too*). Such games are not difficult to construct, and they can give access to some valuable data. However, it is important to use this kind of information only as supplemental data because word games do not always give the same results as ordinary speech. In combination with other data, however, this direct elicitation of structures can make an important contribution to understanding particular features.

Anyone undertaking analysis confronts the problem of deciding when there is enough data. Basically, we want enough data to get to the point where additional data do not add anything new to the understanding. As a guiding principle, some researchers use about 45 minutes to an hour of free conversation as an adequate sample of natural speech for one speaker, if the feature under scrutiny involves a fairly common structure such as the verb *be*. A total of five speakers in a given social category (e.g., middle-class urban Latino teenage males, rural White Appalachian females over age 60, etc.) is sometimes used as a basis for studying the social parameters of speech. Obviously, this amount of data may not always be appropriate, but it is typical of databases that have resulted in valuable research.

VARIATION IN LINGUISTIC SYSTEMS

Patterned group-based differences show up in each of the subsystems that make up a language. This section takes a closer look at what can vary and how.

Box 2.1

Steps in Describing Dialect Features

1. Identify a possible dialect feature for study.
2. Collect data.
   - Listen to casual talk in the speech community to determine that the structure is widely used.
   - Write down actual examples from casual talk.
   - Identify corresponding form(s) in other dialects.
3. Analyze data.
   - Develop hypotheses about the linguistic context in which the form occurs. Hunt for patterns in the data, considering
     - Linguistic forms preceding and following the feature.
     - Various forms the feature can assume.
     - Etc.
   - Check the hypotheses against more data.
   - Accept, reject, or refine hypotheses.
   - Repeat the two previous steps, looking for both differences and similarities with other dialects and testing stereotyped explanations.
   - Stop when no new information appears.

Pronunciation Differences

Pronunciation differences occur in both regional and social dialects. Typically, vowel pronunciation differences distinguish regional dialects, whereas consonant pronunciation differences distinguish the social dialects. (As chap. 1 pointed out, there is an overlap between regional and social differences: The dialect of a social group varies regionally, and within a geographical region, there are different social dialects.)

Dialect differences in pronunciation are widely recognized in our society, but they are not always viewed in terms of rules of pronunciation. Instead, people may use labels such as *drawl*, *twang*, *nasal*, and *flat* in referring to regional pronunciation patterns. In most cases, these terms are used to describe an overall impression, rather than any particular pattern of pronunciation. Here we set out some rules that describe pronunciation patterns more precisely.

Regional Dialects

Several different vowel patterns stand out in regional dialects. One prominent pattern involves the vowels in words like *time* and *ride*. In Northern dialects, the vowel sometimes called long *i* in *time*, *side*, and *pie* is actually a diphthong—the rapid production of two vowel sounds, one something like the vowel *ah* (dictionary *a*) and another something like the sound *ee* (dictionary *e*). The second vowel sound in the diphthong glides off from the first vowel, so that *time* is produced something like "tah-eem," *pie* as "pah-ee," and *side* as "sah-eed." In some Southern dialects (or dialects of Southern origin used in the North), the *e* gliding vowel may be eliminated. Pronunciations such as "tahm" for *time*, "sahd" for *side*, and "pah" for *pie* reflect this regional difference. The quality of the *a* sound may vary considerably from place to place (from dictionary *æ* of *bat* to dictionary *ä* of *father*).

The *y* glides of *boy* and *boil* may be reduced or even eliminated in some Southern dialects, giving a pronunciation like "bô" (ô in the dictionary; also called "open o" after the shape of its International Phonetic Alphabet symbol [ɔ]) and "bôl," respectively. The elimination of the glides following the *a* and *ô* vowels is a fairly well-established characteristic of many Southern dialects of English, and one of the characteristics usually included by the term *Southern drawl*.

Another vowel pattern showing regional variation is the difference between the short *i* sound (as in *bit*) and the short *e* sound (in *bet*). Before a nasal sound such as *n*, these two vowels may sound the same in some Southern dialects. This means that pairs of words like *pin/pen* and *tin/ten* would actually be pronounced the same by these speakers.

The two sets of vowel differences—glide reduction and nasal vowel merger—vary along a Southern/Northern dimension, but other vowels show different kinds of geographic distribution. One of the vowels that is most sensitive to regional variation is the open *o* (dictionary ô) in items such as *fog*, *on*, *water*, and *caught*. Pronunciation of this vowel ranges from the *a* of the vowel in *father*; to the *-o* of *boat*; to the *oo* (dictionary *û*) of *book*, as in the Philadelphian pronunciation of *water* (something like "wûter"); to the schwa (ə) vowel sound, *uh*, in words like *dog* and *log*, so that they sound like *dug* and *lug*. This vowel is probably the most variable in American English regional dialects. The vowel *a* in items such as *bad* or *ran* is also quite sensitive to regional variation, although the range of pronunciation differences is somewhat more subtle than that for the open *o* of *fog*. The production of vowels before *r* is particularly likely to vary regionally, as indicated in dialect differences in pronunciation of words such as *Mary*, *marry*, and *merry*. Some dialects have identical pronunciation of all three items; some pronounce each item differently.

Other vowel patterns come from the influence of another language. Some varieties of English have been influenced by the historical use of

Spanish or a Native American language. A typical case of this kind of influence is the use of the *e* (*beet*) and *i* (*bit*) vowel pattern in some Chicano communities in the Southwest. The vowel of *bit* would be pronounced as the vowel of *beet*, so that there would be no contrast between *e* and *i*. In such English varieties, pairs of words like *pick/peek* and *ship/sheep* are pronounced alike.

Social Dialects

Although consonants are probably more prominent than vowels in distinguishing social dialects of English, there are some consonant contrasts between regional dialects and some vowel differences between social dialects. Moreover, regional and social dialect differences tend to interact with each other. Three areas of pronunciation difference relating to consonants have been widely described—the *th* sounds, *r* and *l*, and consonant blends or clusters. There are many other consonant differences as well. Some that are not discussed here are listed in the Appendix. Works cited in Further Study at the end of this chapter can be consulted for more detail.

th Sounds. Probably the most widely recognized social difference in consonant usage is the pronunciation of *these*, *them*, and *those* as the stereotypical "dese," "dem," and "dose." At the beginning of a word, the *th* may be pronounced like *d*, a stop consonant (Stop consonants involve briefly stopping or blocking the air stream coming through the mouth from the lungs). The *th* sound of *think*, *thank*, and *throw* is different from the *th* of *these*: The *th* in *think* is voiceless (the vocal cords are not vibrating), whereas the *th* in *these* is voiced (the vocal cords are vibrating). To test the voiced/voiceless distinction, lightly clutch your Adam's apple as you elongate the first sound of *think* and *these*, and notice the vibration differences in the two *th* sounds. In some dialects, the voiceless *th* may be produced something like a *t*, which is a voiceless stop (*tink, tank, trow*). In general, the *d* for *th* in *these* is more common than the *t* for *th* in *think*.

An interesting research finding about *d* for *th* at the beginning of a word is the fact that various social groups differ in how frequently they use this pronunciation, rather than not using it at all (Labov, 1966). Middle-class groups may use the *d* for *th* pronunciation to some extent in casual speech, whereas working-class groups simply use it more often. This research finding counters the stereotype that working-class speakers always use *d* for *th* and middle-class Standard English speakers never do. A number of pronunciation differences are manifested in these kinds of frequency differences across social classes in our society.

In positions within a word other than the initial position, the *th* may take on different pronunciation characteristics. In the middle or at the end of a word, the voiceless *th* of *author* or *tooth* may be pronounced as *f*, as in "aufor" or "toof"; in words like *brother* and *smooth* with a voiced *th*, a *v* may occur ("brovuh," "smoov"). This pronunciation is most typically found in working-class African American communities and some Southern rural Anglo American communities, with the *f* pronunciation more common than the *v* pronunciation.

    r and l. A number of regionally and socially significant pronunciations are also found in the *r* and *l* sounds. After a vowel, the *r* may be lost, and an *uh*-like vowel (schwa [ə] or dictionary *u*) may take its place. The "cah" or "fouh" pronunciations for *car* and *four* are typical of this variation. The *l* following a vowel may behave like *r*, so that words like *wool* and *Bill* may be pronounced something like "woou" or "Biu." In some instances, the *l* may be lost completely, including the *l* before *p* ("hep" for *help*) or *f* ("sef" for self). These *r* and *l* differences are linked for the most part with geographical region, and they tend to carry more social significance in Northern urban areas than in a Southern context.

    Consonant Blends. One feature of pronunciation that has been studied fairly extensively in several communities concerns the blending or clustering of consonants at the end of words. Consonant blends in words like *west* (*st*), *find* (*nd*), and *act* (*ct*) may be reduced to a single consonant, as in "wes'," "fin'," and "ac'." For all social groups, the final part of the blend may be absent when the next word begins with a consonant. Thus, many Standard English speakers say things like "wes'side," "fin' time," or "ac' perfect" in casual speech. However, there is considerable difference among groups in the loss of the final consonant of the blend when the following word begins with a vowel. Structures like "wes' end," "fin' apples," and "ac' out" would be much more typical of working- than middle-class speech. This "consonant blend reduction" is particularly prominent in working-class African American communities.

    This reduction pattern does not affect all consonant blends at the end of a word. It is limited to those that end in a stop such as *t*, *d*, *k*, or *p*. So it does not affect items like *sense* or *waltz*, which do not end in a stop (they end in an *s* sound), nor does it affect items like *colt, jump, thank*, or *gulp*, where the first consonant is voiced—*l* or *m* or *n*—and the final member is voiceless—*t*, *k*, or *p*. Finally, it should be noted that this pattern affects words in which the consonant blend is formed by the addition of the *-ed* grammatical suffix indicating past tense, just as it affects words where the blend is part of the base word. So, items like *missed*, pronounced with an *st* blend sound as in *mist*; *talked*, pronounced as "tawkt"; and *banned*, pronounced "band," would all be affected by this rule, making them "mis'," "talk'," and "ban'."

    As with the vowels, there are also regular consonant patterns in the English varieties used by some speakers from other language backgrounds.

One kind of influence comes from differences between the sound system of English and that of the other language. A well-known example occurs in the English of some Mexican Americans in California, where a *ch* sound may be substituted for the *sh* sound (i.e., *shirt* may be pronounced as "churt"). The reverse pattern occurs in New Mexico as well, although it is not as remarked on there ("shursh" for *church*; Fought, 2003). Another sort of difference involves extending the possible sequences of vowels and consonants in the other language into the English language. For example, many languages follow a consonant–vowel pattern within syllables so that consonants do not occur together in clusters, as in English *bread*. Speakers from those language backgrounds may insert a reduced vowel sound between the two consonant sounds (something like "buhread"). The restriction against certain types of clusters in the other language may also result in the insertion of a vowel before the cluster, resulting in the pronunciation of *star* as *estar*.

Still another example involves the lack of contrast between the "n" sound and the "ng" sound at the end of words. In some Hispanic English and Native American English dialects in the Southwest, *sing* and *sin* may both be pronounced as "sin," whereas in other dialects they are both pronounced as "sing." This lack of contrast between the two consonants is related to the fact that the speaker's native language does not contrast these sounds as English does. Many of the pronunciation differences found in ethnic varieties of English are related to influence from the heritage language that has become part of the English variety.

Not all speakers from a particular language background follow identical English patterns. The English of Mexican Americans is different from that of Cuban Americans and Puerto Rican Americans, even though those groups share a Spanish language heritage. Moreover, there is variation in the English spoken within each one of these groups depending on factors such as whether English is the first or second language, age at the time of immigration for non-native speakers, and social class. Variability is also due to where an English language learner stands in the second language learning process. Thus, the dialect situation for English speakers from other language backgrounds is quite complex. In fact, in diverse communities such as that of New York Puerto Ricans, individuals may need to be familiar with several varieties of English (standard and vernacular) and several more of Spanish (Zentella, 1997).

Beyond Consonants and Vowels in Pronunciation. In addition to contrasting consonant and vowel patterns, there are other prominent differences among dialects. Some relate to aspects of pronunciation that affect a whole syllable. Syllables that are not stressed within a word may be eliminated. In casual speech, practically all speakers of English show this pattern to some extent, as indicated in pronunciations such as "'cause" for *because* and "'bout" for *about*. This rule may be extended considerably beyond these common items, affecting items ranging from "'lectricity" for *electricity* and "el'phant" for *elephant* to "'tatoes" for *potatoes* and "'member" for *remember*. There are also cases where the number of syllables in a word is different for various dialects. For example, *baloney* may consist of three syllables in one dialect ("bah-lo-ney") and two syllables in another one ("blo-ney"). In some Southern rural dialects, including Appalachia and North Carolina's Outer Banks, words like *tire, fire,* or *liar* consist of one syllable (pronounced something like "tar," "far," and "lar," respectively), whereas they consist of two syllables in other dialects ("tai-er," "fai-er," "lai-er," respectively; Wolfram & Schilling-Estes, 2006).

Popular discussions of social and ethnic differences in English dialects often include impressionistic references to characteristics such as voice quality, inflection, or lilt. More specific references may include qualities such as voice raspiness, high and low pitch ranges, and general resonance. To a large extent, these qualities are idiosyncratic; however, some features such as voice raspiness may also be molded by community norms. For example, a stylized use of raspiness among African American males has been observed.

Several studies have suggested that the range between high and low pitch used in Black communities is greater than that in comparable White communities. This, of course, would be a culturally learned behavior and totally unrelated to biology. Studies also suggest that women in American society typically have a greater pitch range within their sentences than men do. This kind of pitch distribution over a sentence is what is commonly meant by the popular reference to *inflection*—what linguists refer to as *intonation*.

The rhythm or beats of syllables in a sentence can vary too. English typically gives extra prominence to the stressed words in a phrase and tends to run together the other syllables. So, in the phrase *He 'went to the 'store, went* and *store* usually get greater prominence than the other parts of the sentence (the marks preceding *went* and *store* indicate heavier stress). Other languages may give an equal beat to each of the syllables in the sentence, as in *'He 'went 'to 'the 'store*. This gives an impression of choppiness to those who have learned the conventional English timing system. Speakers of English whose pronunciation is influenced by a language with even stress on syllables may have stress patterns that contrast noticeably with those of other dialects. In Chicano English, a variety spoken by millions of Latinos in the United States, stress patterns contrast notably with those of other dialects. Fought (2003) reports primary stress on the second syllable of *Thanksgiving* in the phrase *Thanksgiving Day* and on the first syllable of *morning* and *sickness* in the phrase *morning sickness*.

Current knowledge about pronunciation is much more extensive with respect to basic consonant and vowel patterns than it is with respect to other aspects of pronunciation, such as rhythm and intonation. More research is needed in this area in order to understand the exact role of these factors in dialect differences, but there is no doubt that they are a contributing factor.

GRAMMAR DIFFERENCES

Dialects also contrast in aspects of grammatical usage. Grammar in this sense refers to the composition of words and the way words are combined in phrases and sentences. For example, the addition of -s to a verb form to mark agreement with certain types of subjects (*it walks* compared with *they walk*) is a grammatical process, as is the contrast in word arrangement that signals the difference between a statement and a question (*You are going* vs. *Are you going?*).

Differences between dialects on points of grammar are generally more subject to social evaluation than those in pronunciation. Vernacular grammatical features more often carry social stigma than do pronunciation features because pronunciation differences tend to be more readily tolerated, particularly in regional accents. Many grammatical differences are more strongly associated with social groups than with regional dialects. These language evaluations match the general patterns of social evaluation in which social class differences are less tolerable than are regional differences.

Suffixes

For the most part, the grammatical systems of all dialects of English are quite similar—there is a large common grammatical core. There are certain areas, however, where divergence is likely to occur. One of them is suffixes—short forms such as plural and past-tense markers that attach to the ends of words. These suffixes indicate certain grammatical meanings on verbs, nouns, and, to a lesser extent, adjectives and adverbs. The language has a much more limited set of suffixes than it had earlier in its history, but there is considerable diversity among dialects in their use of the surviving English suffixes. Incidentally, research on the history of English indicates that variation in the use of these grammatical markers is not a recent development. This kind of variation existed in England long before the settlement of the United States.

Verb Suffixes.   In some dialects, certain verb suffixes that would be expected in Standard English may be absent. Less often, suffixes are used in places where they would not be expected in Standard English. Such fluctuation can be explained more fully in terms of specific suffixes.

Several of the suffix fluctuations affect verbs in the Standard English grammatical system as well as the vernacular English system. One is the -*ed* suffix, which is used to mark past tense on verbs (e.g., *they walked* and *they have walked*). This ending may be absent in speech, to a greater or lesser extent, depending on the dialect in question. As mentioned in the previous section, this difference actually occurs at the level of pronunciation, but it affects a grammatical form. It has been found that all speakers occasionally omit the -*ed* suffix in a sentence like *Yesterday they walk' by the park*. In some socially defined dialects, the suffix may be absent more frequently; and in cases like *Yesterday they walk' in the park*, where the -*ed* absence precedes a vowel sound, it is much more noticeable. This higher frequency and wider distribution of -*ed* absence gives the impression that speakers of these dialects drop the endings of words, and it has even led to claims that speakers of these dialects do not know what past tense is. Research has amply demonstrated, however, that absence of this suffix is typically an English pronunciation feature, not a grammatical one (Fasold, 1972). In some dialects, the –*ed* dropping process is used more frequently than in other dialects. However, because the -*ed* past-tense ending does occur sometimes, clearly the speakers know it.

The other verb suffix that fluctuates is the -*s*, used in the present tense to mark grammatical agreement with certain subjects (third-person singular present-tense -*s*), as in *the dog barks* or *the child plays*. This suffix may be absent in working-class dialects used in some African American communities, where *he go* or *she have a car* may be used. Some absence of this suffix has also been noted for members of Native American communities, although suffix absence is typically more limited there than in African American working-class communities. The –*s* absence is also prominent for speakers who learn English as a second language. For many of them, this absence may result from a lack of grammatical marking rather than a pronunciation rule.

One very widespread item related to the use of this present-tense suffix is the form *don't*. In varieties of English that show no vernacular usage of the third-person -*s* suffix, *don't* may be used with grammatical subjects that in standard use would call for *doesn't*. This results in sentences like *She don't know* and *He don't like it* (Christian, 2000).

The -*s* verbal suffix for the present tense has another interesting variable use. In some Appalachian and Southern communities, the -*s* suffix is heard on verbs occurring with plural subjects as well as with singular subjects, especially if the subject involves a collective noun: *People goes* or *A lot of them goes*. It also occurs frequently in these Southern dialects if the subject is a coordinate noun phrase as in *James and Willis goes a lot*. However, the -*s* tends not to be used in these dialects if the plural subject is a pronoun (*they*).

Other Suffixes. Although the systems of verb endings show more extensive differences between dialects, other suffixes vary too. In the case of nouns, one of the suffixes that fluctuates is the plural marker. In working-class African American communities, absence of the plural suffix has been observed in phrases like *two card* or *all them book*. In some rural Southern or Appalachian dialects, the plural suffix may be absent with nouns that signify weights and measures, particularly when a numeral is used, as in *three pound* or *twenty mile*. Another pattern affects irregular plurals in English—nouns that do not take a suffix, but that form the plural in some other way (*feet, sheep*). Some members of working-class Southern and Black communities apply the regular pluralization pattern to these nouns so that they may say *two foots* or *many sheeps*, for example.

The other noun suffix that shows dialect difference is the possessive *-s* ending. Some speakers from working-class African American communities may omit the possessive *-s* ending, using *my friend jacket* as a correspondence for the standard *my friend's jacket*. A characteristic observed in some rural Southern speech in the Appalachian highlands and in isolated southeastern island communities is the use of the forms *your'n* and *our'n* in places where the standard form is *yours* and *ours* (*his'n* and *her'n* occur as well), as in *This jacket is your'n*.

For adjectives and adverbs, the suffixes that have nonstandard alternate usages are the comparative (*-er*) and the superlative (*-est*) markers. In the standard pattern, these endings are used typically with words of one or two syllables (*stronger, friendliest*). For some words with two syllables, and all words with three or more syllables, the standard pattern uses *more* and *most* preceding the word rather than the suffix (*more efficient, more foolish*). However, this pattern differs across dialects. In some, the suffixes may be added to words that go with *more/most* in the standard patterns, resulting in forms like *beautifuler* and *awfulest*. Also, some forms that are irregular in the standard pattern may be treated differently (e.g., *bad/worse/worst*). Forms built on the basis of analogy with regular form—such as *baddest, gooder, worser*—have also been observed. Forms for comparatives and superlatives like the ones mentioned here have been documented in a wide range of dialects and are not restricted to any particular group.

Suffixes such as these are particularly susceptible to dialect variation for several reasons. In the language system of English, many inflectional suffixes are redundant, so they do not carry much meaning. For example, the *-s* on *he plays* adds little meaning to the present-tense form. It shows that the subject of the sentence is third-person singular, but that information is already apparent from the subject (and English does not typically allow the omission of subjects, as other languages, such as Spanish, do). When this kind of redundancy is found, a form is more vulnerable to change.

Another explanation for dialect variation in suffixes is connected to the fact that English present-tense verbs have been losing different kinds of suffixes for centuries. At one point, English had *I goe, thou goest*, and *he/she/it goeth*—a much more extensive set of suffixes than we have today. But the language has gradually been losing these forms, and the standard variety of English has preserved only the *-s* on third-person singular forms. In some cases, vernacular varieties simply take to completion a process that has been happening to all dialects of English in one form or another.

Changes among suffixes also come from pressure within the language to eliminate exceptions or regularize forms. Thus, a change from *oxen* to *oxes* or *sheep* to *sheeps* can be understood as a natural pressure to make exceptions or irregularities conform to majority patterns. From this perspective, the *-s* on third-person forms (e.g., *he goes*) is an exception to the majority pattern, in which all other present-tense forms are not marked with a suffix (e.g., *I go, you go, we go,* etc.). Eliminating this exception makes the verb system more regular.

Other Differences in the Verb System

Three important kinds of patterned dialect differences may affect verbs: tense marking, agreement marking, and some special characteristics of the use of the verb *be*.

Irregular Verbs.   Many vernacular dialects do not follow the standard patterns for irregular verbs—that is, verbs that do not use the *-ed* suffix to indicate past tense. For instance, the standard pattern for the irregular verb *know* is *knew* and *have known*; for *come*, it is *came* and *have come*. In many working-class communities, differences in the way irregular verbs form the past tenses have been noted, including the following patterns:

Vernacular Past-Tense Formation With Irregular Verbs

Regularization: They *growed* a lot. (*heared, knowed*)

(The general pattern of English verbs is followed.)

Exchange of participle   I *have went* already. (*broke, saw*)
and simple past forms: I *seen* it. (*done, sunk*)

(Simple past-tense forms occur where the standard uses the past participle, and vice versa.)

Unmarked forms: I *give* it away already. (*come, eat*)

(The plain verb form is used.)

Different irregular forms: They *brung* it. (*drug* for *dragged*)

(The different irregular form is not part of standard dialects.)

Some of these forms occur with high frequency among speakers from working-class communities; others occur more rarely or have been found to be more regionally concentrated.

One restricted aspect of verb tense involves the absence of the "helping" or auxiliary verb *have*, especially before *been*, as in *I been there before*. This grammatical pattern actually results from a pronunciation rule that removes the *'ve* after *have* has been contracted (or the *'s* of *has*). Another feature that has been found in Southern working-class communities is the addition of *done* to signal completion of an action, as in *I done threw it away* or *They've done sold it*. It may also be used for emphasis as in *I done forgot it*. This *done* should not be confused with the past participle *done* of the verb *do* (e.g., *I have done it*). Although the forms are identical, their functions are different. The past participle is a main verb (*I've done it*), whereas the feature in question here functions as a helping verb or auxiliary (*I've done sold it*). This structure shows that an additional distinction can be indicated by verbs in certain working-class dialects where there is no directly corresponding form in standard dialects.

Agreement Marking.   We have already discussed subject/verb agreement and the third-person singular *-s*. Another area of subject/verb agreement in which dialects may differ involves the *be* verb forms. The standard pattern for *be* retains many agreement distinctions that other English verbs no longer use (*I am, it is, you/we/they are, I/it/was, you/we/they were*). In many working-class dialects, the agreement pattern allows the use of *is* and *was* with plural subjects (*the dogs is barking, they was barking*). This feature in the agreement pattern for *be* is quite common, and it has been observed in many communities. This adjustment is a kind of regularization: *Is* or *was* is used throughout the paradigm (i.e., *I/you/he, she, it/we/you* (plural)/*they was*). Along the Outer Banks of North Carolina, there is an interesting regularization in which *weren't* is used throughout the negative paradigm: *I/you/he, she, it/we/you* (plural)/*they weren't*. In the affirmative, the regularization pattern is like that in other vernacular dialects, using *was* as the primary regularized form (*I/you/he, she, it/they was*).

Habitual Be.   Another use of the verb form *be* has been noted in working-class African American communities, signifying a meaning distinction not found in other dialects. In sentences like *Sometimes they be acting silly*, the verb form indicates an activity that takes place habitually (it happens at various intervals over a period of time). This habitual *be* form must be distinguished from constructions that look similar but do not carry the meaning of habitual occurrence. Observations of language patterns have indicated that structures like *They be here tomorrow* and *They be here if they could* result from the absence of the auxiliary forms *will* and *would*, respectively, and they are different from the habitual use of *be*. For the most part, the habitual use of *be* is limited to the speech of working-class Black speakers.

Be Absence.   Another characteristic pertaining to *be* is its absence in cases like *She not going* or *They nice*. The forms of *be* involved in this pattern are *is* and *are*. This feature was discussed in considerable detail in the earlier section on describing language patterns, but one additional point is interesting. The patterned absence of *are* has been documented in many Southern White and Black working-class communities, whereas the absence of *is* has been found mainly in Black communities. That is, working-class White Southerners would use sentences such as *We going to the game*, but not *She going to the game*, whereas working-class Black speakers may use both of these structures.

Other Grammatical Differences

Negation is another grammatical structure where significant variation is found in English dialects. The use of sentences negated in more than one place is widely noticed and frequently commented on. Most studies of dialects in working-class communities note the negative patterns in sentences like *We didn't go nowhere*, *They couldn't find no food*, and *It don't never run good*. These patterns have been compared to the standard pattern that allows only one negative to occur. In multiple negation, a negative form is attached to both the verb and the indefinites (*nowhere, no*) or adverbs (*never*) following the verb. Thus, the forms that can carry negation are made to agree with each other. In addition, inversion of subject and auxiliary in negation has been observed in some Southern communities, along with the more widespread pattern in which the negative indefinite word follows the verb: *Couldn't nobody see it* (a statement meaning *Nobody could see it*, not a question) and *Ain't nobody gonna do it*! have been noticed.

Another common but highly stigmatized feature of negation in working-class dialects is the use of *ain't*. This form is used to correspond to the Standard English negative version of *is, are, am, has*, and *have*, in cases like *They ain't here* and *I ain't found it*. In working-class African American speech, it can also be used for *didn't*, as in *She ain't go yesterday*. An interesting pronunciation variation on this form is *ain't*, used by some rural Southern speakers. Despite the highly negative attitude often expressed toward *ain't*, it persists in widespread use in many speech communities.

In studying the grammatical patterns of a community, then, some important areas to check are suffixes, verb usage, and negation. There is notable diversity among dialects of English in these areas, but any extended observation will undoubtedly identify differences in other areas as well for an inventory of grammatical features in a particular dialect. The list of dialect differences in the Appendix includes the features discussed here and provides more detail.

Illustrative Dialect Samples

In doing dialect study, it is important to remember that not all speakers use all of the features of a dialect. Our discussions refer to a composite picture of some dialects, rather than the dialect of any one person. To illustrate the actual use of some variable structures in speech, we present two annotated passages taken from live speech samples. The first example, "Appalachian Ghost Story," comes from an interview with an elderly White woman who lived her entire life in the southern part of West Virginia. The second passage is from a conversation with an 11-year-old African American boy from Baltimore, Maryland. For these samples of vernacular speech, dialect features are noted and described following the samples. Odd-numbered superscripts refer to pronunciation differences, and even-numbered superscripts refer to grammatical differences. We have chosen to use regular spelling for the most part so that the majority of the pronunciation differences are not indicated in the spelling. The punctuation roughly reflects the pausing and intonation patterns in the flow of speech, rather than written language conventions. For frequently occurring features such as *d* for *th* and *n* for *ng*, we only mark the first five instances of the feature in the typescript.

Appalachian Ghost Story

I was always kindy[1] afraid to stay by myself, just me, you know, it was gettin'[3] about time for me to get in, so Ingo, he'd[2] went[4] over to this man's house where we carried our water from, and to get some water, and, ooh, the moon was so pretty and bright, and I thinks[6], heck, hit's[5] dark, I hear him a-talkin',[3,8] a-settin'[3,8] over there in the field where the spring is, I'll just walk down the road and meet him, you know, ooh, it was so pretty and light. I got down there and I hearn[10] something shut the churchhouse door, but I didn't see a thing, and the moon, oh the moon was as pretty as daylight, and I didn't see nothin.'[3,12] And he come[14] on the walk, pitty-pat, pitty-pat, and I just looked with all my eyes, and I couldn't see a thing, come out that gate, iron[7], slammed it and hit[5] just cracked, just like a[9] iron[7] gate, it will just slam it there. And all at once, something riz up[10] right in front of me. Looked like it had a white sheet around it, and no head. I liketa[16] died. That was just a little while before Florence was born. I turned around and I went back to the house just as fast as I could go, and about that time, Ingo come[14] along and he says[6], "I set the water up," and he said, "I'm going down the churchhouse," he said, "I hearn[10] somebody go in," he said, "They went through that gate." And he walked across there and he opened the door and he went in the churchhouse. And they had him a-lookin'[3,8] after the church, you know, if anybody went in, he went down there. He seen[18] something was the matter with me, I couldn't hardly[20] talk. I told him, I said, "Well, something or other, I hearn[10] it, I seen[18] it, whenever I started over to meet you, and I couldn't get no[12] further." So he went down there and he took his lantern, of course, we didn't have flashlights then, took his lantern, had an old ladder, just spokes, just to go up beside of the house, he looked all behind the organ, all behind every bench, he went upstairs and looked in the garret, not a thing in the world he could find. Not a thing. Well, it went on for a right smart little[32] while and one day Miss Allen was down there. Her girls come down there very often and sweep the church and clean it. So one evenin'[3], they come[14] up the house, you know, and I's[11] tellin' them. They said, "Honey, don't feel bad about that," she said, "Long as you live here, you'll see something like that," said "they[34] was, in time of the war, they[34] was a woman, that somebody'd cut her head off and they'd buried her in the grave down there." And they said there'd been so many people[24] live in the house we live in, would see her, and said "That's what it was," said, "it just had a white sheet wrapped around it." And we didn't live there very long cause I wouldn't stay. He worked away and aw heck—I's[11] just scared to death but still Miss Allen told me, she said, "Don't be afraid because hain't[5,26] a thing that'll hurt you."

Wild Life

Boy: And then I went home. And then I was watchin,'[3] um, Wild Life, about animals.

Interviewer: And which animal did you see?

Boy: And a[9] elephant and a rhino was[22] fightin'[3] The elephant kicked the rhino down. And then it start[30] grabbin'[3] its whole body with[21] its, with[21] its.

Interviewer: Tusk, trunk.

Boy: Yeah, thr[13]ow him but he couldn't get him up but it ran. And then it was this little dancin'[3] chickens, that do like this, like Indians, so they were jumpin'[3] up and down doin'[3] a dance.

Interviewer: Why?

Boy: I don't know.

Interviewer: Were they mad at each other?

Boy: No, they was[22] dancin.'

Interviewer: They were happy. Did they have music (makes sound of music)?

Boy: Yeah, with[21] they[36] mouth,[21] they go uh uh uh uh and stuff. It[34] was a whole lot of them doin' it. And then the Indians'll come out and do it with[21] them.

Interviewer: And then the Indians would dance with the chickens? Wow!

Boy: And then we saw a movie with, uh, lions, uh uh cheetah, and um gorillas on it, and they said a, a dog[15] bit the baby and it died.

Interviewer: Bit a real baby?

Boy: (Nods yes)

Interviewer: Oh.

Boy: And then that man had anoth[21]er tiger, a po[19]lice came to the house and shot that one and they got anoth[21]er one.

Interviewer: This is all on Wild Life?

Boy: (nods)

Interviewer: With the elephant and the rhinoceros? All this happened on Wild Life?

Boy: (Nods)

Interviewer: Wow.

Boy: And then another one came on about the, uh, white lions and stuff. Don't you know them[38] white ones?

Interviewer: White lions?

Boy: Tigers I mean.

Interviewer: White tigers. Tigers are orange with black stripes, thank you.

Boy: No, they[40] white too. Uh huh. They got white—they got white, then they got white, I mean, black stri[23]pes goin' down.

Interviewer: That's a zebra.

Boy: Um uhm, it's[34] another one, that's a snow tiger.

Interviewer: Oh, the snow tigers, oh, okay.

Boy: And then that man had one. Then, we went to a black, a black panther. It wasn't[25] no[12] black panth[21]er, it was something, black what you call em, I don't know.

Interviewer: Uh-huh.

Boy: And then, it[34] was a um, we was[22] lookin' at monkeys jumpin' up and down, had—

Interviewer: Monkeys are funny, huh?

Boy: And they were hittin' each other—and then it[34] was one that went to the doctor's and he was uh (makes noises). Cause—

Interviewer: A monkey went to the doctor?

Boy: [27]Cause he ain't[26] want to get his shot. Went in his leg. And he said (noises) and he got a needle shot in his leg and he say[6] (noises). And then the man gave him a peppermint so he could suck on it. And then he was bitin' his glasses. Then he put them on and was lookin' at the camera. And then when he got home he said that lady said he don't[28] like to say no so he had bang[30,42] on the table and all that. And then that lady gave him a sucker and he was suckin' on it.

Interviewer: Just like a little kid, huh?

Boy: And then he had diapers on, had a little jumper.

Interviewer: (laughs) She kept him in her house? Oh, so it was like her pet monkey? Or was it a monkey out in the jungle? Oh.

Boy: And then they'd take him places with[21]em, like a diner and all.

Interviewer: Don't you think the monkey will run away?

Boy: He won't run away.

Interviewer: Did they have him on a leash? Like they do a dog?

Boy: No. And then when they got him home, they were jumpin' on a big trampoline.

Interviewer: All three of them?

Boy: No, just one.

Interviewer: Oh, just the monkey?

Boy: Yeah.

Interviewer: The lady wasn't jumpin' on the trampoline too?

Boy: No, she was watchin' them [27]cause they was[22] jumpin' up and down, walkin' around.

Notes on Transcripts

Pronunciation

1. In an unstressed, final syllable of a word, the schwa sound [ə] can be changed to the high vowel *ee* of *beet*, as in "sofy" for *sofa* or "kindy" for *kinda*.

3. The -*ing* form in a final unstressed syllable may be changed from an *ng* sound to an *n* sound.

5. Before the items *it* and *ain't* an older English *h* may be retained, resulting in items like "hit" for *it* or "hain't" for *ain't*.

7. The sequence *ire* in items like *tire*, *fire*, or *iron* may be collapsed to a single syllable, resulting in pronunciations such as "arn" for *iron*, "tar" for *tire*, "far" for *fire*, and so forth.

9. The form *a* may be generalized to occur before items that begin with a vowel (e.g., *a apple*, *a iron*) as well as those that begin with a consonant (e.g., *a pear*).

11. Initial *w* sounds may be deleted in an unstressed syllable, resulting in forms like "young 'uns" for *young ones* or "we's" for *we was*.

13. Following a consonant, *r* may be deleted before *oh* and *u* so that *throw* becomes "th'ow" and *through* becomes "th'u."

15. Open *o* is centralized to schwa so that *dog* and *Doug* sound the same.

17. When the stop consonant (*t* or *d*) follows another consonant, thus creating a consonant blend or cluster, the final consonant may not be pronounced—so that *happened* (pronounced "happend") may be pronounced as "happen."

19. Stress may shift on syllables of certain words. *Police* is stressed on the first syllable, and the vowel of the stressed syllable becomes *oh* instead of schwa.

21. When it occurs in a medial or final position of a word, the voiceless *th* sound may be pronounced as *f*, as in "deaf" for *death*; and the voiced *th* sound may be pronounced as *v*, as in "mover" for *mother*.

23. The consonant cluster *str* is pronounced as *skr*. *Street* becomes "skreet" or *stream* becomes "skream."

25. Before nasal sounds (*m*, *n*, and the sound spelled *ng*), certain consonants can be altered. Voiceless *th* may become *t* (*nothing* becomes "not'n"), *z* may become *d* (*wasn't* may become "wadn't"), and *v* may become *b* (*seven* may become "sebm").

27. Unstressed syllables may be deleted. *Because* may be rendered as "'cause," *remember* as "'member."

Grammatical Differences

2. A pronoun form may be used after a subject noun, as in *My mother she* … or *The man in the middle, he* …

4. The past form of an irregular verb may be generalized as the past participle form, as in *he had went* or *she had did*.

6. Present-tense forms may be used in animated narratives of past-time events, including an -*s* on non-third-person forms, as in *I says* or *we goes*.

8. An *a-* prefix may attach to verbs or adverbs ending in -*ing* as in *He was a-hunting* or *He makes money a-building houses*.

10. Different irregular verb forms may be used in past-tense forms as in *brang* (for *brought*), *hearn* (*heard*), or *tuck* (*took*).

12. Multiple negatives may include a negative marker in the verb phrase and a negative indefinite form following the verb, as in *I didn't see nothin'* or *She ain't goin' nowhere*.

14. A present-tense root of an irregular verb may be used in past-tense forms as well, as in *She come late yesterday* or *Last year he run in the race*.

16. The special modal form *liketa* is used to mark a significant event that was averted. It may be used in figurative and literal senses.

18. The past participle form of an irregular verb may be generalized to a simple past-tense form, as in *He seen it* or *She done it*.

20. Multiple negation may involve negative marking in the verb phrase and an adverb following the verb, as in *They don't hardly eat* or *She shouldn't never go*.

22. The conjugated forms of *be* may be regularized to *is* in the present tense, as in *We is here now,* or *was* in the past tense, as in *They was there*.

24. Relative pronoun forms can be absent if they are the subject of a relative clause, as in *That's the dog bit me*. In standard dialects, these relative pronouns can only be absent when they are the object of the relative clause, as in *That's the house he was building*.

26. The form *ain't* can be used for *be + not*, *have + not*, and *did + not*, as in *He ain't here*, *She ain't done it*, or *He ain't go*.

28. The third-person singular present-tense form -*s* may be absent from the verb, so that forms such as *she go* or *He don't* may occur.

30. The past-tense maker -*ed* may be deleted: *After the movie, we want to go to that restaurant, but it wasn't open*.

32. The adverbs *right, right smart*, and *right smart little* are used to intensify attributes, such as *She's right tall* or *He took a right smart little while*.

34. For the expletive use of *there* in Standard English (e.g., *There's a new boy in my class*), vernacular dialects may use *it* (e.g., *It's a new boy in my class*) or *they* (e.g., *They's a new boy in my class*).

36. The subject form of the third-person plural pronoun *they* can serve the possessive function: *Let's go to they house*.

38. The demonstrative pronoun *those* may be replaced by *them* to get *Them dogs was barking all night long*.

40. The copula may be omitted, as in *She crazy*.

42. Past participle may occur in place of the simple past: *They went to the game and they had yelled at the umpire*.

Vocabulary Differences

Most Americans can readily cite cases where the word for an item in one region differs from that used in another. When travelers return home from a visit to New England talking about how *frappe* and *cabinet* are used, whereas other regions might use the term *milkshake*, or when Northerners mention that a Southerner says *carry* in the sense of accompanying, as in *He carried her to the movies*, they are referring to basic vocabulary differences in regional dialects. Vocabulary differences can affect all word classes, including nouns (e.g., *hoagie/grinder/submarine/hero/sandwich*), verbs (e.g., *press/mash the button*), prepositions (e.g., *sick at/to/in my stomach*), adverb/adjectives (e.g., *very smart/right smart fella*), and adverbs (e.g., *fell plumb asleep*). *The Dictionary of American Regional English*, which has been in the making for more than three decades, has more than 50,000 vocabulary entries for regional words (Hall, 2002).

A few examples from recent investigation into the language variety used in Ocracoke, one of the islands of North Carolina's Outer Banks, suggest something of the complexity inherent in regional vocabulary differences. There are several kinds of relationships between the Ocracoke vocabulary and that of other dialect areas. First, the Ocracoke dialect, which people who live there call the *brogue*, includes some words that have not been found elsewhere, even on other Outer Banks islands. This is a small set of words, perhaps no more than a few dozen, which includes terms for locations or geographic features, such as *up the beach*, meaning off the island to the north; *down beach*, meaning off the island to the south; and the *ditch*, meaning mouth of the harbor. These Ocracoke-specific words also include terms for games and activities, such as *meehonkey* and *whoop and holler* for local versions of hide-and-seek, *call the mail over* for bring the mail from the mainland, and *scud* for car ride. Although the set of words that are unique to Ocracoke is small, and some words may even be restricted to particular groups within the island community, they cannot be ignored because some of them are used fairly frequently in everyday speech. *Going up the beach*, meaning going off the island to the north, is a fairly common activity that islanders often mention in conversation. If listeners are not familiar with what this phrase means, they might inappropriately expect someone who had gone up the beach to return shortly from a nearby sandy spot. The islander going across the beach, meaning to the shore along the sea, may be back in a short while, but not the one who is going up the beach. Although they are relatively few, the vocabulary words that are found only in Ocracoke are critical to understanding and participating in the daily routines of island life.

Many commonly used words are shared by Ocracoke and other Outer Banks communities, including some of those on the coastal mainland areas immediately adjacent to the Outer Banks, but they are not known to occur elsewhere. This set of words includes items like *mommuck* (hassle), *slick cam* (very smooth water), *dingbatter* (nonislander), *quamish* (upset stomach), and *hard blow* (strong wind).

Some Outer Banks words show regional distribution within the Outer Banks. *Bankers* is an older term apparently used more in northern areas of the Outer Banks than in the southern islands. Similarly, *dingbatters* may not be used in all areas of the Outer Banks. On Harkers Island, *dingbatter* alternates with the term *dit-dot* for outsiders, which used to occur more frequently than *dingbatter*. Despite this variation within the Banks, some of the Outer Banks words have taken on symbolic significance in distinguishing Outer Banks residents from the rest of the world.

Most of the distinctive vocabulary words in Ocracoke are shared with dialect areas throughout the South, including the Appalachian region and the Atlantic South, as well as the Piedmont area that lies between the mountains and the lowland Atlantic South. This list of shared vocabulary is quite extensive and includes many terms popularly associated with the South, such as *fixin' to* (about to) and *reckon* (suppose).

Unlike grammatical differences, most vocabulary differences in regional varieties of English are considered neither good nor bad—they are typically viewed as quaint curiosities. There is little social value associated with saying *spigot* versus *faucet*, *pail* versus *bucket*—these are simply accepted as part of the normal regional variation of English.

Vocabulary Matters Across Dialects

Other dimensions of word choice that are sometimes associated with certain dialects actually occur across language varieties. Malapropism and slang are two salient examples.

Malapropism.   *Malapropism* comes about when two words sound reasonably similar: for example, *I found the discussion very interesting and enervating* (for energizing) or *I caught ammonia* (for pneumonia). In some cases, a less familiar word (*enervating*) replaces a more familiar word with the same stem (*energizing*); in other cases the less familiar word may be replaced by a more familiar, similar-sounding but unrelated word, as in *old timer* for *Alzheimer* as in *She's got old timer's disease*.

Some malapropisms may be stimulated by a situation in which a person feels the need to use more formal, educated-sounding language. The classic example is someone from a working-class background who attempts to use a more formal, middle-class, educated style of speech—one with which the speaker is not entirely comfortable. Although such uses have been stereotyped as humorous, malapropisms arise in natural language situations. The negative evaluation they receive is related to the fact that the speaker is attempting to appear educated but not succeeding at it. But middle-class, educated people also use malapropisms (the sentence with *enervating* was heard at an annual meeting of a professional organization) or they adopt those that have some currency: *There were some incidences of looting* for *incidents of looting*. The motivation in general is the desire to sound educated and erudite. These vocabulary misuses are different from dialect uses that are shared by a group of speakers.

Slang. The term *slang* seems to be used in several senses, as typified in the following examples:

(a) Those people don't speak Standard English: They just use slang.
(b) Young people use a lot of slang words, like *way scary* for *very scary* and *chill* for *calm down*.
(c) Basketball players have their own slang, like *rebo, jumper,* and *chucker*.

In some instances, the term *slang* is used to refer derogatorily to any variety of English that is not Standard English. In the Ebonics debate of 1997, African American English was often inaccurately called slang and broken English. This sense is illustrated in Sentence (a).

Slang is also used to refer to certain words or phrases that have a strong connotation of informality, particularly as compared with the words they replace (Sentence [b]), and that are often associated with the teenage and early adult years of life. A sense of informality is conveyed by using *man* or *girl* as a term of address, in place of a person's name, or saying *No problem* instead of *You're welcome* in response to someone's "Thank you." Many of these uses have a short life span, arising quickly and falling just as quickly into disuse. Other slang items actually last fairly long and become stabilized as a kind of national slang (e.g., *cool*). This interpretation of *slang* is probably the most widely used one and certainly cuts across different dialects.

Finally, *slang* is sometimes used to refer to a specialized vocabulary associated with a particular field of activity, profession, or trade, such as technology specialists or athletes. In some cases, it may refer to secret vocabularies, such as that of drug dealers or prostitutes. This is the usage illustrated in Sentence (c), which most linguists refer to as *jargon* rather than *slang*.

Linguists restrict the use of the term *slang* to the sense illustrated by Sentence (b). Even here, however, there can be disagreement over what words should be designated as slang. Although there may be near consensus on some words (e.g., *freaked* for *stressed, hot* for *attractive*), others are harder to classify (e.g., *bucks* for *dollars, fired* for *terminated*). It appears that there is a set of characteristics for classifying slang rather than a single definition. Furthermore, there seems to be a slang scale because some items appear to be more "slangy" than others. Like other words, terms that fall somewhere in the indeterminate category of slang may differ regionally and socially. Part of the appeal of these words for young people is the fact that they highlight the boundary between the peer group and other age groups (Eble, 1996). Despite its reputation as linguistically marginal, slang shows complex and interesting sociolinguistic properties.

This section has looked within the broad categories of dialect difference—pronunciation, grammar, and vocabulary—where the linguistic processes show distinctive social and regional patterning. There are many more of them, some of which are listed in the Appendix. Linguists' expanding descriptions of dialects can certainly inform educators about the details of particular varieties. Teachers gain fuller understanding of the regularities in students' English language varieties by working to extend the existing dialect descriptions, using the sociolinguistic methods described at the beginning of the chapter.

AFRICAN AMERICAN ENGLISH

One variety of English has received more attention by far in the discussion of dialects over the last several decades. Even before the Ebonics debate, the dialect called *African American English, African American Vernacular English,* or *Black English* was certainly one of the most prominent vernacular dialects of U.S. English. Part of its prominence is due to its difference from Standard English. But African American English is not alone in this regard. Other U.S. dialects also contrast remarkably with Standard English. For example, there are some isolated dialects on the Southern seaboard—such as Tangier Island and Smith Island in Virginia and Maryland, and Ocracoke and Harkers Island on the Outer Banks of North Carolina—that are probably more difficult to comprehend in natural conversation for speakers of other varieties than African American English. However, African American English is certainly the most prevalent native English vernacular dialect in the United States in terms of numbers of speakers. Furthermore, this dialect has received considerable attention in the media, which has focused on everything from teenage rapping to hip hop to Ebonics and Standard English instruction. Often African American English has been misrepresented. In fact, it is a variety of English that has combined a number of vernacular English forms in a unique way. Its uniqueness lies not so much in the distinct language forms that are found only in that dialect, although there are a few, but in the particular combination of forms that make up the dialect.

In the 1960s, this language variety typically was called *Nonstandard Negro English* and *Negro Dialect.* The term *Black English* then replaced these terms for a couple of reasons. First, there was a precedent for designating dialects with color terms (e.g., the terms *Black Bobo, Red Thai,* and *White Rus-*

sian are used for distinct varieties of these languages). Second, the dialect's name change reflected the change in the ethnic label from *Negro* to *Black* that was taking place in American society at the time. Finally, the name change was motivated by the desire to throw off the pejorative stereotypes of terms such as *substandard*, *nonstandard*, and even *dialect*. The ethnic designation should not be applied to the speech of African Americans in general because there are many who do not use this dialect at all or to any great extent. In addition, those of other ethnic groups who learn their language in the context of a Black working-class community may learn this dialect.

The modifier *vernacular* was added to the terms *Black English* and *African American English* to avoid the stereotype that all African Americans spoke this variety, so that it became known as *Black English Vernacular* or *Vernacular Black English* and *African American Vernacular English*. Alternative labels such as *Ebonics*, *Afro-American*, and *Afram* have been selectively used over the past few decades, but these terms have not been widely adopted by linguists. The label *African American Vernacular English* was introduced by African American linguists in the early 1990s, in keeping with the general shift from the label *Black* to *African American* in American society. More recently, they have come to use the terms *African American English* and *African American Language*.

Names and labels can be a tricky business. Often they become symbolic tokens of sociopolitical stances. We can be assured that whatever label is used, it will be somewhat controversial. Two articles, "'What Is Africa to Me?': Language, Ideology, and *African American*" (Smitherman, 1991) and "The Politicization of Changing Terms of Self-Reference Among American Slave descendants" (Baugh, 1991), consider these labeling issues in depth.

The Origins of African American English

The history of African American English may be somewhat different from that of other British-derived dialects of English; and this history, combined with the social conditions under which African Americans have existed in American society, account for the uniqueness of the dialect. According to some linguists, what we call *African American English* today probably started out as a creole language something like the creoles or mixed languages of the Caribbean (e.g., Jamaican Creole). When two groups of speakers do not have a language in common, they often create an intermediary language for communication, with a drastically altered grammar and a modified vocabulary taken from one of the primary languages. This type of language often develops under special social conditions, such as the need to communicate for trade or business purposes. This situation is what probably happened originally on the West Coast of Africa, as Europeans from various countries, including the British Isles, developed trade routes. Over time, this intermediary language (a *pidgin*) became an established means of communication (a *creole*). That pidgin or creole was then brought to the Americas with the importation of slaves. In the American South, it mixed further with Southern White varieties of English. But the change from the prior creole was neither instantaneous nor complete. African American English today is not a creole like the Caribbean creoles, but it still has some traces of its creole past combined with many features of Southern English. The historical origin, the addition of Southern features, and the fact that the dialect developed in a largely segregated society have resulted in a unique dialect of English.

Although the history of African American English was hotly disputed in the 1990s (Bernstein, Nunnally, & Sabino, 1997; Mufwene, 1996; Schneider, 1989), most linguists conclude that current-day African American English is a distinctive vernacular variety. Linguists who do not accept the creolist hypothesis point to the social conditions that have segregated Black and White Americans and a sense of ethnic solidarity among Blacks as the basis for developing and maintaining a distinct variety of English.

The Changing State of African American English

The recent course of change in African American English has also been debated. In a study done among the urban African American working-class in Philadelphia, Labov (1987) reported that African American English was becoming *more* different from other vernacular dialects of English, rather than converging with them as might be expected. As linguistic evidence for his position, he cited some forms that had not been highlighted in earlier studies of African American English; as sociological evidence, he cited the increasing pattern of de facto segregation among urban African Americans that might promote divergence among dialects because social or physical segregation tends to promote divergence.

Labov's contention that African American English is diverging from other vernaculars, rather than converging, has been contested by some of his fellow linguists who also study African American English. Some linguists think that, if anything, African American English is leveling its differences with other dialects, rather than diverging from other dialects. Linguistically, they maintain that the forms Labov offers as evidence have been in existence all along, and that his analysis of their diverging use in African American English is not justified. Sociologically, they cite the increasing educational levels of African Americans and note that general education trends are probably more closely related to change in African American English than segregation (Fasold, 1987). Certainly, the final word on this issue has not been spoken. At this point, we can only say that African American English is certainly not dying out; whether it is diverging or converging with other dialects of English is still an open question.

Dialect or Language?

During the Ebonics debate, the question was raised as to whether African American English is a dialect of English or a language on its own and never entirely resolved. Although the criteria used to distinguish a dialect from a language are sometimes debated by linguists, the kinds of differences that distinguish African American English and Standard English are those that typically characterize dialects rather than separate languages.

When the linguistic characteristics of African American English and Standard English are placed side by side, we find many more shared language features than distinctive ones. Dialectologists tend to focus on the differences between dialects rather than their similarities, and our discussion here has largely concerned differences. However, African American English and Standard English dialects share a large common core of structures and vocabulary. A similar comparison of French and English, Spanish and English, or even Spanish and Italian would make the differences between African American English and Standard English seem trivial. (Compare the degree of difference, for example, in *They're talking*, *They talkin'*, and *Ils parlent*.) Most linguists, then, conclude that the kinds of language differences found between vernacular and standard varieties of English set apart dialects of the same language, rather than separate languages.

The level of intelligibility between speakers of Standard English and African American English also suggests a dialect rather than a language difference. For the most part, vernacular speakers understand what Standard English speakers are saying, and speakers of Standard English who have some exposure to vernacular dialects comprehend what vernacular speakers are saying. This generalization does not rule out some minor problems in understanding each other, but any difficulty in comprehension does not match that found between speakers of different languages.

For schools, the important points regarding African American English are that it does not represent an incorrect way of speaking and that not all African Americans speak African American English. Furthermore, some speakers use some of the forms associated with it without using others. The definition of who speaks African American English depends on what forms are considered to be central to the dialect. Although there are varying opinions as to what forms define the dialect, typical inventories usually include grammatical forms such as suffix -s absence (e.g., *She like school*), the use of habitual *be* (e.g., *Sometimes my ears be itching*), and copula absence (e.g., *He nice*), along with a set of pronunciation features that are largely Southern English. Certainly, the African American working-class population is more likely to use these forms than the African American middle class, just as the White working class is more likely to use vernacular forms; but this is a statistical trend that cannot necessarily be applied to an individual speaker.

FURTHER STUDY

Adger, C. T., Christian, D., & Taylor, O. (Eds.). (1998). *Making the connection: Language and academic achievement among African American students*. Washington, DC, and McHenry, IL: Center for Applied Linguistics and Delta Systems Co., Inc.
This volume, published as a contribution to the Ebonics debate, includes a discussion of key educational issues that were often overlooked or misconstrued in public discussion: dialects in the classroom, teaching students to be bidialectal, dialect awareness for students, dialects in teacher preparation, language policy in schools, and dialects and assessment.

Baugh, J. (1998). *The linguistic legacy of American slavery: Race relations and the Ebonics controversy*. New York: Oxford University Press.
The context for the Ebonics controversy of 1997 is fully detailed here: explanation of the term *Ebonics* and the Oakland, CA, School District's resolution concerning it; historical backdrop and legal considerations; and theoretical considerations that were misunderstood.

Fought, C. (2003). *Chicano English in context*. New York: Palgrave Macmillan.
This careful sociolinguistic study of the English language variety spoken by Latinos goes beyond technical description to explore bilingualism in this community and the role of Chicano English in establishing social identity.

Rickford, J., & Rickford, R. (2000). *Spoken soul: The story of Black English*. New York: Wiley.
Written for a general audience, this account of African American English covers all dimensions of this dialect. It is particularly informative about its value as a social marker.

Schneider, E. W. (Ed.). (1996). *Varieties of English around the world: Focus on the USA*. Philadelphia: John Benjamins.
This book is intended for language scholars, but it may be interesting to others who want to know how U.S. dialects came to be and what they look like now in various locales.

Smitherman, G. (1986). *Talkin and testifyin: The language of Black America*. Detroit: Wayne State University Press.
A readable discussion of language in the Black community that includes the consideration of dialect functions as well as dialect forms. A lively presentation format incorporates dialect into the text at times, as Smitherman integrates a personal community perspective with her discussion of empirical facts.

Wolfram, W., & Schilling-Estes, N. (2006). *American English: Dialects and variation* (2nd ed.). Oxford, England: Basil Blackwell.
This description surveys the social and linguistic factors that account for dialects and the functions that dialects serve. It introduces students and a general audience to the principles underlying language variation. The discussion attempts to limit technical terminology but provides an extensive glossary to assist readers.

3

Social Interaction

Dialectologists have focused principally on regional and social group patterns of pronunciation, grammar, and vocabulary use. But there are also important differences in the way that groups of people use language in social interaction. To understand communication patterns in a particular speech community—individuals who generally share a language and expectations about appropriate ways of interacting—researchers investigate the norms for appropriate interactive behavior in various situations.

Interactive norms may involve the use of particular linguistic forms, such as when people use each other's first names and when they use last names, or more general rules for interacting, such as when to keep quiet, when to talk, and what kinds of things to say. (As with dialect features, the term *rule* applied to communicative behavior refers to norms or observable regularities, rather than prescriptions for deportment.) For example, some speech communities' norms for appropriate behavior favor greeting strangers in most situations. If unacquainted people pass each other in a public place, perhaps a courthouse or hospital hallway, it would be considered appropriate to exchange greetings. In a speech community where this behavior is the norm, greeting a stranger is expected and unremarkable, and not greeting a stranger is remarkable. Someone who follows the rule but is not greeted in return may conclude that something is wrong with the other person—that she or he is rude or uncaring or so deep in thought as to be oblivious to others. If the person who does not greet obviously comes from a different social or ethnic group, then the absence of a greeting may evoke a stereotype about some people's lack of manners; but if that person seems to come from the same group, the lack of a greeting is more likely to be interpreted as a temporary lapse in behavior. People might be more inclined to rationalize some apparently inappropriate communicative behavior coming from someone of their own social group and more likely to attribute bad intentions, moral turpitude, or social ineptness to someone from another group.

A word about terms: The term *speech community* emphasizes the common expectations about language behavior that underlie successful communication within a community (Patrick, 2004). The term *dialect group* is usually used more narrowly to refer to those who use a particular language variety defined by a shared set of linguistic structures. Another term used here—*cultural group* or simply *culture*—applies more broadly: It usually refers to a group that shares values, behavioral norms—including norms for interaction—and beliefs about the nature of the world. There is a significant overlap between dialect groups and cultural groups, especially when social dialects are considered. Members of cultural groups may use a dialect to highlight solidarity and resist assimilation. In fact, anthropologist Fordham (1998) found that in the high school where she did field work, African American students used African American English as one way of refusing to comply with culturally alien aspects of schooling. A similar phenomenon was found among middle-age native islander men on Martha's Vineyard off the coast of Massachusetts and on the Outer Banks island of Ocracoke off the coast of North Carolina. Feeling challenged by tourists from outside the island, these men highlighted and heightened dialect features as a kind of resistance to outside social forces (Labov, 1963; Wolfram & Schilling-Estes, 1995).

Language as a form of cultural behavior and an identifying feature of cultural groups involves more than the basic features of dialect. It involves social interaction. Interaction and dialect are inevitably intertwined in language behavior differences between groups and in contributing to the social attitudes toward those differences.

This chapter outlines some important dimensions of language use in social interaction, emphasizing that cultural groups and speech communities may display unique patterns. Such contrasts between groups can be perplexing to students and teachers alike. As with dialect differences, teachers may find that investigating interaction in their classrooms will help them and their students see some regular patterns associated with cultural groups and understand their meaning.

CONVERSATIONAL POLITENESS

Social interaction is similar to driving in traffic: There are some basic, underlying rules that individuals must follow if the enterprise is going to work. The important consideration is not which side of the road to drive on, but the fact that everyone agrees about it. Although drivers are individually more or less considerate of each other, what people do behind the wheel must be generally responsive to what others are doing, as well as to such basic conventions as driving on the right or left side of the road. Some driving patterns are culturally influenced, and some are fairly universal. Many rules of the road are taught, but others are tacit, and drivers may not realize the extent to which their driving patterns respond to others'.

Several frameworks have been spelled out to explain the ways that people interact through talk. One of them concerns politeness. The prevailing theory holds that people tacitly agree to talk in a way that will save face for themselves and others (Brown & Levinson, 1987). Politeness boils down to maintaining others' face so that they will be kindly disposed toward maintaining our face—as people take turns merging from two lanes into one, letting one car go ahead in the expectation of getting the next turn to merge. Face has two sides: negative face, including the needs people have for territory and freedom; and positive face, including needs to be approved of. Both of these dimensions are respected in conversation.

Although people generally take into account each other's face needs, they sometimes have to say things that are inherently face-threatening. A request or command, for example, threatens hearers' negative face because it imposes on them—their freedom to act is compromised. In this case, there are trade-offs for the speaker between communicating directly and preserving the other's face. For example, if someone steps on your toe, you can use the direct command, "Get off my toe." However, by speaking so directly, you risk threatening the offender's negative face (the need for freedom from censure). In addition, if you grimace at the same time, you also threaten the person's positive face by showing disapproval. You might mitigate your statement by appealing to the offender's positive face: "Hey, you're on my toe," said with a laugh that shows friendliness and no hard feelings. You could use an indirect strategy aimed toward negative politeness (putting your own negative face at risk), such as, "Excuse me, would you mind moving your foot?" phrasing the message as a question rather than a command. Even less direct is, "Oh, my toe!" This scenario suggests that speakers unconsciously weigh their social relationships with those to whom they are speaking and assess how inherently face-threatening the message is. What they say—how they encode the message—reflects their calculation. According to this framework, polite interaction is more than a matter of using certain polite forms (e.g., "Please"): It is strategic.

Cultural differences with respect to what constitutes face and threats to face can make interaction across cultures difficult. For example, a teacher concerned with preserving students' face might say "I like the way Antoine is working" as an indirect demand—a hint that others should get to work. As long as teacher and students have a common basis for interpreting talk, students can understand that a statement can be a directive. However, if students come from a cultural background where authorities are expected to issue direct messages and indirectness is viewed as weakness, then the teacher's effort to preserve their face is ineffective (Delpit, 1995). Because the basic politeness system is subject to cultural variation, people do not necessarily know how others intend their words to be taken.

Another theoretical framework, closely related to the politeness framework, focuses on cultural difference in showing consideration for others. Tannen (2005) has shown that people show consideration for each other in two quite different, general ways, and that cultural groups generally place different values on these approaches. One kind of considerateness stems from a desire for interpersonal involvement that motivates speakers to show friendliness and enthusiasm for each other's talk. Some groups do this by talking fast and loudly, by giving a lot of nonverbal and verbal feedback while the other person is talking—"Yeah, yeah, yeah," "Uh-huh," "Right," "I'm telling you"—by latching their talk immediately onto the previous speaker's talk, or by overlapping it with talk that extends the topic. They may respond to another's story by offering one of their own on the same topic.

The other kind of considerateness is deference-based. Following this principle, speakers maintain some social distance to avoid trampling on each other's conversational toes. They generally leave somewhat longer pauses between turns at talk. For them, overlapping is interrupting. They stop talking if another person overlaps them, or they mark the overlap as competitive by outshouting the speaker who appears to be usurping their turn. They ask leading questions to evoke co-conversationalists' stories. Although individuals observe both the involvement and the deference principles at different times, the cultural group to which they belong may generally encourage one kind of considerateness over the other.

Different turn-taking behavior in classroom discourse is not all due to members' cultural backgrounds, but some patterns are rooted in different traditions. The pace of talk in whole-group instruction may be relatively slow when only one person speaks at a time, but it picks up when more than one student responds. Some African American teachers occasionally encourage overlapping and unison talk that is reminiscent of the call and response style of gospel meeting. In terms of topic, this highly engaging interaction is structured by the teacher, but the students participate in determining who will talk (Adger, 2001; Foster, 1995, 2001). What constitutes appropriate interaction, then, depends to a great extent on one's cultural background.

MAKING MEANING

Sometimes people tell each other to "just say what you mean." People have been led to believe that they can make themselves understood by being clear and logical when they talk and write, as if a message in one person's brain could be fully encoded into language, heard or read, and then decoded in the other person's brain. If that were true, people would only need to speak the same language in order to communicate. Conversational experience suggests otherwise. People often have misunderstandings, or at least conversational rough spots, with others who are native speakers of the same language.

Cooperation in Communicating

In order to be understood, people say and do things that will get others to recognize their communicative intentions, but they do not spell out fully what they want to communicate. They do not need to. Hearing what is said, others fill in the rest, using their store of general information and beliefs about the world, as well as aspects of the context for the communication. Hearers assume that speakers are generally following culturally based rules for conversation. Thus, conversations are meaningful because conversationalists cooperate with each other to make meaning together.

Each participant in an interaction is entitled to assume that everyone is following certain "conversational maxims" (Grice, 1975, 1989):

1. Quantity—Be as informative as is required by the conversation, but not more so.
2. Quality—Be truthful, and do not say anything that you are not sure about.
3. Relation—Be relevant.
4. Manner—Be clear in expressing yourself, brief, and orderly.

Conversationalists either follow these maxims, or they flout them in principled ways. A speaker who is clearly not following a maxim intends that others will recognize that fact and figure out why. In the segment of conversation in Box 3.1, the second speaker followed all of the maxims except Relation. Saying "Okay, I'll call Ann," in response to "It's snowing in Dayton," flouts the Relation maxim because telephoning is not relevant to snow. Here the second speaker signals to the first to fill in the missing information that would make that turn relevant. To understand the second turn as a coherent response to the first one, considerable background knowledge is necessary. If the speakers made explicit all of the assumptions listed in Box 3.1, the conversation would be absurd and tedious, and both speakers might feel insulted at being told the obvious.

The Role of Context in Making Meaning

In making meaning, conversationalists draw on aspects of the context for talk. Another theoretical framework for understanding how conversation works details contextual elements that could well be important to any interaction (Hymes, 1974). These elements, organized under the mnemonic acronym SPEAKING, are useful for understanding communication patterns:

Box 3.1

Ellipsis in Conversation
The following segment introduced a long-distance telephone conversation:

Ron: It's snowing in Dayton.
Barbara: Okay, I'll call Ann.

To interpret this talk as cooperative and meaningful, the participants drew on background information from previous conversations and shared history, as well as general knowledge about the world, such as the following: Ron is in Dayton, and Barbara is not. Ron is about to get on an airplane. Airplanes sometimes get delayed by snow. Because Ron's plane might be delayed, he might not get home as planned. Barbara is going out for the evening. Barbara and Ron have a baby, Meredith. If Ron does not get home, no one will be available to take care of Meredith. Friends sometimes help with child care in emergencies. It is reasonable to ask their friend Ann to stay with Meredith because Barbara and Ron sometimes care for Ann's baby. Although this list is not completely detailed, it suggests that speakers appeal to a broad range of unspoken information when they speak and when they interpret each other's talk.

S—Setting or scene
P—Participants
E—Ends (purpose)
A—Acts of speaking
K—Key (the tone or participants' feelings)
I—Instrumentality (the language or language variety)
N—Norms
G—Genre

The first letter of the mnemonic refers to aspects of the Setting. For example, the fact that talk is happening at school rather than at home or in the doctor's office favors some potential meanings over others. Focusing more narrowly within the school setting, talk in classrooms has a different context from talk in the cafeteria, even when the speakers remain the same. The social identity of the Participants is always an important feature of the context for any talk: Their status will probably be important for figuring out meaning, especially speakers' relative status and their particular relationships to each other. For example, when a teacher says "Jeffrey" in a classroom, it is highly likely that Jeffrey is being asked to respond to a question already on the conversational floor, to do something, or to pay attention. The same word spoken by a peer during a basketball game might carry some of the same meaning potential. It might be a call to get attention, but it would probably not be a way of recycling a question, as it is when spoken by a teacher in a classroom.

Other potentially important contextual elements are the Ends of the interaction—its purpose(s), its goals—and, of course, what is being said—the talk or communicative Actions. What can come next in conversation is predicted to some extent by the previous turn at talk—the act or action that was accomplished through speaking. The teacher's saying "Jeffrey" counts socially as nominating him to speak. We can expect that when Jeffrey hears the teacher call his name, he will be the one to respond, and others will wait for him to do so or risk being reprimanded. Moreover, what he says must clearly be an act of responding. For example, if a question or direction is already on the floor (e.g., "Let's see whether people had trouble with the homework"), then Jeffrey is expected to respond with a statement (e.g., "I couldn't do the last one"), a question (e.g., "Is the first answer 2x–y?"), or some other action that is relevant in that moment.

Key refers to the psychological state prevailing in the situation: If participants are excited, perhaps the one-speaker-at-a-time rule can be temporarily overridden, allowing students to call out responses without being called on. Instrumentality is the language or language variety being used—for example, written language versus spoken, a standard variety or a vernacular variety, or a fairly formal language register, as opposed to a casual one. Norms refers to the underlying interactive rules in play—for example, whether overlapping talk is appropriate; and Genre is the type of interaction—for example, faculty room chat. Thus, it is important to determining meaning in the "Jeffrey" example to know that this exchange occurs in a lesson, not on a basketball court. The acronym SPEAKING does not cover every possible facet of context in a specific way, but it does draw attention to a broad range of contextual elements that are important to understanding how people make meaning.

The importance of context is highlighted when people claim that something they said has been taken out of context, or when people try to tell about an incident that seemed funny or striking in some way, and the telling falls flat. "You had to be there" is the stock response because if you had been there you would have had access to the contextual elements at play. Context is not just a decorative fringe on the tapestry of verbal interaction: Aspects of the context form the very warp and woof as people weave conversational meaning together.

Figurative Language in Context

Not only do people not have to say everything they mean because they know unconsciously that the context contributes to meaning making; they can also say things that aren't intended literally, and context will allow others to understand their intention. Everyone uses figurative language, and most conventional figures of speech (e.g., *at the end of the day*) are understood by other speakers of the same language. But here again, there are culturally based differences at various levels of language use. For example, European Americans may say that someone has died or passed away, and African Americans may say that someone has passed. Conventions regarding literal meaning vary within cultural groups as well. Goodwin (1990) noticed that pre-adolescent African American girls criticized each other for bragging, but African American boys of the same age frequently referred to their abilities and actions in exaggerated terms. In some groups, any mismatch between word and deed is expected to be understated rather than overstated. Underlying cultural values often play a role in determining the situational appropriateness of literal and nonliteral meaning.

LANGUAGE RITUALS

Certain contexts call for highly predictable language forms and behaviors. For example, many cultures have ritualistic behaviors that are considered appropriate responses to death—patterns for what to say and do to console family members, and how to conduct ceremonies that mark the event. Common, everyday occurrences such as greetings are also ritualized. That explains why it can be somewhat difficult to respond when a doctor asks, "How are you?" as part of a greeting sequence. Even sick patients may respond with "Fine." Greeting rituals are governed by cultural norms. In the South, for example, greeting is generally more elaborate than elsewhere and more highly prized. Learning these rituals is an important part of language socialization during childhood.

Other rituals of everyday life that do not have labels have highly predictable interactional patterns nonetheless. Rituals that develop in families, to become part of that small group's unique shared interactional patterns, are likely to have a social group and/or cultural basis. For example, in many middle-class families, children are expected and invited to talk about their day at school over dinner, at length or briefly. Although they may have little to report, the topic is raised day after day because it is part of the family's culturally based patterns. This ritual can have several functions. It reinforces the notion that the child's education is an important family concern. It also serves a practical function. It provides the occasion for children to tell their parents any school news. In addition, when children participate in discussion with adults, they practice an interactive activity that schools value. Thus, the ritual supports the development of communication skills.

A language ritual of certain African American communities that has been widely described is called *sounding* (e.g., Labov, 1972). This game of insults, also known in some places as *signifying, joning,* or *playing the dozens,* usually involves groups of young males and builds from a fairly low-key exchange at the start to a point of considerable verbal creativity. The insults traded usually include slurs on the opponent and the opponent's family. Real proficiency in this verbal game is valued among members of the cultural group. Other examples of stylized language use can be found in storytelling. Distinctive styles of telling stories may characterize the verbal art tradition of a community (Scollon & Scollon, 1981). Their ritualistic qualities make these speech events easy to identify.

Schools observe rituals too, of course. Like families, which may have their own version of a general cultural pattern, classrooms may develop their own routines or their own versions of pervasive school routines, such as some kind of speech event at the beginning of each day (e.g., "circle time" in elementary schools). Some rituals involve both oral and written language (e.g., checking the homework assignment or reviewing for a test in secondary schools). All of these routines are likely to include some highly predictable interactional patterns and even recurring phrases and specific terms, although details may well differ from classroom to classroom. Students come to know the special meanings connected with these rituals and how to participate in them. When a teacher says, "I want you to be responsible for the material on page 243," or a student says, "Do we have to know the perfect numbers?" special meanings are being conveyed concerning what may appear on a test. Participating appropriately in a test review ritual requires understanding these meanings.

Not every communicative situation is ritualized, of course, but implicit norms and judgments about appropriateness guide interaction nonetheless. In less predictable situations, people make appropriate conversational contributions based on what they think is going on. Doing so requires making instantaneous, unconscious assessments of subtle modulations in topic and context. Some features of context that affect these assessments may remain constant throughout a conversation—perhaps the setting and the speakers—but others can modulate from moment to moment. A serious conversation can be punctuated with humorous remarks, or there may be some shift in how new speakers can enter the discourse. For example, teachers often expect students to raise their hands for a turn at talk, but at times they welcome spontaneous student talk. Clearly, something in the context modifies the speaker selection rules.

CONVERSATIONAL MISADVENTURES

Conversation is subject to misinterpretation by its very nature. The fact that talk is elliptical and that conversationalists must share general assumptions about the nature of the world and of the immediate situation to make meaning together opens the door to misunderstandings. In addition, cultural differences can cause difficulty.

Often when things go awry in an interaction, people recognize that there has been a misunderstanding and try to repair it so that they can proceed. For example, consider the following exchange:

Molly: The movers are coming next weekend.
Vanessa: But I won't be here. You know that I'm going to the beach.
Molly: No, not this weekend—next weekend.

The misunderstanding in this exchange results from differences in using *next* to signify the first weekend or the second one from the time of speaking. Such a misunderstanding could lead to considerable inconvenience, but it seems just as likely to get cleared up, as it is here, because people are aware of certain kinds of language use differences.

But misunderstandings are not always identified easily and immediately. Sometimes people realize that something has gone wrong in the conversational flow, but they do not know what it is and they do not know how to repair it. Sometimes they intensify the conversational strategies that they normally employ successfully, but the effect may be to make a bad situation worse. Investigation has shown that employers or school counselors who do not get verbal and nonverbal feedback, including eye contact, at the point in discourse where they expect it according to their culture will repeat or rephrase what they have said. They take the lack of feedback as a sign that the other person is not understanding them. That person, feeling condescended to, may withdraw from the conversation and thus provide fewer indications that she or he is following the speaker. No one stops to think that cultural differences in gaze and head-nodding behavior, along with the type and timing of a verbal response, might be working against them. Such communicative behaviors are so taken for granted that people simply do not guess that they can vary from group to group (Erickson & Shultz, 1982). When interaction runs into trouble as a result of culturally contrasting strategies, people can repair the problem if they recognize it. Often, however, they attribute the trouble not to misunderstanding, but to the other person's ill will or social incompetence.

In her autobiography, *Singin' and Swingin' and Gettin' Merry Like Christmas,* Maya Angelou (1976) gives a hilarious example of this human tendency to do more rather than less of some behavior that is producing interactive trouble—not in talk, but in music. Auditioning for a Broadway show, she realizes in mid-song that she and the accompanist are not in the same key; but instead of stopping and beginning again, she sings louder. The pianist responds by playing louder: "She would get me back on pitch or there would just be splinters left on the piano" (p. 124). The volume increases on both sides until Angelou triumphantly outdistances the piano in yelling the final note. What goes wrong here is much like what happens in conversation when speakers try vainly to get each other to play by their own cultural rules (Bateson, 1972; Tannen, 2005).

CULTURAL STYLES IN THE CLASSROOM

When members of a school community come from different backgrounds, they bring different expectations about language use that can trigger quite different interpretations of behavior. Lisa Delpit (1988), an educational anthropologist, reports an anecdote involving some White teachers who felt that a Black teacher in their school was very authoritarian. Speaking loudly and using direct commands rather than indirect suggestions (e.g., "Talk louder, Paula," is direct; "I don't think people can hear you, Paula," is indirect), this teacher struck her colleagues as displaying her power, rather than striving to create the democratic environment they favored. Delpit points out that the African American teacher was following a different set of interactional norms than the White teachers expected. In that teacher's community, authority is not assumed by virtue of status; it is created in the give and take of institutional life. In the school context, teachers from this cultural group act out their authority status in concert with their students, says Delpit, creating and maintaining a social structure that they lead and that casts children as students. These teachers are authoritative leaders, not authoritarian dictators. Judging from their own cultural perspective on appropriate teacher talk, the White teachers had misconstrued the social identities that the African American teacher was assembling with her students, the purpose of her talk, aspects of her oral language, the key being created, and perhaps even the genre of talk.

Culture creates lenses or frames for interpreting the meanings of interaction. When teachers and students do not all share the same frame, their reactions to each other's behavior can range from feeling that something is slightly out of kilter to gravely misjudging the meaning of events and participants' intentions. Because schools generally align with the cultural traditions associated with the middle class, educators may judge some of the interactional patterns used by students from groups other than their own to be deviant rather than rooted in a different social and cultural tradition and history. Such judgments can place students at risk for failure or make them candidates for referral to special education. The excerpt in Box 3.2 comes from an early, classic sociolinguistic investigation into the ways in which institutional practice may fail children.

Anthropologists and sociolinguists who have studied language behavior in multicultural classrooms have discovered how mismatched patterns of language use can produce discord and also how groups learn to accommodate some of their differences. For example, several researchers have investigated interactive patterns in various Native American communities where children do not participate in the classroom as Anglo teachers expect them to. Mohatt and Erickson (1981) noticed that in an Odawa community, turns at talk in group interaction were not controlled by one person. At school, however, Anglo teachers were accustomed to controlling the flow of talk in teaching and learning. The cultural mismatch between students

Box 3.2

Excerpts from *"The Logic of Nonstandard English,"* by William Labov (1969). Reprinted with permission.

In the past decade, a great deal of federally sponsored research has been devoted to the educational problems of children in ghetto schools. In order to account for the poor performance of children in these schools, educational psychologists have attempted to discover what kind of disadvantage or defect they are suffering from. The viewpoint that has been widely accepted and used as the basis for large-scale intervention programs is that the children show a cultural deficit as a result of an impoverished environment in their early years. Considerable attention has been given to language. In this area, the deficit theory appears as the concept of "verbal deprivation": Negro children from the ghetto area receive little verbal stimulation, are said to hear very little well-formed language, and as a result are impoverished in their means of verbal expression: They cannot speak complete sentences, do not know the names of common objects, cannot form concepts or convey logical thoughts.

Unfortunately, these notions are based upon the work of educational psychologists who know very little about language and even less about Negro children. The concept of verbal deprivation has no basis in social reality. In fact, Negro children from the urban ghettos receive a great deal of verbal stimulation, hear more well-formed sentences than middle-class children, and participate fully in a highly verbal culture; they have the same basic vocabulary, possess the same capacity for conceptual learning, and use the same logic as anyone else who learns to speak and understand English.

The notion of "verbal deprivation" is part of the modern mythology of educational psychology, typical of the unfounded notions that tend to expand rapidly in our educational system. In past decades, linguists have been as guilty as others in promoting such intellectual fashions at the expense of both teachers and children. But the myth of verbal deprivation is particularly dangerous because it diverts attention from real defects of our education system to imaginary defects of the child; and … it leads its sponsors inevitably to the hypothesis of the genetic inferiority of Negro children, which it was originally designed to avoid.

Box 3.2 (continued)

Verbality

The most extreme view that proceeds from this orientation—and one that is now being widely accepted—is that lower class Negro children have no language at all. … On many occasions, we have been asked to help analyze the results of research into verbal deprivation in … test situations.

Here, for example, is a complete interview with a Negro boy, one of hundreds carried out in a New York City school. The boy enters a room where there is a large, friendly White interviewer who puts on the table in front of him a block or a fire engine and says, "Tell me everything you can about this." (The interviewer's further remarks are in parentheses.)

[12 seconds of silence]
(What would you say it looks like?)
[8 seconds of silence]
A space ship.
(Hmmmmm.)
[13 seconds of silence]
Like a je-et.
[Like a plane.]
[20 seconds of silence]
(What color is it?)
Orange. [2 seconds] An' whi-ite. [2 seconds] An' green.
[6 seconds of silence]
(An' what could you use it for?)
[8 seconds of silence]
A je-et.
[6 seconds of silence]
(If you had two of them, what would you do with them?)
[6 seconds of silence]
Give one to some-body.
(Hmmmm. Who do you think would like to have it?)
[10 seconds of silence]
Cla-rence.
(Mm. Where do you think we could get another one of these?)
At the store.
(Oh ka-ay!)

(continued on next page)

Box 3.2 (continued)

We have here the same kind of defensive, monosyllabic behavior that is reported in [a psychologist's] work. What is the situation that produces it? The child is in an asymmetrical situation where anything he says can literally be held against him. He has learned a number of devices to <u>avoid</u> saying anything in this situation, and he works very hard to achieve this end. … If one takes this interview as a measure of the verbal capacity of the child, it must be as his capacity to defend himself in a hostile and threatening situation. But unfortunately, thousands of such interviews are used as evidence of the child's total verbal capacity or, more simply, his "verbality."

The view of the Negro speech community that we obtain from our work in the ghetto areas is precisely the opposite from that reported by [psychologists]. We see a child bathed in verbal stimulation from morning to night. We see many speech events that depend on the competitive exhibition of verbal skills: sounding, singing, toasts, rifting, louding—a whole range of activities in which the individual gains status through his use of language. We see the younger child trying to acquire these skills from older children—hanging around on the outskirts of the older peer groups and imitating this behavior to the best of his ability. We see no connection between verbal skill at the speech events characteristic of the street culture and success in the schoolroom.

and teachers meant that when teachers called on their Native American students, the students frequently remained silent or responded in ways that struck the teacher as awkward. In group work, by contrast, Odawa children spoke to each other about the academic task with ease. In this instructional arrangement, children's community-based norms for communication matched those of the school. Similarly, Philips (1993) found that in classrooms on the Warm Springs Indian Reservation, teachers faulted students for not asking questions and for not interrupting each other to get the floor. But outside of school, Philips observed, children who asserted themselves in the way that teachers wanted them to do in school were viewed as pretentious and bold.

Mismatched styles can cause trouble across educational levels. Thomas Kochman (1981), a sociolinguist, noticed that the students in his university classes used a variety of different interactive strategies in discussions, as did his colleagues in faculty meetings. When African American students and faculty members wanted to establish a point, they often did so with passion, using hyperbole, figurative language, repetition, increased volume, and a wide intonational range; but most European American students and faculty attempted to make their points dispassionately, outlining their reasoning, and speaking more quietly and with a narrower range of intonation. Not only did the two groups not see that their contrasting participation styles were a matter of cultural difference, but they also assumed malevolent intentions on the part of the other group—the kinds of intentions that they would harbor if they were speaking in that way. African Americans believed that Whites were hiding their feelings about the topic and thus attempting to mislead people and camouflage the truth. Whites felt that African Americans had lost emotional control and could not reason clearly when they were out of control. The one group interpreted passion as irrationality; the other group interpreted lack of passion as deviousness.

Patterns of verbal participation that have been learned in the cultural context of the home community predispose interaction in the classroom. Communicative behavior may be misinterpreted by those who do not share that cultural background.

Understanding Students' Language Behavior

Studies of language use in various cultures, such as those just cited, can be helpful in raising people's awareness of communication patterns and helping them look for cultural contrasts. Heath (1986) cautions that descriptions of middle-class children's language behavior do not necessarily apply to other children. Her study of working-class African American and European American children's language practices in the Piedmont, mentioned in chapter 1, does not necessarily generalize in all details to language behavior of other working-class children of other cultural groups or from other regions (Heath, 1983). However, it does raise the possibility that what teachers mean by *story* or other important classroom activities may be different from the meanings that children have acquired in their communities. It also shows that children have learned sophisticated language skills in their communities that may be different from those that school requires.

Profiles of cultural behavior associated with various groups have been prepared by professional organizations such as the American Speech-Language-Hearing Association and the National Council of Teachers of English (NCTE), and by school districts, but these must be used with caution. Examples and generalizations are unlikely to apply to all members of any group. Like studies of talk at school, these profiles can suggest ways in which language use can vary, but they should not be treated as predictive in any specific way or for any specific student. Moreover, children's language use repertoires expand. In research on African American children's narratives, Champion (2003) found that over time children learned to tell and write stories in ways that combined the variety of narrative structures and styles to which they were exposed in school and in the community.

Heath's work, and that of other anthropologists, linguists, and educational researchers, can be useful for opening up new possibilities. For instance, *Children of Promise* (Heath & Mangiola, 1991) outlines four programs that accommodate children's language backgrounds while involving them in stimulating literacy activities. Lee (1995) has worked with African American high school students on ways to use their expertise at signifying for writing and for engaging in literary criticism.

RESEARCHING CLASSROOM INTERACTION

To gain insight into their own students' language use patterns, which may include cultural or other group differences, teachers can conduct research in their own classrooms. Suppose a teacher becomes concerned that boys as a group seem to participate more in whole-class instruction than do the girls. In this case, gender, rather than ethnicity, may be the relevant basis for language use patterns. Concerned about gender equity and the history of girls having lower test scores in some subject areas, the teacher wants to identify the speaker selection patterns in the class. It seems that boys and girls get called on about equally, but by the end of a lesson, boys seem to be doing the talking, and many of the girls seem to be uninterested.

It is quite possible for teachers to study classroom participation and quite likely that contextual explanations for the patterns will present themselves in what is observed (Acheson & Gall, 1997). Patterns can be compared with what others have found about general tendencies of boys to engage competitively in public talk and girls to contribute more cooperatively in smaller groups (Sadker & Sadker, 1994). Studying classroom talk requires systematic observation and analysis. Of course, doing that and teaching at the same time is practically impossible. Partnering with another teacher or staff member is one way to make space for such inquiry.

Data Collection

Two good possibilities for data collection are videotaping the class or inviting a colleague to observe and take running notes about who is talking and what they are saying. Each method has pros and cons. Teachers who are accustomed to being observed only for evaluation may find peer observation stressful at first, and colleagues who are not accustomed to observing their peers may not know what to look for. But collegial observation is part of peer coaching, and many teachers have learned how to do it successfully. Without a peer observer, however, the teacher can experiment with videotaping by simply setting up a camera in a corner, focused broadly on students' faces, and letting it run. Students and teacher may be uncomfortable for a time, but once they grow accustomed to the camera, people will relax. No one else need see the tapes; if the teacher never comments on them, students are likely to accept the taping as routine. In any event, videotaped data is potentially so valuable as to be worth a bit of inconvenience.

Data Analysis

With dialect study, the investigator needs to look for instances of particular linguistic features; but in studying interaction, stretches of talk are of interest. When the research question concerns interaction patterns across lessons, the whole lesson will need to be reviewed in order to find those patterns. The teacher already knows that girls and boys talk approximately equally at the beginning of the lesson, and boys talk more at the end, but what happens in the interim? How does the teacher, as the general controller of turns at lesson talk, contribute to the shift?

Basically, investigators who use videotaped data watch their tapes carefully and repeatedly, noting evidence that could be relevant to their research questions. Watching the tape for the first time, the teacher makes notes about anything interesting, jotting down the time code on the tape to facilitate rechecking these segments. Watching it again leads to preliminary conclusions that can be checked by watching certain sections again. Videotaping another lesson or two will help to confirm, disconfirm, or, more likely, refine the original understandings.

Suppose that a teacher is concerned about David, a seventh-grade student who often seems to be disengaged. David never volunteers to participate, often mumbles something irrelevant when called on, usually turns in classwork that is only half done and mostly incorrect, and rarely does homework. The teacher is not succeeding in reaching this student, who seems to fade into the background. Are cultural differences playing a role in this student's poor performance? In videotaping the class, the teacher focuses on David, hoping to gain some insight into how he manages to remain invisible.

In reviewing the tape, the teacher notices that David slouches down into his seat further and further. Not once does he get involved in group interaction at his table, regardless of whether those activities are official ones. Occasionally he talks to the student sitting next to him, however, and the teacher wants to follow up on this. The next time through the tape, the teacher notices that David acts as if he doesn't know what's going on. When directions are given, most students look at the teacher, but David does not. As other students begin activities, David is sometimes still day-dreaming, sometimes rifling through papers on his desk, sometimes leaning on the table watching other students. When he finally does get around to the task, he leans over to his neighbor, who seems to explain the activity to him. The teacher wonders why David's significant lack of attention to the task was not more noticeable before. Another viewing of the tape allows her to compare David's participation to that of other students. Most do attend to teacher instructions, and when they are lost or off-task, their behaviors are eye-catching. They get involved in off-task behavior with others or they call out to the teacher. They wave their hands and lean into the interaction, but David shrinks away from it.

This example of the analytic process involves first noticing something as simple as David's posture and then making comparisons with other students' behavior to identify how he opts out. Noticing that he is not working raises the question of whether he knows what to do, which leads the analyst to locate a point in the tape where directions are being given and to focus in on David's behavior there. There is every suggestion that he is not attending to directions: He gazes into space, slouches further, taps his pencil on his desk. Having found a trouble spot, the teacher consults with a colleague who is more familiar with David's background. She learns that he has not acquired strong academic language skills in English, his second language. Other teachers have suspected a learning disability, but the school has not been able to test him appropriately.

As a result, the teacher resolves to insist on drawing David into class activity. She modifies the way she gives directions. She captures everyone's attention, including David's, by using more direct strategies and repeating them: "Look at me, everyone. Put your pencils down. Sit up straight, and listen while I tell you what to do." Although such directness may seem overbearing and even face-threatening to the teacher, direct attention-getting is appropriate and expected for students from David's background.

In this case, the analyst focuses on the structure of lessons (teacher direction-giving, followed by student lesson activity). In another case, finer details of interaction might be important. In a study of a student who had poor reading comprehension, some of the student's miscues seemed to be due to the teacher's turn-taking behavior. Whenever the student paused during oral reading, the teacher immediately offered prompts that often provoked outlandish responses from the student. The teacher's culturally based turn-taking behavior depended on shorter pauses than the student expected, based again on cultural background (Adger, 2001).

When conducting action research in one's own classroom, there are opportunities for informal data gathering. The teacher can become more observant of certain kinds of classroom happenings with or without videotapes. In the gender-based response example, the teacher might begin to sense the point at which girls stop volunteering or to see the more assertive body language accompanying boys' requests for a turn. The data-gathering task might shift as a search for solutions starts to take over. The teacher may observe that girls are more active in cooperative learning groups than they are when class members are competing for the one chance to respond in whole-group instruction. With this realization, the teacher can try out some different social structures for learning, such as having students work in pairs on short tasks or in groups on longer ones. Videotaping can be resumed at any time—or not. It is wise to save tapes and analytic notes, however, in case different questions arise later on.

The analytic path may take various turns in action research, as is typical of descriptive study. The general route is to pose a question, gather relevant data, examine it in as open-ended a manner as possible, look for recurring patterns, gather more data, and refine the pattern descriptions. Action research is practically oriented, but it requires careful, thorough investigation (Mills, 2000). Practitioners must strive to view their own communicative behavior as an element of the action, rather than a fixed feature. A particular challenge is to view one's own behavior objectively. Action research questions arise in practice, and the analysis motivates change.

For teacher research to be successful, it is important to have a clear objective in mind, allowing for change as understandings grow richer. The SPEAKING classification of contextual factors can encourage the analyst to take into account the broad range of elements that contribute to communication. Figuring out what aspects of the setting are important can be useful. For example, it may be that students in one part of the room are more active than those in another. Repeated viewing may reveal that the teacher turns toward that side of the room more than to the other.

Action research need not be a solitary enterprise. Published studies on language use in the cultural group of interest can be helpful—not because they will directly answer the research question, but because they may suggest direction. Action research is frequently conducted by teachers working together. Conferring with a colleague during the research process can be stimulating and helpful. In fact, teacher research on contrasting language use patterns within a school can be a productive professional development activity, either on its own or in concert with school renewal projects. Those who choose that work are likely to gain considerable insight into their students and their own professional practice, and they may be willing to share their knowledge and research skills with others.

LIVING WITH LANGUAGE BEHAVIOR DIFFERENCES

In the face of diverse communicative styles, schools may try to identify some basic guidelines for classroom interaction that all students need to follow. The following list, which was posted in an elementary classroom, exemplifies.

CLASSROOM RULES

We will:

1. Enter the room quickly and quietly and take our seats.

2. Look and listen for instructions.
3. Begin work on time.
4. Work carefully and quietly.
5. Respect others.
6. Raise our hands and wait if we have a question or contribution.

These formal guidelines are different from the unconscious interactional rules of culture with which this chapter has been concerned. For one thing, these rules are prescriptive rather than descriptive of the patterns that actually underlie social interaction in most classrooms. They are intended to restrict student talk rather than to facilitate interaction. They predict that students will talk only when the teacher calls on them. Actually, in successful, exciting, teacher-led lessons, teachers are likely to reward spontaneous student contributions. Certainly, there are some basic interactional guidelines for school behavior that all students have to follow, but if such guidelines aimed at repressing talk were actually enforced, they would restrict the communication that is central to learning. Many educators say or show through their interactions with students that a more effective way to diminish communication difficulties due to cultural differences is to foster trust and respect. The checklist in Box 3.3 is useful for gaining insight into how students actually do talk in the classroom.

Although culturally based interactional style differences do get in the way of understanding, it is also true that not every difference is jarring. In one multicultural first-grade classroom, it became clear that two friends—an African American and a Vietnamese American—had quite different argument participation strategies, but that their styles seemed not to conflict (Adger, 1986). The African American boy protested forcefully when other students offended him and continued protesting vigorously to win the argument, whereas the Vietnamese American boy used language to defuse a confrontation. The fact that the boys seemed to have different conversational goals may have made it possible for each to find satisfaction in their arguments with each other. The African American boy could always get the last word because the Vietnamese American boy did not want it, and the Vietnamese American boy could defuse the argument by not seeking to win it. There was also evidence that the children gradually accommodated to the contrasts in each others' interactional style.

Recognizing the human propensity to prefer the familiar and be wary of the strange, it is no wonder that people often evaluate others' cultural styles negatively. Members of dominant sociocultural groups typically have less experience with the interactional ways of the nondominant groups, and they may feel uncomfortable, bewildered, and dismayed in social settings where they are in the minority—whereas members of nondominant groups are more likely to have facility with the cultural language use conventions

Box 3.3

Checklist for Language Use in Classrooms

Culturally based differences in communicating may exist in many areas of language use. This list suggests some important ones. Categories overlap.

Objective: Determine whether there is a possibility for misunderstanding based on cultural contrasts in the following areas:

Classroom Speech Acts
Explaining: giving an account
Reporting: giving information
Requesting: asking for actions, items, or information
Directing: telling someone to do something
Commenting: volunteering a remark
Greeting: acknowledging another's presence
radicting
ining to take action
nmitting to an action
g: expressing approval
egretfully acknowledging an offense
cting to an offense

propriately in Interaction
is defined within cultures according to social factors such as the relative age and role status of speaker and hearer, situational factors such as setting, and communication factors such as speakers' intentions and immediate linguistic environment.

Attending
Gaze and other nonverbal behavior
Verbal feedback ("Uh-huh," "Um")
Remaining silent

Responding
Volunteering relevant talk
Replying when nominated
Requesting clarification
Producing a speech act or other act appropriate to the preceding speech act

(continued on next page)

Box 3.3 (continued)

Turn-taking
　　Talking at appropriate points in discourse
　　Providing wait time

Maintaining and changing topics
　　Producing talk that is relevant
　　Introducing topic change; picking up on topic change

Narrating
　　Producing a story

Giving reports
　　Presenting known information
　　Presenting novel information

General Sociolinguistic Considerations
Directness/indirectness
Address terms
Nonverbal behavior
Paralinguistics: volume, pitch, tone, voice quality, and so on
Relative focus on passion versus dispassion
Appropriateness of topics

of the majority. People can increase their understanding of others' ways through formal study and informal observation of their own interactions in the multicultural society.

FURTHER STUDY

Heath, S. B. (1983). *Ways with words: Language, life, and work in communities and class-rooms*. New York: Cambridge University Press.
　　An ethnographic study of two different Southern communities and how language functions in the community and in the school, this classic study provides important background for understanding many of the attitudes and approaches to language revealed by children from vernacular-speaking backgrounds, with significant implications for the role of educators.
Morgan, M. (2002). *Language, power and discourse in African American culture*. New York: Cambridge.
　　This volume focuses on ways in which speakers display power relations and cultural identity in a number of kinds of talk and text. The author makes a point of demonstrating that language and language use is quite variable among African Americans.

Tannen, D. (1986). *That's not what I meant! How conversational style makes or breaks your relations with others*. New York: William Morrow.
Using scenes from everyday life, Tannen explores the communication ups and downs that everyone experiences and traces them to desires for both closeness and distance and different groups' ways of maintaining relationships. Although she does not specifically treat language in school, her insights hold for communication there as well.

4

Interpreting Language Difference

Federal regulations require schools to collect data on students' performance, analyze it according to various demographic categories, and report the results. Many schools elect to examine their data further, find explanations for the patterns that emerge, and use these findings to modify their programs. In the context of such efforts to improve schools, there are opportunities to consider the role that language and language variation play in students' performance, instructional practice, and school policy. As a result of interpreting their data, schools may decide that they need to align their procedures and practices with scientific knowledge about dialects.

Where does the responsibility lie for considering the influence of language and language variation? Traditionally, attention to language and responsibility for promoting students' language development has been vested primarily in English language arts and English language development departments. But the importance of speaking, listening, reading, and writing in all of the content areas is now acknowledged. For example, the content standards for math developed by the National Council of Teachers of Mathematics (NCTM) emphasize that students need to be able to explore ideas collaboratively and to explain their thinking as they do math. Furthermore, the National Council of Teachers of English (NCTE) and the National Council for the Social Studies (NCSS) both list dialect knowledge in their standards for what students should know and be able to do.

Clearly more attention is being paid to language and language variation in school than in the past. A greater focus on talk in doing math creates the need for math teachers to consider variable patterns in their students' speech and to examine their own attitudes toward students' language. More attention in the social studies curriculum to dialect as an essential feature of culture creates the need for social studies teachers to learn about language variation and language attitudes in the society. The same is true for English language arts teachers. With this increased focus on language in the curriculum, it makes sense for schools to coordinate attention to language across all of the content areas. Working together across disciplinary areas, teachers and administrators can identify the language use goals and the language development goals in the content area standards, and devise ways to share responsibility for addressing them. In doing so, they can focus on language variability in their own school.

This chapter and those that follow focus on the ways in which students' dialects can affect their school careers and thus become an important consideration in school improvement. In this chapter, we examine prevailing interpretations of language difference, especially the perception of language difference as language deficit. The view that variation is a problem—a pervasive, established perspective—depends on the illusion of a unitary English: the mistaken notion that there is one logical, correct form of English and that all other varieties are imperfect approximations of it. This attitude leads to the conclusion that speakers of vernacular dialects have a deficit in their language skills. That notion has permeated various aspects of education with serious consequences. When schools do not systematically accommodate different language varieties, some groups of students do less well in the gate-keeping activities that determine program access, placement, and progress. Standardized tests assume that test-takers are proficient in Standard English, and proficiency in other dialects may be defined by standardized measures as a disability. The deficit perspective on language variation affects many aspects of schooling, several of which are examined in the following sections.

PERCEPTIONS OF LANGUAGE STANDARDS

There is a widespread feeling that the English language is under siege and needs to be protected from public use and abuse. One recent guardian of the language was John Simon, who served as theater critic at *New York Magazine* for many years and frequently offered critique on people's use of English. In the PBS program, *Do You Speak American?* (2005), Simon tells host Robert MacNeil that the state of American English today is "unhealthy, poor, sad, depressing, and probably fairly hopeless."

The notion that English is declining is also articulated by others in positions of influence, including some teachers, professors, and other educators. Because these people's own use of language is generally accepted and even admired, they may be considered to be language experts even if they have not actually studied language structure. Thus, their opinions carry weight.

Concerns about the state of the language are not at all new. Periodically, there are major outcries about the supposed misuse of the language, part of a long and very human tradition of insecurity about language. Thomas Sheridan wrote in the 1780 *General Diction of the English Language* (unpaginated) that "some of our most celebrated writers, and such as hitherto passed for our English classics, have been guilty of great solecisms, inaccuracies, and even grammatical improprieties" (cited in Battistella, 2005). At one time, only Latin was considered to be a worthwhile language by scholars and European society at large. The vernaculars spoken in various areas of Europe (which developed into languages such as French and Spanish) were considered to be vulgar forms of speech and certainly not fit to be written down.

Today's critics also decry what they see as a failure to maintain the rules of Standard English in the speech and writing of various segments of our society. Those who take this stance lack an understanding of two basic characteristics of language (all languages, not just English). First, there are a number of different dialects of the language, all of which have been shown to be equally logical and patterned, but they are not all standard dialects (i.e., they are not all equally valued by society). Typically, speech and writing that do not reflect the rules of Standard English are governed by the rules of some other dialect. Language performance that reflects the rules of vernacular dialects does not signal decay in the language; rather, it signals the health of vernacular varieties of the language.

The second characteristic of language that critics overlook is that languages are constantly changing. Evaluation of various language varieties is part of that process. Research on the history of language shows clearly that language change is inevitable. Just as today's English has evolved from the English of Shakespeare's time, which evolved from the English of Chaucer's time and earlier, the language is evolving right now toward some future form that will be just as different from today's version. One typical reaction to change is resistance. Speakers may feel that the new alternatives being introduced are not as good as the old ones. Change, in itself, however, is neither inherently good nor inherently bad.

Critics also see language decline in evidence related to directness/indirectness in language use. When an indirect usage arises, it may exist along with another expression (as *physically challenged* and *physically disabled*), or it may even replace another term in people's language use (*crippled* has become highly stigmatized). In the vast majority of cases, however, the resources for saying things in different ways remain available, and thus the language is not diminished. If our language limited us to saying *previously owned vehicle* rather than *used car*, for example, we might say that the power of the language had been lessened when the new term arose because we could no longer express the concept directly. Far from reflecting decline in the language, indirectness shows linguistic resources being used imaginatively.

The possibility of speaking indirectly enables speakers to send meta-messages about their stance toward their topics and their listeners/readers. For example, the term *handicapped children* was changed to *individuals with disabilities* with the federal reauthorization of special education in 1992 as the result of efforts by disabilities rights advocates to put more focus on the individual than on the disability. The term *disabilities* avoided negative connotations associated with *handicapped*. Because both terms still exist in the language, using the less direct *individuals with disabilities* allows the speaker to show solidarity with those who prefer that term. Using *handicap* is also meaningful: It can show lack of familiarity with the politics of disability or distrust of "politically correct" language.

ARE STUDENTS' LANGUAGE SKILLS DECLINING?

Critics sometimes claim that the nation's schools are not teaching students to read and write as well as they used to and as well as they need to. But The National Assessment of Educational Progress (NAEP), dubbed "The Nation's Report Card," shows that 8th graders' reading performance on this important test actually improved between 1992 and 2003, and there was no difference during that time for 4th graders. For writing, fourth and eighth graders' performance improved between 1998 and 2002, and there was no change for twelfth graders (http://nces.ed.gov/programs/cos/2004, retrieved February 26, 2006).

Another widely watched measure of literacy skills, the Scholastic Aptitude Test (SAT), showed declining scores between 1960 and 1993, when the average score on the verbal test dropped 53 points out of 800 total points, from an average score of 477 in 1960 to 424 in 1993 (Bennett, 1994). In 1995, the scores were recalibrated, and since that time scores on the verbal test have remained fairly stable. In 2005, scores on the test of verbal skills were four points higher than 10 years before (www.collegeboard.com/press/article/0,46851,00.html, retrieved January 7, 2006).

DIVERSITY AND TEST SCORES

Although the overall results of literacy indicators such as these do not support criticism of American educational standards, it is important to look at the performance of subgroups. On the 2003 NAEP, the average reading performance of European American and Asian/Pacific Islander students in 4th and 8th grades was higher than that of American Indian, Hispanic, and African American students. The writing performance of Asian/Pacific Islanders and European Americans in Grades 4, 8, and 12 exceeded that of African Americans and Hispanics. Nevertheless, an analysis of the NAEP data found that African American students' reading scores improved at a greater rate than those of European American and Asian/Pacific Islanders between Grades 4 and 8. It is not the case, then, that students' language and literacy skills are declining. That claim oversimplifies a complex situation.

An important consideration in the issue of the relationship of test scores to ethnic and cultural diversity is that tests are not always appropriate for all the groups to whom they are administered. The practice of using standardized, norm-referenced tests arose when the school population was more homogeneous than it is now and when there was more tolerance for imposing the dominant group's language and culture on other segments of society. Although test-makers have endeavored to accommodate diversity, there is still a strong expectation of linguistic and cultural uniformity in test development, validation, and norming. Rather than measuring what they claim to measure (such as intelligence or aptitude), test items sometimes measure instead test-takers' knowledge of standard forms of the language (Wolfram, 1976, 1983). This means that the standardized test may contain biases against various groups of students in the test population, resulting in somewhat lower scores for those groups. For example, this practice SAT item is intended to indicate the test-taker's ability to identify sentence errors: "The other delegates and him immediately accepted the resolution drafted by the neutral states" (www.collegeboard.com/student/testing/sat/prep_one/sent_errors/pracStart.html, retrieved June 18, 2005). For speakers of a standard dialect, the preferred response is obvious, based on the knowledge of language that they have acquired unconsciously. For speakers of other dialects, however, this sentence might reflect a linguistically well-formed language pattern, in that it follows a regular pattern of the test-taker's dialect. To respond correctly to the question, these students must suppress an answer that is based on their own knowledge of language and appeal instead to knowledge of external language norms.

Do such items measure students' educational aptitude? If *educational aptitude* means ability to learn, then a test of Standard English can in no way be construed to be an appropriate measure. Around the world, students learn in many different languages and dialects. If *educational aptitude* means ability to perform in institutions whose norms call for Standard English, the test might predict future success. However, considerations of educational equity demand that test-takers' Standard English proficiency be tested separately from their ability to learn.

DIFFERENCES AND DISORDERS

A mismatch between standard tests and students' language can put children at a disadvantage quite early in their academic careers. Young children who use vernacular grammatical forms—including, for example, multiple negation—or vernacular pronunciation—such as *d* for voiced *th* at the beginning of a word (pronouncing *they* as "dey")—may be found by screening procedures to have developmental delays. Children from Standard English-speaking communities may also use some of these same forms in the early years, but for them these forms indicate only immature language when they persist past the age of 5 or so. In other words, identical linguistic features give different evidence about children's language development depending on which dialect they are acquiring. Features that are developmentally inappropriate for standard dialect speakers may be developmentally appropriate for nonstandard dialect speakers. Educators of young children who do not recognize the details of language variation risk misinterpreting students' language structure, with negative consequences for their school biographies.

The key consideration in distinguishing between a language difference and a disorder is the language norm of the student's own speech community. Recall (from chap. 3) that a speech community is a group of speakers who share norms for language use. In a multicultural society, a community may actually subsume several speech communities. Individuals whose speech and language are not appropriate according to the norms of their own speech communities are the ones who may be showing genuine disorders. The most effective basis for discriminating dialect difference from language disorder comes from an understanding of normal language variation and specific knowledge about local dialects.

Teachers may need to be able not only to discriminate difference from disorder, but also to react to classifications and possible misdiagnoses on the part of others in the schools. For example, a student from an African American working-class community or from a rural Southern working-class European American community may use the form *f* to correspond with what other speakers pronounce as a voiceless *th* sound, when they say "birfday" (*birthday*), "toof" (*tooth*), and "baf" (*bath*). If this student were to be diagnosed as having a pronunciation disorder, the dialectally knowledgeable teacher could make certain observations that would clarify the situation. First of all, the teacher might notice that in the student's speech, the *f* pronunciation is used only in the middle and at the ends of words, never in the beginning (e.g., never "fick" for *thick*). Thus, there is a restricted pattern to the student's pronunciation, not a general substitution of *f* for *th*. Second, other speakers from the speech community in which the child lives have a similar pronunciation pattern in their speech. Considering these facts in conjunction with other knowledge about dialect differences, the teacher could conclude that the student was using a regular rule of the speech community's dialect and could argue against a diagnosis of disorder.

Speech and language assessment does not always take dialect differences into account. Therefore, scores on standardized tests used to diagnose language disorders may be a problem. Some subtests may contain items specifically designed to examine Standard English features; responses that reflect a nonstandard feature in speech would be considered wrong. Thus, a speaker of a vernacular dialect might get more responses wrong than a Standard English speaker simply because of the dialect acquired, not because of any disorder.

Other aspects of testing may put non-middle-class children at a disadvantage. Some of the most innocuous-appearing procedures for getting children to produce a language sample for diagnostic purposes may be fraught with sociolinguistic values that discriminate against their speech. For example, a friendly invitation by an adult to a child to "tell me everything you can about the fire engine on the table" is laden with implicit values about verbosity (the more you tell, the better), telling obvious information (describe the object even though you know the adult knows all about it), and the consequences of information sharing (what a child tells the adult will not be held against the child).

In addition to the items on tests and diagnostic tasks, bias may be introduced at the level of the norming of a standardized test. When a test is normed on a Northern middle-class population or on a population in which these speakers predominate, for instance, these norms may not be at all appropriate for students from a Southern working-class community due to language and culture differences. Some tests do provide alternative scoring guidelines to accommodate vernacular speakers. However, these norms are intended to account for speakers of that social group nationwide, and not all responses are locally appropriate. Bias at both these levels—social group and geographical region—is part of the reason that it is difficult to rely on standardized test results for diagnosis of oral language disorders.

Language at Home and at School

For all students, the school experience is quite different from the home experience. All children have to learn new ways of interacting with language in school. Typically, however, the home language socialization experiences of middle-class children prepare them to ease into school language patterns. But for children whose background is not middle class, language socialization at home is different, and consequently their language abilities are not as relevant for schooling. The reason for this bias, as suggested earlier, is that middle-class expectations and practices generally pervade schools.

Question asking and answering is one kind of classroom interaction for which early language learning may put some children at a disadvantage. In this case, the problem lies not so much with language form as with the function and use of certain types of questions. Mainstream children are usually prepared by their home experiences to deal with questions that ask for a display of knowledge that the questioner already knows. Consider a typical question from early childhood educational settings, "What color is this?" asked in reference to an object that is in full view of the questioner. Responding appropriately to such questions is considered an important academic language skill. But some students do not have much practice in this form of questioning at home because in their communities adults' questions more typically ask for information that is not shared (e.g., "Where did you leave your coat?") or they function as something other than a request for information (e.g., "Where do you think you're going?"). Children from these communities must acquire new responding skills once they get to school. Teachers who do not share their students' backgrounds and who are unaware of speech community differences in interacting through language may not provide appropriate help. They may even suspect that children have language processing problems. In schools with large populations of children from nonmainstream communities, early referrals for language testing are common. Problems inherent in testing such as those mentioned earlier make it more likely that the referring teachers' perceptions will be reinforced.

Early Literacy

Another area of school/community language use contrast that presents problems in the early school years relates to literacy. Many classroom activities build on literacy skills that children are assumed to have acquired at home (see chap. 6). Middle-class children may have many experiences with reading and writing before they come to school. For example, reading stories aloud to young children is usual in middle-class homes. However, in some communities, storytelling is more common than reading aloud. As a result of different experiences with narrative forms, children may have different ideas about the structure of narratives.

In the early school years, an important literacy activity is "sharing time" (or "show and tell"). In this speech event, students practice producing cohesive text, considering the audience, and using other skills that figure in literacy development. Students may not all be able to profit equally from this experience. In a study of sharing time in urban elementary school classrooms, researchers found that children's storytelling styles affected their success in the sharing time activity and their chance to gain literacy skills from it (Michaels, 1981). Specifically, European American, middle-class teachers expected a linear narrative style, like that used in books where events are linked sequentially. The presentation style of European American children generally matched this expectation much more closely than that of working-class African American children. As a result, the European American students received helpful feedback for refining their narrative style, but the African American children often experienced frustration. Their stories were likely to include several episodes rather than one, with shifting scenes, and they used more narrative markers, such as "and then" (meaning *also*). European American teachers treated these episodic narratives as poorly formed and attempted to guide the students toward the literate discourse model by telling them to talk about "just one thing" (topic-centered discourse). Such judgments illustrate the general problem of viewing some culturally based practices as deficient rather than different. Misunderstandings like this may serve to widen the gap between home and school experiences. As children learn that their language skills are less valuable at school, they may learn to devalue their own abilities and distance themselves from school experiences.

To test for an ethnic bias in teacher reactions to children's stories such as those that Michaels reported, other researchers prepared recordings of episodic and topic-centered stories told in Standard English and played them for students at the Harvard Graduate School of Education. As anticipated, European Americans preferred the topic-centered stories and found the episodic stories hard to follow. They believed that the episodic stories were told by low-achieving students with language problems or even family or emotional problems. African American graduate students did not make this distinction. Although they appreciated the topic-centered stories, they remarked that the episodic stories displayed good use of detail and description. A story that had suggested serious language problems to the European American graduate students was viewed by the African American graduate students as likely to have been produced by a highly verbal, bright child (Cazden, 1988).

Children's background experience with language and literacy remains a crucial variable in educational success, but one that may not be adequately explored in teacher education (Meier, 1999). Teachers encounter a wide range of language and cultural differences in early childhood and primary classrooms. When they share cultural identity with their students, teachers are more likely to perceive students' language use as appropriate and to know how to support development of the academic language skills that count for success at school and in other mainstream institutions. When teachers and their students are ethnically different, it becomes crucial for teachers to investigate the possibility that their students' classroom performance is rooted in community practice. Investigation, including teacher research as outlined in chapters 2 and 3, can help educators ascertain whether students' performance is due to cultural norms with which they are unfamiliar, or whether there might be a developmental delay.

DIALECT DIFFERENCES AND CURRICULUM CONTENT

Fields of study typically develop specialized language uses. All students, regardless of dialect background, must acquire the "language of mathematics" or the "language of science," in the sense that they must learn the crucial special conventions of language use peculiar to the field. Neither standard dialect nor vernacular dialect speakers go around uttering comparisons such as "one fifth as many as" or "the sum of five squared and three cubed is equal to" in ordinary conversation, yet such language structures must be processed and produced in learning fundamental math operations.

Recognizing that all students must learn a special set of language conventions for the various content areas, it is still reasonable to expect that the differences between math language and ordinary, everyday language are probably greater for the vernacular speaker than they are for the standard speaker (see chap. 1). But the differences are a matter of degree rather than kind, and at this point we do not know whether the extent of the dialect difference is great enough to become a significant obstacle. Only careful, matched, comparative studies of vernacular and standard dialect speakers processing the special conventions of math language and science language, for example, can answer this question.

Given the importance of language in math and science learning, some educational researchers have devised materials to teach minority language students the conventional uses of math and science language (Crandall, Dale, Rhodes, & Spanos, 1987). These materials systematically introduce the language conventions used to convey operations and functions in these subject areas. Box 4.1 shows an exercise for use by student pairs. The student who takes a tutoring role helps the other student phrase algebraic expressions in common terms. Anecdotal reports from using these strategies are encouraging. Such materials should also prove helpful to majority language students who need to grasp these specialized language conventions.

Information about language and dialect differences is crucial for educators in every content area because language plays such an important role in learning. Whether it is a focus of attention—as in English language arts and social studies classes—or simply the vehicle for discussion, reading, and writing, language is central to the school curriculum. Students' language is on parade when they take part in learning and testing activities, and the stakes are high. Because of the possibility that features of students' language use may be interpreted as abnormal or incorrect when they are actually quite regular, schools would do well to examine their treatment of dialect differences and enhance staff understandings of what is normal.

Box 4.1

Sample Exercise on Language for Math (Crandall, Dale, Rhodes, & Spanos, 1987, pp. 130–132). Reprinted with permission.

TUTOR: Help your partner match the algebraic expression or equation with the phrase that best translates it.

EXAMPLE: What does x • 5 represent if x stands for the number of pounds George weighs now?

> A) George's weight after he gained 5 pounds.
> B) George's weight before he lost 5 pounds.
> C) 5 times George's weight.

1. If h is the height of the Washington Monument, what do you suppose h/2 represents?
   A) Twice the height of the Washington Monument.
   B) The quotient of the height of the Washington Monument.
   C) One half the height of the Washington Monument.

2. What can c + .40c represent if c is the wholesale cost of a wristwatch?
   A) The cost of a wristwatch after a discount of 40%.
   B) The product of the wristwatch and 40% of the cost.
   C) The cost of a wristwatch after a 40% markup.

3. If Harry has only dimes and nickels in the cash register, what can d(.10) + n(.05) represent?
   A) The number of dimes in the cash register.
   B) The number of nickels in the cash register.
   C) The amount of money Harry has in the cash register.

4. If an airplane can fly coast to coast, 2,400 miles, in 4.5 hours, what can the equation 4.5x = 2,400 be used to find?
   A) The time it takes to fly coast to coast.
   B) The average speed per hour the plane flies.
   C) The distance traveled from coast to coast.

5. On a suit priced at $180, the sales tax is 6%. Based on this information, what can the equation $180 • 6% = x be used to find?
   A) The amount of sales tax on the suit.
   B) The price of the suit.
   C) The sales tax rate.

FURTHER STUDY

Adger, C. T., & Schilling-Estes, N. (2003). *African American English: Structure and clinical implications*. Rockville, MD: American Speech-Language-Hearing Association.
CD-based materials provide an inventory of structural features of African American English for speech/language pathologists' use in diagnosing speakers of this dialect.

Cooper, E. J. (1995). Curriculum reform and testing. In V. L. Gadsden & D. A. Wagner (Eds.), *Literacy among African-American youth: Issues in learning, teaching, and schooling* (pp. 281–298). Cresskill, NJ: Hampton.
This chapter discusses the links between high-stakes testing and curriculum, research on poor test performance by some groups of students, and instructional and testing practices that would improve education for children from minority groups.

Craig, H., & Washington, J. (2000). As assessment battery for identifying language impairments in African American children. *Journal of Speech, Language and Hearing Research, 43*(2), 366–379.
This important article sets forth procedures for differentiating dialect differences from disorders.

Craig, H., & Washington, J. (2006). *Malik goes to school: Examining the language skills of African American students from preschool–5th grade.*
The authors' significant contributions to understanding oral language development and literacy skills among African American children is summarized. The book is useful for teachers, policymakers, and speech/language pathologists.

Fair Test Examiner
National Center for Fair and Open Testing
342 Broadway
Cambridge, MA 02139
http://www.fairtest.org
The quarterly publication addresses issues in K–12 assessment and other testing topics, emphasizing equity. The Web site offers fact sheets, articles from the *Fair Test Examiner*, resources, and links to other relevant sites.

Linguistics and Education. An International Research Journal.
This journal, published quarterly by Elsevier, covers all aspects of language and education, including dialects. Volume Seven, 1995, included two special issues on Africanized English and education.

5

Oral Language Instruction

Although all language varieties are complete and coherent linguistic systems, many people argue that the social realities of American society dictate that all students be proficient in Standard English. This position invokes central educational issues concerning language differences between groups of students. If it were possible to teach Standard English quickly and successfully to members of communities where other dialects are used, doing so might provide a rather simple solution to all the problems involving language diversity mentioned in this volume. If there were truly a clear-cut social advantage to speaking Standard English, then, after a short time, all students would share the same advantage. Problems of language interference in test-taking, writing, and reading would be eliminated. However, as might be expected, the answer to questions about how schools should address dialect diversity is not nearly as simple as teaching all students to speak Standard English. This chapter explores the issues related to Standard English and suggests some principles for program development.

STANDARD ENGLISH AND SOCIAL REALITY

A central question in any discussion of teaching Standard English concerns the broad-based influence of the home dialect. Can classroom instruction in the standard dialect succeed despite the influence of the speech of parents, siblings, and friends outside of school? There is evidence to suggest that it should. Children in families that move from one English-speaking area to another often adapt quickly to the regional dialect spoken in the new location, even when their parents maintain the original dialect of their backgrounds. Similarly, children whose home language is not English can succeed in learning English and using it at school and with friends while maintaining a different language with their family. The language context outside of school does not override the language context inside school.

But the social situation inside the school can be an important factor in dialect learning. If tensions between standard and vernacular speakers are high, then vernacular-speaking students have reason to resist the standard variety. If relationships between groups are harmonious and if the vernacular dialect and the associated culture are not devalued in the school and classroom, students may not experience a disjunction between home and school in terms of language. In this case, studying Standard English may not have a negative symbolic value that interferes with learning.

For years, debate has ebbed and flowed in education and linguistic forums, and in the popular press, on the topic of teaching Standard English. Just as interest in dialect issues seems to be waning, debate flares up again when a school district introduces an instructional program or policy related to dialects, as happened in 1996 and 1997 when Oakland (CA) Unified School District drew attention to its program through a school board action.

Some observers have opposed teaching Standard English, arguing that doing so is discriminatory because certain students would be singled out for instruction—those who do not already speak Standard English. Because Standard English instruction would look like remediation, others would assume that these students had some sort of deficit. These observers point out that there is no linguistic reason to ask people to change the way they speak. The only solution, they maintain, is to change society's attitudes toward various dialects so that all varieties of English are accepted.

Proponents of teaching Standard English, in contrast, argue that given society's attitudes, Standard English must be regarded as a necessary tool for success at school and in the workplace, and that schools should be held responsible for providing students with this tool. Because attitudes are extremely difficult to change, schools should provide high-quality instruction in Standard English, rather than waiting for social attitudes to be altered. Parents from vernacular-speaking communities typically expect that schools will teach Standard English because they are likely to hold some of the entrenched and unjustified language prejudices found in the society at large. They recognize the instrumental value of Standard English and expect schools to equip their children with the tools they need for economic success.

GROUP REFERENCE AND DIALECT LEARNING

For many years, schools have attempted in one way or another to ensure that all students speak Standard English. Yet many people who have gone to school continue to use vernacular forms in situations that call for a standard variety. We need to confront the relative lack of success that has typified both formal and informal strategies of teaching

Standard English. Why hasn't instruction in Standard English been more successful?

As with all learning, the factor that is probably most responsible for success (or lack of it) in teaching someone to speak a standard dialect is relevance. People are motivated to learn a dialect that they need for daily interaction. Group reference becomes a key element when need is understood from the speaker's perspective, rather than from the observer's. The desire to belong to a group whose members speak a particular language variety is a critical motivational factor for learning another dialect. If students from vernacular-speaking communities identify with Standard English speakers, the chances are good that they will learn Standard English; but if identifying with Standard English speakers and learning Standard English leads to rejecting the home culture, undesirable consequences can occur for the individual, the community, and the society. Students who have no desire to identify with Standard English speakers will probably resist attempts to teach them Standard English. African American students in an urban high school were found to resist speaking Standard English and other behavior that they saw as "acting White" (Fordham, 1998).

Showing solidarity with one's social and/or ethnic group can be an important motivation for using a vernacular dialect. In fact the power of language choice in conveying solidarity is so strong that people who are not fully proficient in a vernacular dialect may use certain of its highly salient structures, intonation patterns, vocal quality, or vocabulary to signal their social loyalties. For example, people of Southern origin living outside the South may continue to use regional dialect vocabulary (e.g., *y'all* for the plural *you*; *fixin' to*, instead of *about to*) to show affinity with other Southerners.

Students' relationships with their home communities, then, play an important role in language learning and language resistance. They must continue to interact and participate appropriately in the home setting and with peer groups. To maintain these important ties, they need to retain the ability to interact in the native dialect.

POSITIONS ON DIALECTS AND DIALECT EDUCATION

In light of all these issues, several professional organizations have issued position statements in an effort to help educators take action with respect to dialect differences. A subdivision of the National Council of Teachers of English (NCTE), the College Composition and Communication Conference (CCCC), adopted a strong position on students' dialect rights, which was modified and adopted by the larger group. The NCTE statement follows:

> Resolved, that the National Council of Teachers of English affirm the students' right to their own language—to the dialect that expresses their family and community identity, the idiolect that expresses their unique personal identity;
>
> That NCTE affirm the responsibility of all teachers of English to assist all students in the development of their ability to speak and write better, whatever their dialects;
>
> That NCTE affirm the responsibility of all teachers to provide opportunities for clear and cogent expression of ideas in writing, and to provide the opportunity for students to learn the conventions of what has been called written edited American English; and
>
> That NCTE affirm strongly that teachers must have the experiences and training that will enable them to understand and respect diversity of dialects. ...
>
> That NCTE promote classroom practices to expose students to the variety of dialects that comprise our multiregional, multiethnic, and multicultural society, so that they too will understand the nature of American English and come to respect all its dialects.
>
> (www.ncte.org/about/over/positions/level/gen/107502.html, retrieved June 26, 2005)

Although the statement asserts the rights of students to their own language and dialect, it also asserts that teachers will give them the opportunity to learn written *edited American English,* which is another term for Standard English. Here the need for linguistic adjustment falls disproportionately on vernacular speakers. But the mainstream population bears the responsibility to alter its prejudices and respect dialect differences for what they are—a natural manifestation of cultural and linguistic diversity.

Other language-related organizations have also issued position statements regarding dialects. The American Association for Applied Linguistics (see Box 5.1), the American Speech/Language/Hearing Association, the Linguistic Society of America, and Teachers of English to Speakers of Other Languages all affirm that language variation is normal and natural.

The right of individuals to maintain their own dialect must be balanced with the need for language standardization in the society. This conclusion comes not just from examining the situation in the United States or in English-speaking areas, but from surveying language situations throughout the world (Fasold, 1984). In all speech communities, there is a drive for standardization and a tendency toward social evaluation based on language differences. Resolving the Standard English debate involves balancing the

Box 5.1

AAAL Position Statement

American Association for Applied Linguistics
Resolution on
Application of Dialect Knowledge to Education

WHEREAS, The American Association for Applied Linguistics recognizes the legitimacy of African American language systems, variously referred to as African-American Vernacular English, Black English, or Ebonics, and their pedagogical importance in helping students acquire standard English;

WHEREAS, Public discussion of the Oakland School Board's decision on the legitimacy of Ebonics and its usefulness in teaching Standard English demonstrates a lack of public awareness and understanding of the nature and naturalness of different varieties of language; and

WHEREAS, Students' competence in any dialect of English constitutes an important resource for learning Standard English as an additional dialect;

THEREFORE BE IT RESOLVED at the general business meeting of the American Association for Applied Linguistics, convened on this 11th day of March, 1997:

1. THAT, All students and teachers should learn scientifically-based information about linguistic diversity and examine the social, political, and educational consequences of differential treatment of dialects and their speakers;

2. THAT, Teacher education should systematically incorporate information about language variation and its impact on classroom interaction and about ways of applying that knowledge to enhance the education of all teachers;

3. THAT, Research should be undertaken to develop and test methods and materials for teaching about varieties of language and for learning Standard English; and

4. THAT, Members of the American Association for Applied Linguistics should seek ways and means to better communicate the theories and principles of the field to the general public on a continuing basis.

inevitability of dialect diversity, the benefits of language standardization, and the sociopolitical realities that lead to negative evaluations of nonstandardness and vernacular-speaking groups.

POLICY DEVELOPMENT

A school's response to dialect differences in the student population ultimately depends on the values, goals, and resources of the school district, the school, the teachers, and the community. Each link in this chain is vital to implementing any programmatic decision about teaching spoken Standard English. Some school districts have developed Standard English instructional programs that use children's implicit knowledge of another dialect to teach the standard dialect. More often, however, Standard English instruction has proceeded from outdated curricula that treat vernacular dialect features as errors and attempt to eradicate them. This approach is problematic for reasons related to social identity, political power, and pedagogical effectiveness. To break this curricular mold, educators and communities need to examine current dialect policies and instructional programs and develop new policies that are scientifically based and socially equitable. Toward this end, several general recommendations can be made.

It is likely that school districts have implicit policies on teaching Standard English, although policies and practices may be different for oral versus written Standard English. These policies typically derive from the states' content area standards, many of which in turn have been built on or at least influenced by the NCTE standards (NCTE/IRA, 1996). These standards mention that students must be able to speak and/or write Standard English. At times, policy on teaching Standard English becomes a focus, as it did during the Ebonics controversy, and there is debate about whether to teach a standard variety and how to treat vernacular dialects. Obviously, these conversations may be difficult because language variation is linked to ethnicity, social class, and power—topics that communities may find hard to discuss. Nonetheless, policy development calls for discussion, and various stakeholders should be involved, including administrators, teachers, principals, parents, students, and employers. Whatever decision is reached about teaching Standard English, those who establish policy and set curriculum goals should be aware of the facts of their local language and culture situation and the consequences of dialect instruction.

Policy discussion about dialect curriculum should take into account the two perspectives on speakers from different dialect groups—the deficit position that sees dialects other than the standard as inadequate, and the difference position that sees them as equal and different. The fact that language differences do not represent deficiencies is an important premise for any educational program, regardless of whether the choice is made to teach spoken Standard English.

Policy development should also consider curricular priorities. Because vernacular grammatical forms are perceived much more negatively than most variations in pronunciation, a school district might decide that grammatical structure, not pronunciation, should be the focus for oral language instruction. Alternatively, the focus for Standard English instruction might not fall on oral language at all, but on writing, because the ability to speak a standard dialect may not be as crucial for students' success as the ability to use standard forms in writing. The following list suggests general language skills that students need to succeed in school and their relative importance (from highest to lowest). It takes into account the social consequences of using a vernacular dialect in a Standard English setting:

1. Ability to understand the spoken language of the teacher.
2. Ability to make oneself understood to the teacher.
3. Ability to read and understand conventional written English.
4. Ability to speak with standard grammar.
5. Ability to write with the conventions of standard written English.
6. Ability to speak with standard pronunciation. (Burling, 1973)

Considering the relative importance of oral Standard English for a given district, school, and community is an important step in deciding how, or if, it will be emphasized in the educational program.

Whatever decision a district makes with respect to teaching Standard English, the policy must apply to all content areas. It is confusing to students and ultimately counterproductive to demand one set of language standards in one classroom and another set in other classrooms, unless the reason for doing so is established as school policy and is sensible and explicitly explained. If the decision is made to teach Standard English in English language arts, as has usually been done, that dialect can be reinforced in other classes if all teachers share knowledge about the dialects represented in their school and all take responsibility for implementing the school language policy.

CURRICULUM DEVELOPMENT

If the policy decision is made to teach spoken Standard English, it is important to develop an explicit, articulated curriculum. General principles for curriculum development reflect the considerations outlined earlier:

1. *Teaching Standard English must take into account the importance of the group reference factor.* Students will not be motivated to study a dialect that they cannot imagine themselves using; but if they see that their own social group uses that dialect for certain purposes or that groups they would like to belong to use the dialect, they are more likely to regard dia-

lect learning as a natural objective. Attempting to provide external sources of motivation for the students (e.g., they will need Standard English to get a good job) is another way of dealing with this factor, but convincing students to study a dialect with which they do not identify at present is a tall order. One possibility is to organize a program of instruction in Standard English that is optional, so that some motivation could be assumed for those who enroll. However instruction is organized, the group reference factor must be acknowledged in order for it to succeed.

2. *The instructional program for teaching spoken Standard English must proceed from explicit curricular goals.* Two opposing goals are bidialectalism—adding Standard English while maintaining the native dialect—and eradicationism—learning Standard English to replace the native dialect. The ability to use two dialects to interact in different settings, called *bidialectalism* by analogy to *bilingualism*, is often presented as the most reasonable goal for an oral language instruction program that deals with dialect differences. Speakers of vernacular dialects learn a standard variety of English in school and maintain their home dialect as well. It is safe to assume that many students are still being socialized with the eradication perspective, but bidialectalism is the more rational and humane goal.

Developing an instructional program to foster bidialectalism is not simple, however. Such a program needs to demonstrate the value of different dialects and their appropriateness for different contexts—probably by including contexts where the vernacular dialect is more appropriate (e.g., talking with a peer about a problem related to a social relationship), as well as those where the standard dialect might be expected (e.g., explaining a proof in a geometry class). Exemplifying dialect shift according to context shows students that standard and vernacular dialects already coexist in their lives, including within the school setting, and it encourages them to note dialect shifting in contexts outside school.

3. *A Standard English instructional program should incorporate information on the nature of dialect diversity.* Any focus on dialect learning needs to counter the misinformation about language variation that often goes unchallenged in schools by including a robust, scientifically based program of dialect knowledge in the instructional program. It is essential in teaching another dialect to establish that both the native and the target dialect are full-fledged constituents of the American English family, with social and political histories and large numbers of users. To ground second dialect teaching and learning, teachers and students need a solid understanding of the natural sociolinguistic principles that lead to the development and maintenance of language varieties. Furthermore, students, like teachers, need to un-

derstand that a dialect difference in no way represents an inherent linguistic or cognitive deficit.

Providing students with background information on dialect diversity will underscore the social basis for evaluation of speech patterns and strengthen the pragmatic rationale for developing skills in a standard variety. Furthermore, because most people find dialect diversity inherently interesting, including information about a variety of dialects will engage students. Having students investigate different ways of speaking, including their own, can amplify their understanding of dialect diversity and demonstrate the integrity of their own and others' dialects as full-fledged language systems. Accumulating accurate information about dialect diversity is necessary to confront the myth that some dialects are deficient. An outline of a language awareness program, with sample activities, appears in chapter 8.

4. *Teaching Standard English should help students understand that there are systematic differences between the standard and vernacular forms.* Although younger learners seem to benefit from just being exposed to a variety of dialects, older learners profit from approaches that highlight some of the structural contrasts between the standard and vernacular varieties. Teaching materials for this age group should juxtapose contrasting vernacular and standard features.

5. *Instruction should begin with heavily stigmatized features.* More stigmatized features should be addressed before less stigmatized ones—both highly diagnostic features, such as "aks" for *ask* in African American English, and general rules that affect many items, such as negation (vernacular *I can't find none* vs. standard *I can't find any*). Similarly, because the deletion of the *-s* suffix on third-person forms of verbs (e.g., *She go*) affects almost all verbs and is highly stigmatized, it should be addressed early in the program. Less heavily stigmatized rules, such as the "in'" pronunciation instead of "ing," could be addressed much later.

6. *The dialect of spoken Standard English that is to be taught should reflect the language norms of the community.* Any program must be tailored to the community in which it will be used, so that it accurately presents local dialect norms. Standard and vernacular English varieties vary regionally. Thus, it becomes crucial to identify the local norms for both standard and vernacular dialects in order to present students with accurate, credible information about the language they hear around them. In chapter 2, we outlined a method for investigating local dialect features.

The goal of instruction should be learning the informal standard dialect of the local community, not some formal dialect of English that is rarely used in the area. This is particularly true for pronunciation features, where local standards may exist along with standards for grammatical features that characterize a wider area. Thus, the standard model of pronunciation for eastern New England will be different from that in Chicago, Illinois, or Raleigh, North Carolina. In eastern New England, the standard variety may include the absence of *r* in words like "cah" for *car* and "pahty" for *party;* in many Southern dialect regions, the lack of contrast between words like *pin* and *pen* or *tin* and *ten* are part of the regional standard, as is the ungliding of the vowel in *time* ("tahm") and *tide* ("tahd").

7. *Language instruction should address interactive norms that typify mainstream speakers, at the same time that it respects culturally based differences in interactive style.* Speaking a mainstream language variety includes using particular conversational strategies (see chap. 3) as well as the linguistic forms that distinguish standard from vernacular dialects. In particular, conversational routines for specialized uses of language, such as business telephone conversations and costumer service exchanges, involve behaviors that extend beyond language structures per se. In other words, using a standard language variety in a business telephone conversation involves more than just using standard grammatical and pronunciation features. It also requires that speakers know other conventions, such as answering the phone with one's name rather than "Hello." Thus, how a person uses language to communicate particular messages must be considered an essential part of language deportment along with the use of particular standard forms. At the same time, culturally based interactive styles must be respected for use in other settings.

A final issue for developing a Standard English instructional program concerns when to introduce it. The optimum age for second dialect learning to begin has not been established. Studies conducted on foreign language learning may provide some guidance. Because of the common assumption that children can learn some aspects of a new language system more easily than adults can, many programs advocate beginning second language instruction as early as possible. However, results of research studies have shown that this assumption is not always an appropriate guideline. There may be some language learning advantage in early childhood due to certain characteristics of brain development, but there are other significant factors that affect language learning in which older learners are at an advantage. For example, the influence of peer groups, particularly strong among adolescents, may be an important factor in inhibiting or favoring the acquisition of Standard English. The duration of contact with a second language system is an important factor, regardless of the age at which the contact began. In some situations, adults may actually be more efficient language learners. Older learners can be more analytic and may be better able to monitor their speech. Some investigators advocate postponing instruction in a second dialect until students can appreciate the social significance of different dialects of English, at about Grade 4 (Burling, 1973). However, if this approach is taken, there is the risk of negative evaluation when children use the vernacular, especially in writing, unless teachers are well aware of school policy.

Language awareness instruction in the primary grades can provide a good basis for Standard English instruction in upper elementary. In kindergarten, children can begin to pay attention to different dialects in the stories that they hear and read. They can talk about the general notion of suiting language to the situation and identify ways that language varies from situation to situation in the stories that they hear and read. From that stage, they may be introduced to learning Standard English for some situations.

METHODS OF TEACHING SPOKEN STANDARD ENGLISH

In the past, some approaches to teaching spoken Standard English as a second dialect borrowed heavily from that used for teaching foreign languages. In some ways, teaching a second dialect and teaching a foreign language are similar because in both cases the aim is to support students' access to another language system for use in certain circumstances. The learning contexts differ significantly, however, in that two varieties of English have almost everything in common, whereas two separate languages may have little in common. There is no need to learn an entirely different language system in second dialect programs as there is in learning a new language. Standard dialect instruction should focus on the particular areas of difference between the standard and vernacular varieties used in the school's community. This approach is called *contrastive analysis* because it involves analyzing the contrasts between the varieties. A systematic comparison of the local vernacular variety with the local standard dialect will reveal particular areas of difference.

In second language acquisition studies, an important distinction is made that is relevant to second dialect teaching and learning. This is the distinction between *language acquisition*, which involves the tacit knowledge of language rules that accumulates through simple exposure to another language, and *language learning*, the explicit knowledge of language rules that derives from the overt teaching of particular structures of language. Knowledge acquired through language learning comes into play primarily when language structures are the instructional focus, whereas knowledge from acquisition comes into play in natural communication where language structure is not a primary focus. In acquiring a second language, communicative fluency is the primary goal; whereas in second dialect acquisition, the consistent use of a limited set of language structures is typically the goal because fluency in the language has already been achieved.

The fact that native dialect items are thoroughly habituated has implications for instruction. It is sometimes more difficult to modify a small set of thoroughly habituated items within a pattern of overall similarity than it is to learn an entirely new pattern because modifying habituated items may involve unlearning as well as learning. Thus, there may be little alternative but to focus on the structural differences in the systems. If nothing else, specific attention to the structural details of dialect differences may prove useful when conscious attention to speech is heightened. Thus, attention to contrasts, either directly through contrastive analysis or indirectly through some other approach, is likely to be useful in second dialect instruction.

Instruction is likely to be most effective when it is clearly tied to situations of authentic Standard English use, and when it is part of short mini-lessons intended to promote expert performance in real situations. Consider a situation in which middle school students are preparing oral presentations. Several students use the vernacular "Here go my speech." Regardless of whether anyone mentions the structure during class critique of the practice session, the teacher can seize the opportunity for a mini-lesson contrasting vernacular "Here go" with standard "Here is" or "Here's." A direct focus on language structures is more likely to be effective when it is embedded within such situations.

One method of teaching spoken Standard English that does not work is "correcting" vernacular features. Piestrup (1973) found that vernacular speakers who were corrected when they used vernacular features actually used more, not fewer, vernacular features over time.

A more positive strategy is reinforcing and augmenting students' existing knowledge of the standard dialect. Activities can include role play and dramatization—having students practice using appropriate dialect patterns as they act out a part. They may plan scenarios in advance, or they may act them out on the spur of the moment. They can assume adult roles like that of a teacher, school administrator, salesperson, doctor, newspaper reporter, or office worker in which they must try to approximate the speech styles of people from different backgrounds as realistically as possible. Scenarios may come from real life or from texts the students have read. This activity gives the student the opportunity to vary verbal styles and deliberately switch to alternate dialect patterns. It also gives students practice for real-life contexts outside of school where the use of Standard English forms may be crucial, such as in a job interview.

From a bidialectal perspective, realistic role playing might also include situations where a vernacular dialect is called for, such as in peer group and family conversations. Identifying these situations calls for observational research because intuitions are likely to turn up language ideals that do not match language practice. When role play uses both kinds of English, the important function of each is demonstrated realistically, along with the fact that they coexist in the community. Students tend to be more willing to learn a standard variety when they see clearly that the solidarity functions of their vernacular variety are not necessarily threatened by the addition of a standard variety. One caution is in order: In instructional settings that include students who are monodialectal in Standard English, those students should not be asked to speak in a vernacular dialect. There is a likelihood that they will produce stereotyped structures that are not grammatical in that dialect. The use of role playing and dramatization, combined with a small amount of explicit instruction in Standard English structures, is a practical approach to giving specific attention to the use of spoken Standard English.

Identifying situations in which students naturally use Standard English features can show them that Standard English is already an important medium for them. Students can be involved in identifying Standard English situations at school—probably those in which they speak with authority on some topic (Adger, 1998). Identifying natural sites for Standard English in the classroom has several instructional implications. The teachable moment occurs in situations where students implicitly agree to use standard features, but encounter difficulties. Because no one likes to be interrupted with edits, the teacher can note potential problem structures and then conduct mini-lessons at an appropriate future time.

Teaching oral Standard English should incorporate several components. Some activities should be directed at sharpening students' awareness of the nature of dialects and developing motivation for enhancing their proficiency in a second dialect. Other activities involve learning which structures have standard and nonstandard alternates, and practicing their use in appropriate social contexts.

PROMOTING LANGUAGE DEVELOPMENT

All children need linguistically rich classrooms in all subject areas to develop expertise in literacy and in academic talk, the genre of language used in teaching and learning, and in business and professional settings. This genre contrasts with the language of interpersonal communication in that academic talk is often more decontextualized—less elliptical, less dependent on the surrounding talk and other aspects of the context. Meanings are usually made more fully explicit through words in academic talk. Language may also have different functions in academic interaction than in family and community interaction. For example, the request for a display of known information (the teacher requests the students provide information that the teacher already knows) may be more common at school that elsewhere (see Box 3.2). Some explicit instruction about academic language conventions may be necessary, especially in the early years and especially for children from nonmainstream communities. It is important, of course, to teach academic language conventions as an addition to community language use and to ground instruction in actual communicative situations.

Linguistically rich classrooms provide many opportunities for children to talk on academic topics. To make this possible, social interaction structures need to be varied. Whole-class instruction is generally not the most linguistically productive structure because it is dominated by teacher talk, in terms of both the number of turns at talk and the amount of talk that children usually do. Moreover, certain students tend to participate more than others even when the teacher does not privilege their participation by calling on them. Pacing in whole-group instruction depends on getting appropriate information into the lesson at the appropriate point. Students who are adept at doing this become more likely candidates for lesson talk with teachers (Erickson, 1996). With time, other students become less and less likely to self-nominate, and they may pay less and less attention so that when the teacher does nominate them they have little to say. For these students, classroom communication is a listening occasion at best.

Students have more opportunity to be active during whole-group instruction when the teacher varies the participation patterns. The typical classroom interchange involves some version of a basic routine—teacher elicitation/student response/teacher praise—in which the teacher has two turns and one student has one turn. An alternative is Think/Pair/Share (Lyman, 1992). After the teacher poses a problem, students take 30 seconds or so to think about it and a minute or two to consult with their partners. Then several pairs report their results to the group. The linguistic advantage to this arrangement is that because every student must engage in academic talk, each gets practice. A cognitive advantage comes from actively involving every student in the lesson, and a social advantage comes from involving students in constructing lessons together rather than listening passively.

Alternatives to whole-group instruction, such as various cooperative learning structures, allow students to practice academic talk. No particular dialect is associated with this genre. In small-group structures, vernacular speakers are likely to use vernacular features in discussing academic topics, although expectations can be set for them to use standard features when the sociolinguistic situation calls for it.

FURTHER READING

Dyson, A. H., & Genishi, C. (Eds.). (1994). *The need for story: Cultural diversity in classroom and community*. Urbana, IL: National Council of Teachers of English. This collection looks at reading, writing, and oral stories and storytelling as personal, cultural, and social practice. Chapters are organized into sections: Connections Between Story, Self, and Others: Why Do We Tell Stories?; Ways With Stories: Whose Stories Are Told? Whose Stories Are Heard?; and Weaving Communities Through Story: Who Are We?

Hynds, S., & Rubin, D. L. (Eds.). (1990). *Perspectives on talk and learning*. Urbana, IL: National Council of Teachers of English.

This collection includes several articles on dialects in school along with detailed discussions exploring the role that oral language plays in education.

Wheeler, R. S., & Swords, R. (2006). *Code-switching: Teaching Standard English in urban classrooms*. Urbana, IL: National Council of Teachers of English.

In this book, university professor Rebecca Wheeler and urban elementary teacher Rachel Swords describe a method of teaching about contrastive analysis and code switching as a way to foster Standard English mastery among African American dialect speakers.

6

Dialects and Writing

Teaching students to write is seen as one of the most important functions of schools. But teaching writing is hard work. Students bring a range of language skills to this task. For speakers of vernacular dialects, there are some special factors for teachers to consider in writing instruction largely because the contrasts between the language of speaking and the language of writing are greater for them than for speakers of standard varieties. This chapter considers a range of issues in teaching writing to vernacular dialect speakers.

ORAL AND WRITTEN LANGUAGE

The contrast between the spoken language medium and the written language medium presents several kinds of challenges for all writers regardless of their dialect. One challenge concerns the need to distinguish between features that are particular to writing and those that are generally restricted to speaking. Another is the more general challenge of accommodating the special communicative demands associated with the writing situation.

Developing written language expertise involves learning to make choices about style at different levels of language, including vocabulary, grammar, and text structure. One element of the stylistic contrast between spoken and written language relates to formality. School writing is generally more formal than both the speech style that students use most often and the writing style that they use in other settings. For example, the phrase *a good deal of difficulty* might be preferred in an essay or report over *a lot of trouble*, which is appropriate for a note or an e-mail message and more common in informal speech. The use of conversational features like *you know* and *like* is quite restricted in writing. In some school writing, it may not be considered appropriate to use the

113

first-person perspective: Rather than using the form *I think soccer is very popular*, a writer might say, *Soccer seems to be very popular*, or *It seems that* ... , and so forth. To become successful writers, students must eventually master such contrasts and understand the connotations of alternative ways of expressing the same thought.

A second dimension of the contrast between written language and speech is inherent in the circumstances surrounding the acts of writing and speaking. The two media place differing demands on the communicator. The fact that writing is received visually means that the kind of information that can be conveyed orally through vocal shifts in stress and intonation has to be provided in another way. For example, in speech, the difference between a compound word (e.g., *a blackbird*) and a phrase (*a black bird*) is conveyed by stress; in writing, it is conveyed by spacing. Similarly, questions can be indicated by intonation in speech, but they have to be marked by punctuation in writing (e.g., *Malcolm took the train?*). Writing involves a set of conventions unique to this medium—the mechanics of writing—that govern when to capitalize, place periods, insert commas, and so forth. These conventions are quite arbitrary, as indicated by the fact that writing systems vary around the world and different languages use different mechanical conventions, but learning to use the conventions of American English is a necessary aspect of learning to write in American schools.

The most significant contrast between writing and speaking situations lies in the role played by the recipient. In face-to-face interaction, the hearer (or viewer, in the case of sign language) provides feedback to the speaker through facial expressions and body orientation, through listening behaviors like *Uh-huh* and *Yeah*, and by commenting and questioning. The speaker and hearer align to each other in a kind of conversational ballet, each following the other's lead, getting and giving news about whether the interaction is succeeding (Johnstone, 2002; Tannen, 1993). If something goes wrong, they can adjust appropriately. In writing, in contrast, the receiver of the communication is not present in the same way, and immediate feedback is unavailable. Thus, the writer must take care to consider the perspective of this absent reader. If the reader is not well known to the writer, assumptions about shared knowledge that is crucial to interpreting the message may turn out to be ill-founded. Both for the child who is beginning to write and for the experienced writer, taking the perspective of the absent reader into account can be one of the most difficult aspects of writing. A young writer might report on vacation activities with *We went to visit grandma. Ginger went too ...*, without making it explicit that Ginger is a dog. One of the central tasks of writing instruction is helping children develop an awareness of the reader's needs and ways to accommodate them.

VERNACULAR DIALECT AND WRITING

Speaking a vernacular dialect probably has less direct influence on development of writing skill than was once thought. Speakers of all dialects encounter the challenges mentioned earlier as they develop writing skills. This does not mean, however, that the student's dialect can be ignored in writing instruction. In fact, vernacular speakers may have trouble in several areas due to differences between their language skills and those that writing requires.

Vernacular Influence in Writing

Although the research base is limited in terms of the role that a student's dialect background plays in the writing process (but see Ball, 1995; Smitherman, 1994), some observations on the dimensions of dialect influence may be useful for teachers. Vernacular dialect speakers may encounter at least three different types of problems in writing.

Organization or Progression of an Argument or Narrative. Organization problems may relate to culturally based expectations for how to tell a story or make an argument. Chapter 3 describes Michaels' (1981) research on African American children's episodic narrative style, which White teachers took to be illogical. If children write in an episodic style or follow other culturally based styles of oral narrative or argumentation, teachers may fault the organization of their writing.

Grammar. Grammatical differences between Standard English and the student's dialect may interfere in writing. The use of nonstandard verb forms, as in *The girl knowed the answer,* may come from a spoken dialect that regularly uses these grammatical rules. A student may write *a* as the form of the indefinite article before both a consonant and a vowel (e.g., *a teacher* and *a aunt*) if this is how the article is spoken. Similarly, the use of expletive or existential *it* for *there* in sentences such as *It was a new student in the class yesterday* in writing may come from a vernacular speaker's normal use of this form in spoken language. Vernacular grammatical forms in written language are highly stigmatized.

Mechanical Aspects of Writing. The fact that English spelling does not map onto the sounds of the language consistently in a one-to-one relation makes spelling difficult for everyone. Dialect differences, however, introduce an additional set of possibilities for spelling errors. For example, spelling the first vowel sound of *tinder* and *tender* the same way may be related to the fact that these words are pronounced the same in Southern dialects.

This would be quite similar to a Standard American English speaker confusing *t* and *d* spellings in a word like *therapeutic* (*therapeudic*) because the *t* and *d* are pronounced similarly in this position. This confusion would not arise for speakers of British English who pronounce *t* and *d* between vowels (as in *latter* and *ladder*) differently.

Difference and Error in Written Language

In the strictest sense, the examples given previously are not errors, but rather the reflection in writing of differences in verbal expression, grammar, and pronunciation between the student's dialect and the standard dialect against which writing is judged at school. One of the dangers of teachers treating the predictable reflection of verbal expression as error is that students may infer that their writing skills are inadequate and hesitate to use them. Also, they may make real errors in an attempt to avoid certain usages from their spoken dialect, a phenomenon known as hypercorrection. For instance, after numerous experiences with correction in their use of indefinite articles, a student might begin using structures like *an car* or *an city*. Such usages, which may also occur to a lesser extent in speech, represent an effort to catch potential errors.

The following paragraph, composed by a ninth grader from an African American working-class community, shows the influence of vernacular dialect. It was written in response to a teacher's question on a reading passage:

> I would prefer living the way the Hunzakuts live. because they live a whole lot longer and they don't have no crime and they don't get sick and if you are the age of 60, or 80 you still can play many game like you the age of 6 or 9 and don't have to worry about Cancer or Heartattacks. Its would be a whole lot better living their way.

Given detailed knowledge about the student's spoken dialect, we can identify some instances of direct influence in this passage. For example, *they don't have no crime* is an instance of multiple negation, a common feature in vernacular dialects of English. The absence of the plural ending in *many game* is also a candidate for dialect influence, as is copula absence *like you the age of 6 or 9*. These dialect influences can be contrasted with mechanical errors. For example, if the writer had written *your* for *you're*, as in *your the age of 6*, this would be a mechanical error. All speakers of English share the problem of writing words that sound alike but are spelled differently in various uses (*your* and *you're* are like *break* and *brake* or *to, two,* and *too* in this respect).

This sample of student writing also shows indirect influence from spoken dialect. Hypercorrection is suggested in the construction *its would be*. A fairly common feature for speakers with backgrounds like that of the writer is the absence of the *are* and *is* forms of the verb *be* in sentences like *they nice* or *she here*. It may be that this feature had appeared previously in the student's writing and was corrected rather frequently, resulting in the student becoming sensitive to the problem of leaving out those verbs. The unnecessary addition of *s* on *its* in the case of *its would be* may represent an unconscious effort to avoid the mistake of leaving *is* or *are* out, but without a full understanding of the structure in question. This example of hypercorrection illustrates that a dialect can influence production of written forms indirectly.

Writing samples from vernacular dialect speakers reflect only selected features from the spoken dialect; other equally frequent characteristics of speech are seldom found in writing. Some of those that do occur are apparently related to general writing development patterns. A study that compared a large amount of spoken and written data from both standard and vernacular dialect speakers at all age levels found that all writers, regardless of dialect background, omitted certain grammatical suffixes to some extent in early writing (Farr & Daniels, 1986). These included the verbal *-s* ending (e.g., *he walk*), the plural ending (as in *many game* from the sample composition), and the past ending *-ed* (*last summer she move to Texas*). For all groups in the sample, the suffixes were sometimes absent, but the frequency was much higher for vernacular dialect speakers, who also use these features in their speech to varying extents. Thus, the influence from dialect combines with a general tendency in writing development to produce a pattern involving nonstandard structures in early writing.

Paradoxically, some of the vernacular features that count as errors in school writing are typical features of the instant messages (IM) that have become a popular mode of communication. This practice lends a certain flair to IMing, which follows the tradition of using vernacular features to indicate distance from the mainstream. The language of IMing has been characterized as a threat to acquiring proficiency in written Standard English for students, but it is unlikely that writers would become proficient in this genre and not in others.

TEACHING WRITING

How can teachers support the development of writing skills in their vernacular-speaking students? Farr and Daniels (1986) suggest a set of key factors in effective writing instruction for secondary school students from vernacular dialect backgrounds, which appear to be readily adaptable for students at any level. Students should have

- Teachers who understand and appreciate the basic linguistic competence that students bring with them to school, and who therefore have positive expectations for students' achievements in writing.

- Regular and substantial practice in writing, aimed at developing fluency.
- The opportunity to write for real, personally significant purposes.
- Experience in writing for a wide range of audiences, both inside and outside of school.
- Rich and continuous reading experience, including both published literature of acknowledged merit and the work of peers and instructors.
- Exposure to models of the process of writing and writers at work, including both teachers and classmates.
- Instruction in the process of writing: that is, learning to work at a writing task in appropriate phases, including prewriting, drafting, and revising.
- Collaborative activities involving other students that provide ideas for writing and guidance for revising works in progress.
- One-to-one writing conferences with the teacher.
- Direct instruction in specific strategies and techniques for writing.
- Limited instruction in grammatical terminology and related drills, and ample use of sentence combining activities.
- Instruction on writing mechanics and grammar in the context of producing compositions, rather than in separate drills or exercises.
- Moderate marking of surface structure errors, focusing on sets of patterns of related errors.
- Flexible and cumulative evaluation of student writing that stresses revision and is sensitive to variations in subject, audience, and purpose.
- Experience in using writing as a tool of learning in all subjects in the curriculum, not just in English. (Farr & Daniels, 1986, pp. 45–46)

Several important conclusions can be drawn from these guidelines for teaching writing. One is that writing instruction for vernacular speakers should include all of the elements of effective writing instruction, and that attention to vernacular forms should be embedded within it. Another conclusion is that decontextualized skills-based instruction in written Standard English should be avoided, just as with teaching spoken Standard English. It does not lead to competent writing, and it alienates students who seek to improve their writing. The process approach to writing, which emphasizes language skills that all students can be presumed to have in rich abundance, deals with grammar and mechanics only after the writing is drafted.

We do not mean to suggest that teachers should not teach Standard English forms to students who use vernacular forms in their writing. There is fairly widespread agreement among educators and researchers that the ability to use Standard English for written work is an important skill (Smitherman, 1995). But writing instruction for speakers of vernacular dialects should not be limited to a focus on contrasting forms. Furthermore, dialect differences should not be disproportionately weighted in the evaluation of students' ability to express themselves in written form.

EDITING

The writing process approach postpones attention to form until the later phases of writing so as to encourage students to write thoughtfully and at length. Because vernacular features such as the absence of suffixes do not signal lack of conceptual knowledge, writers can make changes during the revision phase rather easily if instances of dialect interference are pointed out to them. As a practical matter, it may be difficult for teachers who learned to write in a sea of red ink to postpone editing, and students may be concerned with dialect features in their own and others' writing when they are supposed to be focusing on content. However, commitment to producing authentic, high-quality writing, rather than writing for display or remedial skill-learning purposes, suggests that editing be relegated to the back burner during the composing phase. This recommendation should not be interpreted as advice to ignore or downplay editing, but to convey to students that attention to the form of language is distinct from and secondary to conceptualizing and drafting.

Approaches to Editing

The classification scheme suggested earlier—text structure, grammatical features, and spelling—may be useful in identifying the kinds of dialect interference that may arise in students' writing. It might be adopted by students as they learn the process of self-editing. Understanding precisely what kind of difficulty a writer is experiencing with respect to stylistic and dialectal contrast, students and teachers can move more deliberately toward achieving proficiency in appropriate written forms. Teachers and students might, for example, prioritize their difficulties and systematically focus on different kinds of writing misfires at different points in the process of developing proficient Standard English writing skills.

Another technique is to focus on a set of related items rather than on every dialect error and technical mistake in each piece of writing. If possessives become a target of attention, for example, then attending to both singular and plural forms makes sense because these items are related.

To help vernacular speakers learn to edit their writing into Standard Written American English, teachers need to know the structure of their students' home dialect so that they can understand the reasons for the forms that students produce and help their students understand them as well. For example, a teacher in a Southern setting might have to teach the spelling of *tin* and *ten* like other homophonous words such as *two, to,* or *two*. The problems associated with sounding out words to arrive at their spellings do not appear to be that much greater for speakers of vernacular dialects than for other speakers. All speakers are faced with the conventions of English spelling where the sound and spelling relationship is not regular: For example, *could, tough*, and *though* cannot be spelled on the basis of sound. It seems likely, then, that a child who pronounces *toof* can adjust to the standard spelling *tooth* as well as another child who says *tuff* learns to spell it *tough*. Vernacular dialect speakers may make different mistakes in attempting spellings at various stages, which may draw undue attention to a spelling "problem." This potential difficulty can be avoided when teachers know the dialect contrasts that are likely to arise in their schools. The Appendix offers a compendium of vernacular features that teachers can use in developing a profile of the local dialect(s).

Peer Editing

Peer interaction can contribute to developing writing skills when students have been trained to critique each other's writing and to help edit out errors, when the purpose and the nature of the evaluation task is clear, and when editing is directly tied to a whole-class project. Peer editing can generate topics for targeted instruction on mechanics and standard dialect features. For example, if it becomes clear to students from peer editing sessions that many of them have trouble with possessives, as in writing *John hat* for *John's hat* (a problem shared to some extent by both standard and vernacular speakers at certain stages of writing), then this feature can become the focus of direct instruction and student attention for a time. This approach has at least two advantages: Contrasting dialect and mechanics conventions are explained in context, and students share in identifying their writing problems for explicit instruction.

WRITING IN THE VERNACULAR DIALECT

Teachers are being urged to give their students frequent and varied writing activities for different purposes across the content areas. Not all of this writing needs to be refined through the writing process. Jotting down ideas for a structured discussion, annotating written text, and taking class notes are all important kinds of writing that do not need to be refined into a final draft for publication. There is no need to demand that these forms of writing avoid vernacular features. Extensive experience with various forms of writing can help make students comfortable with writing and, perhaps, more likely to feel capable of producing polished written text with Standard English.

Choosing the Vernacular

There may also be occasions on which students are invited to write in the vernacular dialect if they wish to do so and to preserve these features through the editing process. For example, in writing personal narrative, students may find that vernacular features lend authenticity, just as they do in the writing of accomplished authors such as Alice Walker. By inviting students to use vernacular features in this kind of writing, teachers reinforce the notion that writers suit language style to genre (Bean et al., 2003).

In an account of a writing course that involved occasional writing in the vernacular, Irvine and Elsasser (1988) explain that they first created a climate that helped students understand the value of vernacular writing. Their method involved building students' awareness that their dialect was structured, not deficient, and providing direct instruction in some of the structural contrasts between the vernacular and standard dialects.

Dialogue Journals

One strategy to encourage writing without dwelling on form that has been found to work with both mainstream and nonmainstream children is the dialogue journal (Peyton & Reed, 1990). A dialogue journal is a bound notebook in which a student and teacher communicate regularly in writing over a continuous period of time. Students can write as much as they want about topics of their choice. The teacher writes back each time the student writes—often responding to the student's topics, but also introducing new topics, making comments and offering observations and opinions, requesting and giving clarification, asking questions, and answering student questions. The teacher adopts a role as a participant with the student in an ongoing, written conversation, rather than an evaluator who corrects or comments on the writing. There is no overt correction of the student's writing, although the teacher may model particular linguistic features or probe for missing information. The advantage of this method is that students experience writing as an interactive communicative experience in a nonthreatening atmosphere. They also write about topics that are important to them and explore topics in a genre that is appropriate to their current level of proficiency in writing. Many teachers have found that this opportunity encourages students from quite different backgrounds and with quite different experiences in terms of traditional academic success to feel confident in expressing themselves in writing (Peyton, 1990). Students who believe that they have something to say in writing tend to be much more motivated to develop writing skills that are commensurate with academic success than those who have not overcome the initial hurdle of finding something to write about.

ASSESSMENT OF WRITING ABILITY

Although errors in writing stemming from dialect features may be minor in terms of the communicative goal of writing, they often are accorded major importance in formal evaluation. Points of mechanics and Standard English usage are sometimes used as a measure of writing ability in state high school exit exams, putting the speakers of vernacular dialects at a disadvantage. For example, students' writing ability may be assessed in part by their ability to distinguish between the use of *good* and *well*, or the usage of *come* (*Yesterday he come to school*) and *came*. Such items privilege Standard English speakers and discriminate against speakers of vernacular dialects. In recent years, the multiple-choice, grammar-based tests that examine students' ability to recognize errors in Standard English usage and grammar have been balanced with writing samples. However, the grammar-based tests continue to focus precisely on those areas where there is likely to be influence from a vernacular dialect. Preparation materials for the SAT II: Writing test include the following sentences as typical items. Students are to determine whether the italicized portion is correct usage.

- By the time Nick arrived at the campsite, the tents had been set up, the fire was lit, and there *wasn't hardly* anything to do except relax and enjoy the mountain air.
- Both novels deal with immigrants from Africa, who, overcoming obstacles, advance *themself* in America in spite of society's unjust treatment towards Black people. (Ehrenhaft, 1994, p. 29)

Note the focus on double negatives in the first sentence and the singular plural (*themself* for *themselves*) in the second sentence, both regular vernacular features.

Bias in standardized tests of writing may come from other sources. Items written in a highly literate style, such as the following from the same SAT review manual, may be systematically more difficult to evaluate for students from some social groups:

- Although I wish it were otherwise, by this time next week I will have had surgery on my knee, which was injured during a hockey game last winter. (Ehrenhaft, 1994, p. 32)

Those who have less experience with text may have trouble detecting that the verbs in this sentence are considered correct.

Differing conceptions of what constitutes good style according to different cultural groups also may have an effect on students' test performance. For example, an item in which the correct answer requires the choice of "reach my destination" over "get there" appeals to a value on the use of a kind of superstandard English in writing. Thus, objective tests of usage and mechanics may be harder for students from vernacular dialect backgrounds because these tests tend to focus on points of dialect differences in usage. Alternatively, they may require choices based on language experiences that are not shared by all groups.

One might conclude that tests involving samples of student writing are more fair for vernacular speakers than those focusing on particular forms, but there are problems with this approach too. It may be inappropriate to judge an individual's writing ability on the basis of a limited sample of one or two short essays produced in a short time frame. Although this limitation applies to all students, there may be an even greater effect on students who must attend to dialect choices in their writing. If students do not have time to edit written work, they run the risk of including vernacular features. Depending on who is scoring the writing, the writer's use of certain structures that the scorer regards as errors may lead to a lower overall score being assigned, despite scorer training. For example, a rater who considers a feature like suffix absence to be a severe problem may be unable to see positive qualities in a passage when it contains such dialect influence.

There is also some possibility of cultural bias in the topics assigned by the test. For example, a writing prompt for 13-year-olds on the NAEP asked students to describe for a friend a reproduction of a Dali painting. If students could not imagine themselves ever doing such a task, they might not be able to display their writing skills to full advantage.

More holistic approaches to assessing writing skill avoid the unreasonable attention to dialect contrast, but they do not solve the dilemma of assessing writing development in a dialectally diverse population. They also do not necessarily counter the tendency of evaluators to assign lower scores in their overall assessment simply based on the occurrence of some nonstandard dialect forms in writing. Thus, the common but unjustified association of the appearance of dialect features with an inability to express oneself must be recognized and countered by those who engage in holistic assessments.

The classroom teacher is probably in a much better position to assess student writing development than the scorer of a large-scale test—both because of being able to track individual progress across time and because of knowing precisely which dialect differences the student is managing. Informal classroom diagnostic assessments serve to help teachers particularize writing goals for students and plan subsequent instructional activities. Portfolio assessment, a more structured approach, has gained a wide following. Students select some of their writings for teacher evaluation and defend them in a conference with the teacher, stating why they value these writings. Evaluation often involves rubrics, which may include items particular to the student's particular goals. When this approach is used as intended, students play an active role in assessing their own work and articulating their personal view of excellent writing, and teachers can track individual development.

As schools and school districts wrestle with accountability requirements, teaching writing becomes a more public and consequential issue. Students are writing across the curriculum, and their writing in subject matter tests can determine their educational pathways. As the stakes are raised, vernacular dialect speakers are at increased risk for losing out unless writing instruction explicitly addresses the contrast between their language and Written Standard English. The onus is on schools and districts to develop policies and practices that support writing skill development coherently across the school years and take students' diverse language into account in doing so.

FURTHER READING

Ball, A. F., & Lardner, T. (2005). *African American literacies unleashed: Vernacular English and the composition classroom.* Urbana, IL: National Council of Teachers of English.
  The focus here is on the college composition class, but the recommendations for teachers of writing are broadly applicable. The authors show how teachers can help African American students capitalize on their linguistic skills.
Farr, M., & Daniels, H. (1986). *Language diversity and writing instruction.* Urbana, IL: National Council of Teachers of English.
  This resource offers both a theoretical framework and practical suggestions to educators who wish to improve the teaching of writing to secondary school students who speak vernacular dialects.
Hampton, S. (1995). Strategies for increasing achievement in writing. In *Educating everybody's children: Diverse teaching strategies for diverse learners: What research and practice say about improving achievement* (pp. 99–112). Alexandria, VA: Association for Supervision and Curriculum Development.
  Clear and practical, this summary of current thinking on writing instruction does not focus on students' dialect, but it does concern teaching writing to students from outside the mainstream.
Haussamen, B., Benjamin, A., Kolln, M., & Wheeler, R. S. (2003). *Grammar alive! A guide for teachers.* Champaign-Urbana, IL: National Council of Teachers of English.
  NCTE's Assembly for the Teaching of English Grammar developed this resource, which concentrates on grammar in the context of teaching writing. It addresses dialect issues.
Shaughnessy, M. P. (1977). *Errors and expectations: A guide for the teacher of basic writing.* New York: Oxford University Press.
  This classic provides a helpful approach to the systematic study of writing errors. It is not specifically targeted for writers from vernacular dialect backgrounds, but there are many aspects of the approach that will prove useful to teachers of these students.

7

Language Variation and Reading

A correlation between social class and reading failure seems to be indisputable: On the 2002 National Assessment of Educational Progress (NAEP), "students from lower-income homes lagged behind their more affluent peers" in reading despite schools' efforts to close that gap (*The Washington Post*, June 20, 2003, p. A12). On the 2003 NAEP test of reading, the higher the level of poverty in a school, the lower the test scores in Grades 4 and 8 (the only grades for which data were available; http://nces.ed.gov/programs/coe/2005/section2/indicator09/.asp, retrieved January 10, 2006). We infer from this pattern that the likelihood of developing reading problems is increased if a person is a member of a vernacular English-speaking population because vernacular speakers tend to cluster in the lower socio-economic classes.

Despite this correlation, it should not be concluded that speaking a vernacular dialect is the primary cause of reading failure. There are many successful readers who come from vernacular English-speaking backgrounds. Research has indicated that African American children having higher familiarity with Standard English performed better on tests of reading achievement (Charity, Scarborough, & Griffin, 2004), but not all Standard English speakers are proficient readers. Speaking a vernacular variety does not inevitably lead to reading failure, and speaking a standard variety does not guarantee reading success. However, because the correlation between social class and reading achievement has persisted for some years, it is important to consider how dialect differences may relate to the reading process and how reading specialists, teachers, and other practitioners can take the differences into account. This chapter addresses questions about what teachers need to know and do to help vernacular dialect speakers develop reading proficiency.

WRITTEN LANGUAGE AND SPOKEN LANGUAGE

Learning to read involves learning skills beyond the oral language skills that young children acquire unconsciously, but readers automatically apply their general linguistic skills to the task of reading. To get meaning from the printed page, readers must be able to recognize the words they see there and employ their tacit understandings of grammar and semantics. Reading involves interpreting the grammatical relationships among the words on the page and figuring out the meanings of sentences and longer stretches of text, drawing on both implicit linguistic knowledge and general background knowledge. Theorists have disagreed about just how linguistic knowledge and oral language skills are applied in the reading process. There is disagreement about the role that relating print to sound plays in the process of reading, although it is clear that it does play some role.

Because the language of most reading materials is closer to Standard English than to other varieties, we might predict that it would be easier for a Standard English speaker to learn how to read these materials. However, the language of the printed text is not as similar to the spoken language of Standard English speakers or as different from the spoken language of vernacular English speakers as is commonly assumed. There are differences between written and spoken English that transcend dialect. Certain constructions used in early reading materials are unlikely to be used by English-speaking children in natural conversation. For example, adverb phrases are sometimes placed at the beginning of the sentence in books for young children, both basal readers and trade books, as in this sentence from *The Hungry Giant of the Tundra*: "On the other side of the river stood a crane dancing on her long legs" (Sloat, 2002, unpaginated). Similarly, primers sometimes show peculiar patterns such as the repetition of noun phrases, as in *The boy has a boat. The boy likes the boat. The boat is red*. This construction is quite unlike spoken discourse, where pronouns and other anaphoric devices are used for successive references (e.g., *The boy has a boat that he likes. It's red*). Regardless of their spoken dialect, then, everyone learning to read English encounters language structures that differ somewhat from the structures of speech.

It is still true, however, that the language of reading materials may differ more for the speaker of a vernacular variety than for the speaker of a standard variety. The vernacular speaker will find that written language consistently uses certain structures that are spoken only occasionally in vernacular dialect, if at all. For example, beginning reading materials use standard negation (*He didn't hit anything*) rather than multiple negation (*He didn't hit nothing*), which is frequent in spoken vernacular dialect. Thus, there is a contrast between spoken and written language for all readers, but the contrast is greater for the speaker of a vernacular dialect.

WHAT DO TEACHERS NEED TO KNOW ABOUT DIALECTS TO TEACH READING?

What particular knowledge about dialect differences is necessary for a reading teacher to work effectively with students from a spectrum of regional, ethnic, and social class communities? Researchers who have looked at language variation and reading have suggested, either explicitly or implicitly, several types of information. First, general knowledge about the nature of language diversity is required. Without understanding the systematic and patterned nature of differences, it is difficult to appreciate dialects for what they are—natural subgroupings within a language. A second requirement is insight into how cultural differences in background knowledge can affect reading comprehension.

Language Form

Knowledge about particular structures in the dialects that students speak, whether they are standard or vernacular forms of English, is as necessary for teaching reading as it is for teaching writing. This kind of information helps teachers understand why certain forms occur, where they occur, and how they should be viewed in the context of teaching and assessing reading skills. For example, understanding a student's oral reading performance might require knowing about the vernacular pronunciation rule that explains why a speaker would pronounce *tint* and *tent* the same (the absence of contrast between *i* and *e* sounds before *n*) and the grammatical rule that explains why *done* may be used as a simple past-tense form (as in *She done a good job*). Consider the following example of oral reading by a child who speaks a vernacular variety of English:

Text: Ruth's brother missed a game, and the coach doesn't like it.
Oral reading: Ruf brovuh miss' a game, and da coach don't like it.

Several items are noticeably different in the oral rendition of the passage: the pronunciations of *Ruth* and *brother*, the absence of the possessive -*s*, the absence of the -*ed*, and the form *don't* for *doesn't*. All of these contrasts are perfectly predictable in terms of the reader's spoken dialect. Thus, this rendition could signal appropriate decoding and accurate comprehension because none of the differences changes the meaning of the text. It is important for reading teachers to know how dialect differences might be manifested in oral reading so that they can anticipate dialect miscues that do not affect comprehension.

Information about dialect differences is also important for interpreting responses in student worksheets and tests that teachers use in teaching reading and English language arts. Consider, for example, the following items:

(1) *Choose the words that sound the same*: pin/pen, reef/wreath, find/fine, their/there, here/hear
(2) Choose the correct word to complete the sentence:
Yesterday he *come/came* over to the house.
He *done/did* what he had to do.

Because *pen* and *pin*, *fine* and *find*, and *reef* and *wreath* sound the same in some dialects, all the word pairs in (1) might be perceived as identical. In some dialects, *come* and *done* are the appropriate grammatical responses for (2). Students who make those choices could be reflecting regular patterns in their spoken language varieties. If teachers know about students' group-based pronunciation and grammatical patterns, they will realize that some of these responses reflect dialect features and will not penalize students for errors.

If teachers are not well versed in the specifics of how vernacular dialect-speaking children draw different sound/print correspondences than Standard English speakers, they may conclude that there is a decoding problem and place students in low reading groups. Once they are placed in low reading groups, children may fall even farther behind. The nature of the reading experience in those groups may actually make it more difficult for students to learn to read. Children in low reading groups are more likely to receive phonics skills instruction exclusively, rather than the phonics and comprehension strategy instruction that higher groups receive, and to be corrected for "errors" that are often attributable to dialect influence instead of decoding or comprehension difficulty (Collins, 1988). Interrupting reading to target a dialect pronunciation works against the development of reading fluency, a critical dimension of skilled reading that underlies comprehension (National Reading Panel, 2000).

Furthermore, the teacher may be more likely to be distracted by other activities in the classroom when working with the low group because other students recognize the low social status of poor readers (Borko & Eisenhart, 1989). As a result, children in the lower reading groups may experience reading as fragmented and boring, and progress at a slower rate than children for whom reading is more interesting. These students are often ones who are assumed to have less experience with print outside of school and, as a member of a low reading group, they may have less rich experiences with print inside school as well. In this unproductive pattern, vernacular dialect speakers may find themselves repeating skills lessons and basal readers, falling further and further behind other students. Eventually they may be diagnosed as learning disabled.

Knowledge about dialect differences, then, affects instruction and assessment in reading for those who do not speak standard varieties of English. In fact, this conclusion has been supported by the judicial system. In a landmark court decision in Ann Arbor, Michigan, in 1979, the presiding judge ruled that a school district was at fault for not taking the dialect of students from vernacular-speaking backgrounds into account in teaching reading. As part of the ruling, the district was required to implement a program that would educate reading teachers about dialect difference and to devise a reading program that would incorporate information about spoken language varieties into effective reading instruction for students from certain communities (Smitherman, 2000). This judicial decision underscores the importance of understanding dialect differences for those who teach reading.

Beyond Language Form

Information about children's cultural backgrounds can be indispensable in teaching reading as it is in teaching writing, especially when there is a cultural or social class difference between the teacher and the students. Cultural and linguistic differences are closely intertwined in distinguishing vernacular and mainstream communities. Two areas of contrast are noteworthy.

First, the background knowledge that students bring to reading can affect their performance because of the role it plays in comprehension. Researchers investigating this connection asked urban African American children and rural White children to read a passage about a sounding episode—an African American speech event involving ritual insults (Reynolds, Taylor, Steffensen, Shirey, & Anderson, 1982). Clearly, the reading was culturally biased in favor of the African American readers: As anticipated, the African Americans scored considerably higher in comprehension than the rural students—an outcome that suggests that some reading problems may relate to differences in background knowledge. As the researchers discussed the experiment with the African American readers, they explained that some of the rural students might not understand the story. An African American student exclaimed, "What's the matter? Can't they read?"

Another study showed that even highly proficient readers of English—graduate students—made mistakes in comprehension when they read a text set in a different culture. After reading a passage that dealt with an agreement about gifts that a bride's family would give the groom's family, graduate students said that the passage concerned an agreement about gifts to be exchanged (Steffenson, Joag-dev, & Anderson, 1979). Those students' own culturally based expectations about the tradition of mutual gift-giving between bride and groom certainly might have encouraged their misreading. Teachers need to examine assumptions about children's background knowledge that are embedded in texts and compare them with the experiences that students actually bring with them.

One approach to bridging cultural differences between teachers and students involves teachers actively interacting with families outside the school. Some teachers whose cultural backgrounds are different from their students' have been getting first-hand experience with the "funds of knowledge" in their students' homes and communities to improve their understanding of the background knowledge that students bring to reading and other school tasks (Gonzalez et al., 1993). Investigating funds of knowledge involves teacher-researchers visiting some of their students' homes to talk with parents and other family members. Their goal is to become acquainted with the knowledge and skill areas that families possess and the social networks in which they participate. Teachers engaged in this research meet in study groups to compare findings from their visits and reflect together on the match between students' background knowledge and classroom practices.

A second domain of cultural contrast concerns the fit between reading at school and the culturally influenced language and literacy patterns of the home and community. Some researchers have focused on emergent literacy—the abilities and orientation toward literacy that children develop along with other language skills before they go to school that form a basis for reading instruction. Purcell-Gates (1995) told the story of one urban Appalachian family in which the parents' lack of literacy had given the children different experiences with reading than their schools anticipated. In this family, reading books involved inventing stories to match the pictures. As a result, the children did not understand the cuing function of print. Early reading instruction that assumed this knowledge did not meet these children's needs. Understanding the role that reading and writing play or do not play in students' homes and communities can help a teacher to make reading experiences more congruent with students' expectations and thus more meaningful and successful.

Teachers need general knowledge about linguistic and cultural differences among the students they teach and detailed knowledge about their students' dialects and culturally based literacy practices. Beyond that, they should be aware of the status of each student's emergent literacy. To this end, school districts need to provide continuing professional development about the role of language in students' school performance.

TEACHING CHILDREN TO RELATE SOUND AND PRINT

Teaching beginning readers to relate written language to the sounds of oral language may be more complicated because of dialect variation. But the implications of dialect differences are somewhat different for different instructional approaches.

There are two general approaches to teaching children the relationship between the sounds of oral English and the alphabetic symbols on the printed page: the explicit and systematic phonics approach and the nonphonics approach. Phonics instruction focuses students' attention on the relationship of print to sounds, with the intent of helping students learn to decode the combinations of printed letters and blend the sounds to make words (e.g., Open Court Reading). It uses children's phonemic awareness as a foundation (Adams, 1990; Chall, 1996). Nonphonics instructional approaches include meaning-based reading (whole language) and learning sight words (Routman, 1991). These approaches integrate phonics instruction into meaning-based activities or address the sound/print connection after children have learned sight words (Weaver, 1994). Sight word instruction emphasizes understanding words both individually and in the context of the sentence.

Controversy over these two general approaches to teaching reading has not been fully resolved (National Reading Panel, 2000), but it is clear that understanding the relationship of sound and print is essential to reading. At the same time, phonics is only one part of what children need to learn, and teachers need to teach about the reading process.

Effects of Dialect Differences on Reading Aloud

Phonics-based approaches to teaching reading are likely to highlight the connection between sound and print. When students deviate in reading aloud from what the teacher expects, it may be thought to signal a failure to decode and comprehend what was read. But in approaching such deviations, it is important to draw a distinction between dialect influence and dialect interference. *Dialect influence* refers to an oral rendition of text that deviates from the written form in line with certain vernacular features, but has no consequence for meaning; *dialect interference* refers to renditions in which dialect contrast may affect comprehension of the passage. For example, in dialects with identical pronunciations for different words (e.g., *find* and *fine*; *send* and *sinned*; or *Mary, merry, marry*), not differentiating the words has the potential to interfere with meaning in oral reading, but in most cases the reader does not misinterpret the meaning, so the effect is limited to an *influence* on oral reading (i.e., pronunciation).

Dialect differences in grammatical forms also have the potential for influence or interference. In oral reading, producing the text *five cents* as "five cent" shows dialect influence, but probably not interference: It is unlikely that the basic meaning of the text would have been lost by the omission of the final -*s*. However, some deviations from the text are actual reading errors because they do not preserve the author's meaning. If a student sees *He's done trying to please everyone* and reads it as "He done tried to please everyone," the meaning of the text is not preserved, and it is likely that the student has misunderstood. In the written sentence, the verb indicates present completed action. The text might be interpreted as *He's done trying to please everyone for the time being, but he'll resume again later.* But in the substituted sentence, the reader seems to have comprehended a completed past action (signaled by the meaning of *done*).

When a student substitutes a vernacular structure in oral reading, it is not always possible to distinguish dialect influence from true interference. In research being conducted by William Labov at the University of Pennsylvania, a process for estimating whether a vernacular substitution is a reading error or simply a case of dialect influence is being developed (http://www.ling.upenn.edu/~wlabov/Papers/WRE.html, retrieved April 15, 2006). The method involves observing what follows the substitution. If the reader has made a reading error, then what follows may be in error too. But if a substitution is only a case of dialect influence, what follows is likely to be consistent with the text. For example, a third grader read *I played it cool and took a sip of my coke* as "I play it cool and took a sip of my coke." It appears that the reader deleted the final sound of *played* (and thus also the past-tense marker -*ed*), but understood it as a past-tense verb: The next verb in the sentence, *took,* was not altered. Understanding the past tense of *played* seems to have contributed in some way to reading *took* correctly.

Labov's study found that certain dialect substitutions were more likely than others to be errors (i.e., interference, not just dialect influence). This varied according to the reader's ethnolinguistic group. For example, deletion of the plural marker by African American English speakers was unlikely to be a reading error, but deletion of this feature by Latino vernacular dialect speakers was likely to be an error. But comparison between group speech patterns and reading substitutions revealed uneven patterns. For example, the more a group deleted the agreement marker on a verb in speech (e.g., *Kevin usually go__to work early*), the more likely that its deletion in reading would not constitute an error. But the more a group deleted the possessive marker (e.g., *Kevin__cat is missing*), the more likely that its deletion in reading *would* constitute an error. Thus, how vernacular dialects affect oral reading is quite complex and still not fully understood.

One goal of Labov's research program is to find ways to improve the decoding skills of speakers of vernacular dialects. Among the recommendations offered is that teachers of struggling readers who are vernacular dialect speakers should provide direct instruction on certain grammatical features that strongly correlate with reading errors: the possessive marker, the copula (e.g., *Kevin's late today*), and irregular past-tense verbs.

Dialects and Meaning-Based Reading Instruction

Meaning-based instruction, or whole language, integrates reading with writing and speaking, uses trade books, and embeds phonics instruction in these activities. In this approach to teaching reading, the teacher's role is to facilitate students' experiences with literacy by providing materials and opportunities for rich, authentic encounters with written and spoken language. This approach has been criticized on several bases. Some claim that in rejecting explicit and systemic phonics instruction, some whole-language practitioners have adopted a haphazard approach to reading skills, rather than one that presents reading as an authentic, interpretive experience and presents skills as secondary but still important processes (Adams, 1990; Clay, 1987). Delpit (1988) criticizes the approach for disadvantaging vernacular speakers in another way: Because middle-class children are more likely to have acquired literacy skills outside school, instruction that deemphasizes phonics puts those who need to learn sound/print skills at a disadvantage. Critics from outside of education contend that whole-language instruction that encourages children to invent spellings as they write encourages a disregard for standard written language conventions.

Whether instruction addresses phonics systematically (as in the phonics approach) or incidentally (as in the whole-language approach), dialect differences are likely to influence learning sound/symbol relationships unless the teacher's dialect matches that of every student in the class. Dialect pronunciation may not be as problematic with the sight-word approach to early reading (also called *look–say*) in which children begin to read by learning to recognize 50 to 100 words and then learn details of the alphabetic principle—that print relates to sound. Sight-word instruction emphasizes understanding the words both individually and in the context of the sentence. But it is important for teachers using this approach to be aware of dialect-specific pronunciations that differ from Standard English. For instance, when the printed word is *then* and the student pronounces it like "den" or "din," or when the student who speaks African American English pronounces *stream* as *skream*, it should not be assumed that the word has been misidentified. It is unlikely that vocabulary differences between dialects would affect students' performance in word identification exercises in the sight-word approach; that would be more likely to occur in reading extended text. For example, if a student's native dialect uses *sack* to refer to what the text calls a *bag*, this difference may occur in the student's oral reading.

TEACHING CHILDREN TO COMPREHEND TEXT

Comprehension, of course, is the point of reading. For expert readers, comprehension usually occurs effortlessly as long as the text is clearly written and the reader is at least somewhat familiar with the topic and vocabulary. Adult readers may not realize that comprehension is a skill that beginning readers need to learn. Teaching this skill also needs to be sensitive to the potential influence of language differences.

Vocabulary

Getting meaning from text is a cognitive process: The reader processes chunks of text thoughtfully using knowledge of language and the world, and constructs some meaning for them. The meaning of words plays an essential role in constructing the meaning of texts. But in this domain, dialect differences may interfere with the automatic comprehension of text that practiced readers take for granted. Encountering words that are unexpected, including those that result from dialect vocabulary differences, interrupts the fluent flow of reading. For example, readers outside of Louisiana may not be familiar with the term *lagniappe* (meaning *small gift*), or those outside of the Southwest might not be familiar with the term *arroyo* for a type of gully. Again, the teacher needs to be knowledgeable about students' dialects and watchful for potential vocabulary mismatches that cause readers—especially young readers who may not recognize such variants—to stumble. Teachers might want to preteach such dialect-contrasting terms in advance of reading and ensure that children see and hear them repeatedly, while being careful not to imply that the new variant is correct and the familiar one incorrect.

Comprehension Strategies

Teachers are well aware of the need to actively teach new vocabulary to enhance students' facility with text. They also employ various strategies to help students comprehend as they read, strategies that mimic aspects of comprehension or function as aids to comprehension. For example, teachers may describe their own practices in comprehending a piece of text by reading and "thinking aloud" about their inferential processes, and they may ask students to do the same, to strengthen the understanding that reading involves thought, prediction, speculation, and rereading. In thinking aloud about a piece of text, teachers of vernacular speakers could mention predictable dialect influence on the reading process. For example, teachers might analyze the sentence considered earlier, *He's done trying to please everyone*, anticipating possible dialect interference and referring to context to resolve ambiguity. This sort of demonstration has the effect of demystifying the reading process for children who may have had less exposure to reading or different experiences with it before coming to school.

Strategies to support reading comprehension often call for students to write or talk about their understanding. If in doing so they use vernacular features, "correcting" these features could well confuse them. The point of activities such as summarizing and mapping out story elements is understanding the text, not producing Standard English.

Background Knowledge and Comprehension

Texts that assume background knowledge from mainstream culture can make reading comprehension problematic for readers from other backgrounds. For example, urban students having little direct experience with mountain biking or mowing lawns might find passages that presume knowledge about these topics somewhat difficult (just as students living in tropical climates might have trouble understanding blizzard conditions).

Teachers can accommodate students' background knowledge in a number of ways when they recognize what their students' funds of knowledge consist of. There are any number of excellent trade books from which teachers may select that closely match students' cultural background. Including work by authors who share the students' cultural background and who incorporate vernacular dialect in their writing can entice children who might otherwise experience literacy as focusing exclusively on other people's cultures and other people's language.

Teachers can also select strategies to build the background knowledge that students need to comprehend text. Thematic approaches to reading can build up an informational store so that children have the resources they need to become interested in a text and to write and talk about the content of texts that may be distant from their experience. Prereading experiences for students of any age can help them activate and build relevant knowledge. After reading, students may do response-to-literature tasks that lead them into the text again from a different perspective. For example, they may rewrite a part of the story or enact a sequel to it.

Reciprocal teaching (Palincsar & Brown, 1987), a strategy that groups children with diverse abilities and achievement levels for reading and writing tasks, is often mentioned as being particularly appropriate for children whose language and cultural backgrounds may be different from their teachers'. Teachers work with the groups, helping children talk and write about what they have read and how they understood the text. This process engages students in talk about literacy and literature in order to scaffold reading development. It invites vernacular dialect speakers to use their oral language abilities in literacy activities.

Expert teachers have a repertoire of instructional strategies that is continually refreshed through professional development experiences. When teachers understand and value students' language abilities and previous literacy learning, when they acknowledge and accommodate low literacy levels, they are able to continually adapt reading instruction to their students' needs. In their classrooms, students engage with text in ways that build reading abilities throughout the school years.

READING MATERIALS AND DIALECT DIFFERENCES

One of the issues that has been raised by linguists and educators alike with respect to dialects is the nature of the reading materials used in schools in teaching children to read. Are the same reading materials appropriate for students from middle-class, standard-speaking communities and for vernacular-speaking students from non-middle-class communities? In light of the fact that the language of texts is closer to Standard English than it is to a vernacular dialect, should any adjustments be made so that reading materials are more accessible for vernacular speakers?

Two basic positions have been taken regarding the language of reading materials that are written especially for beginning readers (texts with controlled vocabulary and sentence structure). Some researchers have advocated changing the language in the text because it is a poor match for speakers of vernacular dialects; others maintain that texts written in Standard English can be used for everyone because speakers of other dialects can accommodate to them. Both positions acknowledge a concern about the mismatch between those students' oral language and the language of reading materials, but the strategies for dealing with this issue differ. The alternatives also seem to be based on different assumptions about the significance of the mismatch.

Matching Materials and Dialects

Those who advocate changing the materials focus on reducing the mismatch between reader and materials by making the language of the materials more closely resemble the student's language. This change can be accomplished in several ways. One strategy is to remove (or avoid) constructions that are points of dialect difference. For example, in standard varieties, an indirect question can be formed as *He asked if he could go*; other dialects might use *He asked could he go*. In striving for more dialect-neutral materials, this structure would be avoided. A structure common to all dialects of English could be used instead (in this case, a direct question such as *He asked, "Can I go?"*). Such grammatical changes in the texts are intended to make the materials as neutral as possible with respect to dialect differences.

Dialect Readers

Another text modification approach advocated by some researchers involves incorporating vernacular English constructions. Thus, an indirect question formed as *He asked could he go* would be used instead of *He asked if he could go*. Similarly, multiple negatives (e.g., *He didn't do nothing*), vernacular subject–verb agreement patterns (e.g., *We was here*), and alternate tense markings (e.g., *In those days, we went to the fiesta and we have a good time*) would be used in texts designed for communities where these patterns are the norm. Such texts would be used to build literacy skills using beginning readers' oral language skills. They would not be intended to replace other reading materials.

In the dialect reader approach illustrated next, a child who speaks a variety such as African American English uses a reading text written in that dialect (as in Version 2) rather than one written in Standard English (as in Version 1). The African American English passage, taken from an early experiment with dialect readers, represents a deliberate attempt to incorporate grammatical and vocabulary features of this dialect. Changes in spelling to capture pronunciation contrasts are generally considered nonessential.

Version 1: *Standard English*
    "Look down here," said Suzy.
    "I can see a girl in here.
    The girl looks like me.
    Come here and look, David.
    Can you see that girl?"

Version 2: *Vernacular Black English*
    Susan say, "Hey you-all, look down here!"
    "I can see a girl in here.
    The girl, she look like me.
    Come here and look, David!
    Could you see the girl?"

                                  (Wolfram & Fasold, 1969)

Once decoding skills are well established, the learner begins a transition to reading Standard English, using texts in which vernacular and standard dialect versions of a passage appear side by side. Subsequent texts gradually eliminate vernacular constructions, and reading materials eventually conform to the patterns of Standard English.

The original intent was that dialect readers would be written for a variety of vernacular English dialects, but the only materials ever prepared are in African American English.

The use of dialect readers has always met with mixed reactions. Many people, including educators and community leaders, view anything that is written for children in a dialect other than Standard English as educationally unsound and socially offensive. They consider dialect readers patronizing and unnecessary educational accommodations (Labov, 1995). But a small group of people have enthusiastically advocated the use of dialect readers.

Some research was conducted on the effectiveness of dialect readers as compared to traditional reading materials. *Bridge: A Cross-Cultural Reading Program* (Simpkins, Holt, & Simpkins, 1977) was field-tested with secondary students receiving remedial reading instruction. Gains of these students in the Iowa Test of Basic Skills exceeded those of students who used the regular reading materials (6.2 months of gain for a 4-month period for students using the *Bridge* program vs. 1.2 months gain for those using the regular reading materials). Nonetheless, research on the effectiveness of dialect readers has been limited. Negative reactions from a wide range of people virtually eliminated that approach as a serious alternative to traditional basal reading texts for a long time.

More recently, however, linguist John Rickford and educational researcher Angela E. Rickford have contended that it was a mistake to discard dialect readers prematurely, and that experimental research on their effectiveness should be resumed (Rickford & Rickford, 1995). They recommended experimenting with new ways of introducing and using dialect readers that would allay doubts about them. Because dialect readers are so different from basal readers and because they use language that is unexpected and even sometimes proscribed at school, communications with stakeholders would be critical so that they understand the rationale for the use of this approach. Parents and other community members would need to be convinced that dialect readers represent a scaffolded approach to reading Standard English, and that teachers share with parents the goal of supporting children's Standard English development. The Rickfords and their students have conducted research on a small scale with dialect readers that include both vernacular and standard versions of the text. Their work, which is still quite preliminary, suggests that vernacular dialect readers may be most effective with middle school boys.

Language Experience

Dialect readers attempt to be true to the general language patterns of a particular group of speakers. In the Language Experience approach, teachers record what a students says, and those texts are used as reading materials. Thus, the texts reflect the language patterns of an individual speaker. The rationale for this approach is that the greatest asset of beginning readers is their ability to use and understand language. In using a Language Experience approach with vernacular dialect speakers, transcribing can become problematic. If teachers edit students' stories into Standard English, the written version is not a fully accurate rendition of what the child said. In translating the children's stories into what the teacher considers proper English or school language, she or he communicates an attitude about the worth of the children's language. The message for students is that their language is wrong or inadequate. Teachers who are knowledgeable about dialect differences may decide to write down what students say and use this text as one source for reading instruction. The language of the written text is closer to the child's own language experience than that found in either basal reading texts or reading materials written for vernacular dialect speakers. Moreover, the content reflects familiar contexts and activities.

Despite the differences between them, dialect readers and student-created texts that incorporate dialect differences may be lumped together when people react negatively to the use of nonstandard linguistic patterns in print.

Vernacular Dialect for Rhetorical Purpose

People seem willing to suspend their objections to printed vernacular dialect in literature where it is used to evoke cultural identity or social reality. The audience in this case is all readers rather than only those who are vernacular speakers, and the works are selected for their literary value rather than their language form. Reading work by established writers such as Sandra Cisneros, Richard Wright, and Zora Neale Hurston can present the opportunity for high school students to extend their knowledge about language in society and for teachers to introduce language study into the study of literature. Although this is not a method for making the language of reading materials more familiar at early stages of learning to read, it can help older students more about dialect differences.

Discussion might focus on the authors' purposes for using vernacular features in writing, a medium in which readers are more accustomed to seeing standard dialect. Students could consider whether the features seem to be an accurate rendition of speech or a general means of conveying a character's social identity. They might investigate whether the language of the text matches dialects in their own area. They might compare vernacular dialect in fiction with that in poetry and recent works with older ones. How does Alice Walker's use of vernacular in the novel, *The Color Purple,* compare to Paul Laurence Dunbar's in the poem, "When Malindy Sings"? Is dialect used similarly in Richard Wright's *Native Son* and Toni Morrison's *Beloved*, important novels written 50 years apart? How does Lee Smith, who uses versions of Appalachian English in her novels, represent the dialect of some of her mountain personalities in *Oral History*? Studying the dialect of written text can be a valuable route to enhancing students' knowledge about their own dialects as well as those of others.

READING AND THE ACQUISITION OF STANDARD ENGLISH

It has been suggested that young vernacular dialect speakers might find it easier to learn to read if Standard English were taught first. If this strategy worked, then the question of dialect mismatch and reading would be moot. But there are several reasons that making Standard English a prerequisite for reading instruction is unadvisable. In the first place, mismatch between speaking and reading would remain: All speakers of English confront differences between written and spoken language, regardless of their dialect. Furthermore, many speakers of vernacular dialects show little difficulty in overcoming the mismatch. There is no clear-cut indication that learning Standard English will, in itself, increase the ease of learning to read. On top of that, there is little evidence that spoken Standard English is being taught successfully to young children. Most important, however, is timing. If Standard English could be taught successfully, and reading instruction were postponed until children achieved Standard English fluency, learning in other academic areas that are dependent on reading skills would be significantly delayed.

Another possibility would be to teach Standard English simultaneously with teaching phonics by "correcting" a student's vernacular English response to a Standard English response during phonics instruction. But Piestrup (1973) found that correcting students' reading actually led to more "errors," not fewer. Such a practice has serious pedagogical flaws (Scott, 1992). It is confusing to mix teaching Standard English with teaching reading because the two goals are not necessarily linked. If an African American English speaker reads *find* as *fin'*, a rural Appalachian dialect speaker reads *cliff* as *clifft*, or a southwestern Hispanic or Native American student reads *sing* as *sin*, there is no reason to suspect a letter/sound correspondence problem. Such a problem would be indicated, of course, if the same students read *cup* as *sup* or *big* as *dig*. The first set of examples involves accurate reflections of sound/letter correspondences in particular dialects, whereas the second set does not reflect the patterns of any of the dialects. Correcting both types of production as if they were the same phenomenon can only confuse the learner because readers depend on their tacit knowledge of language to figure out sound/print relationships. A New England child might similarly be confused if told that the only correct way to read *car* is with an *r* at the end or that *caught* and *cot* must contain different vowel sounds to be read accurately. Learning a spoken Standard English dialect requires different skills from those involved in learning the sound/letter correspondence. If the two sets of skills are addressed at once, students are unlikely to learn either one very well.

THE SOCIAL CONTEXT OF READING

Cultural and social values about the role of reading in community life, school, and work play an enormous role in children's learning to read and developing reading proficiency, as do different beliefs about how children learn to read (Westby, 1995). In fact, Purcell-Gates (1995) notes that such cultural and social values appear to correlate highly with reading success. Research has shown that the literacy-related experiences that children have in their homes and communities may differ from those presumed by school programs, which more easily accommodate the literacy experiences of White middle-class children (Hammer, 2001; Labov, 1972).

Expert teachers of children from backgrounds different from what schools assume often organize instruction in ways that create a literacy-rich classroom culture that supports children's transition into the school culture. There is frequent, informal writing tied to reading; regular journal writing; literacy activity across the curriculum; silent reading; oral story reading; and story performance: in short, a highly participatory, highly literate environment. Obviously this is not a remedial program, but one that builds literacy for all children.

One study showed the value of such classrooms for children from vernacular dialect-speaking backgrounds who came to school with limited literacy experiences of the type the school expected. By the end of first grade, the students were performing in reading on par with children who had been read to extensively at home. They also scored higher than other children from similar backgrounds in skills-based curricula (Purcell-Gates, McIntyre, & Freppon, 1995).

Other teachers use practices that reduce the discontinuities between home and school. Teachers at the Kamehameha Early Education Program in Hawaii have incorporated a language strategy from students' home culture (Au & Jordan, 1981). In an attempt to address the problem of poor reading by Hawaiian students, they made reading lessons more like important language events in Hawaiian culture, "talk story" and "storytelling." Rather than taking turns at talk during teacher-led discussion to support comprehension, children jump in to extend each other's ideas in talking about the text. They volunteer responses, rather than waiting for the teacher to call on them. The program also incorporates forms of classroom organization that lead to informal learning situations. Students work together in small groups at learning centers. By responding to narrative and social conventions of the students' background, this approach helps to narrow the gap between home and school learning and promote text comprehension.

Reading performance, reading problems, and reading failure for different dialect and cultural groups have a complex explanation. The kinds of materials that children read play a role. Language structure, text content, and readers' background knowledge and cultural values regarding literacy all may influence reading success. Teachers will want to continue observing their students' performance, reflecting on their practice, and refining instruction. Researchers will want to focus specifically on the role of dialect differences in learning to read and to work with practitioners to bring their research to bear on practice.

READING TESTS AND DIALECT DIFFERENCES

A final issue regarding the correlation of low reading scores and vernacular-speaking populations concerns reading assessment. There has been debate for some time as to whether standardized tests, especially standardized reading tests, reflect the linguistic and cultural realities of vernacular English speakers (Hilliard, 1999). Some test takers who score low on these tests do, in fact, have genuine reading problems of one type or another, and this diagnosis holds up through multiple measures of reading ability. Concern about the quality, form, and context of the tests is not meant to deny the seriousness of actual reading problems. The question is whether the tests accurately reflect the nature or existence of reading problems for all students.

In some cases, serious misclassification may occur on the basis of test scores; some students may be classified as overall poor readers even if they are not, due to the kinds of language and cultural items included in the test. In other cases, particular reading problems may be indicated by scores that are really a function of language differences, and certain speakers may be penalized because their native dialect is different from that used as the norming sample on standardized tests. For example, a deficiency in word recognition skills might be diagnosed when, in fact, the test-taker has simply applied the pronunciation rules of the native dialect in responding to test items. The possibility of language bias in standardized reading tests must be taken into account along with other factors in order to make an accurate assessment of reading skills.

Pronunciation, Grammar, and Vocabulary Differences

There are several ways in which dialect differences may affect scores on standardized reading tests. First, some reading tests may contain sections that depend on Standard English pronunciations. The decoding exercise mentioned earlier that relies on the ability to distinguish *pen* from *pin* and *death* from *deaf* clearly contains a bias against speakers of Southern-based dialects, in which these pairs of items may be pronounced the same. In responding to test items, the child sounds the words out according to the dialect's pronunciation rules and does not note a difference. Because the norms for the test reflect the Standard English pronunciation distinction, the child's responses are marked as incorrect, even though they accurately follow precise rules of the native language variety.

In some elementary level tests, students may be required to choose the correct word to complete a sentence. For example, a test item may ask for a choice between *them* and *those* in a sentence such as *I have read (them, those) books* or between *no* and *any* in a sentence such as *I didn't hear (no, any) noise*. According to the Standard English norm, one correct form is predicted (*those* and *any*) in these sentences, but the grammatical rules of the test-taker's home dialect may predict the other choice (*them* and *no*). Responses that follow native dialect rules show accurate word recognition and thus demonstrate reading skill. If those responses are judged to be wrong, dialect differences may lead to faulty assessment of reading ability.

In another testing task, students are asked to match words to pictures, demonstrating their word recognition skills. For example, for a drawing that shows trees with falling leaves, students are asked to select the word that appropriately labels the picture. The options in the test are *aunt, autumn, summer,* and *town.* This test item holds several potential difficulties. First, the term *autumn,* which the test developers consider correct for this scene, may not be thoroughly familiar to some children because it is associated more with written language than spoken language. Children with less written language experience may expect the word *fall.* Thus, this item may be more difficult for them than for others.

Another difficulty with this item concerns students' cultural experiences with seasons. Elementary schools typically emphasize seasons as a school topic, thus establishing the relationship between leaves and *autumn* as background knowledge that is relevant to school tasks. For children in rural and suburban areas regions in the North, this emphasis is congruent with out-of-school experience. But for children living in the inner city, wearing jackets may have a stronger association than falling leaves with autumn/fall. In areas that do not have deciduous trees, such as South Florida and Southern California, or where seasons are marked in a different way, such as rainy and dry seasons in the U.S. Virgin Islands, the test item makes a different semantic demand than it does for children in the East and Midwest.

Tests assume that vocabulary items have the same meaning associations for all readers, but that is not the case. A test can inaccurately assess a reader from a region, social class, or cultural group that uses a vocabulary form different from the response required by the test. The vocabulary test in Box 7.1 is intended to demonstrate what can happen when a reader's skill is assessed using unfamiliar test items. In this instance, the vocabulary is from a historically isolated island dialect spoken on the Outer Banks of North Carolina. It includes items discussed earlier in chapter 2.

Background Knowledge

Tests of reading comprehension entail language processes beyond the literal meaning of a passage. It is virtually impossible to construct a reading comprehension test that pertains only to literal meaning. Comprehension tests assess the student's ability to make inferences—the ability to connect explicitly stated information with other information believed to follow naturally from it.

Background knowledge is among the factors that contribute to inferring meanings from text. We have pointed out that what constitutes a person's background knowledge is constrained to an enormous extent by consider-

Box 7.1
(from Wolfram & Schilling-Estes, 1997, pp. 50–153)

An Ocracoke Vocabulary Test (or How to Tell a Dingbatter From an Ococker)

1. *dingbatter*
   a. baseball player in a small boat
   b. a husband
   c. a wife
   d. an outsider

2. *up the beach*
   a. by the sea
   b. north of the island
   c. the national parkland area
   d. Oyster Creek

3. *meehonkey*
   a. a call used in hide-and-seek
   b. a call made to attract ducks
   c. the call of an angry person
   d. an island marsh plant

4. *quamish*
   a. an upset stomach
   b. a fearful feeling
   c. a bad headache
   d. an excited feeling

5. *pizer*
   a. a small boat
   b. a deck
   c. a porch
   d. a small Italian pie with cheese

6. *mommuck* (also spelled *mammock*)
   a. to imitate someone
   b. to bother someone
   c. to make fun of someone
   d. to become close friends with someone

Box 7.1 (continued)

7. She's *to* the restaurant.
   a. She ate at the restaurant twice.
   b. She's been to the restaurant.
   c. She's at the restaurant.
   d. She's going to the restaurant.

8. *fladget*
   a. gas in the alimentary canal
   b. an island men's game
   c. a small island bird
   d. a small piece of something

9. *puck*
   a. a small disk used in island hockey games
   b. a sweetheart
   c. a kiss on the cheek
   d. a mischievous person

10. *Ococker*
    a. a derogatory term for an Ocracoker
    b. an outsider's mispronunciation of the term *Ocracoker*
    c. an island term for a native Ocracocker
    d. an island term for bluefish

11. *token of death*
    a. a coin needed for admission to Hades
    b. a sickness leading to death
    c. a fatal epidemic
    d. an unusual event that forecasts a death

12. *louard*
    a. lowering an anchor
    b. an exaggerated exclamation, as in "louard have mercy"
    c. moving away from the wind
    d. a fatty substance

13. *Russian rat*
    a. a unique island rodent
    b. an island gossip
    c. a vodka-drinking narc
    d. a mink

(continued on next page)

Box 7.1 (continued)

14. *Hatterasser*
    a. a storm that blows in from Hatteras
    b. a ferry ride from Ocracoke to Hatteras
    c. a person from Hatteras
    d. a fishing trip in Hatteras Inlet

15. *skiff*
    a. a large boat
    b. a small boat
    c. a strong wind
    d. a light wind

16. *scud*
    a. a dirty person
    b. a tire mark in the sand
    c. a ride in a car or boat
    d. a missile

17. *dost*
    a. sick, especially with the flu
    b. a square dance step
    c. a small crab
    d. toast, especially wheat bread

18. *fatback*
    a. bacon
    b. an overweight Hatterasser
    c. an island pig
    d. menhaden, a type of oily fish

19. *goaty*
    a. a small beard on the chin
    b. smelling foul, like a goat
    c. having the appearance of a goat
    d. silly

20. *slick cam*
    a. a well-oiled engine part
    b. greased-down hair
    c. a glossy picture
    d. very still water

Box 7.1 (continued)

Ocracoke Vocabulary Score

0–5 = a complete dingbatter
6–10 = an educable dingbatter
11–15 = an average Ococker
16–20 = an island genius

Answers:

1.	d	11.	d
2.	b	12.	c
3.	a	13.	a
4.	a	14.	c
5.	c	15.	b
6.	b	16.	c
7.	c	17.	a
8.	d	18.	d
9.	b	19.	b
10.	c	20.	d

ations of culture and ethnicity, social class, gender, race, age, geographical location, and other factors. Consider the following description of redwood trees in terms of the background information that a child from New York City and a resident of Northern California near the Redwood Forests might bring to the test:

> They are so big that roads are built through their trunks. By counting the rings inside the tree trunk, one can tell the age of the tree. (From the Metropolitan Reading Test for third graders, cited in Meier, 1973)

If an urban child is less familiar with the use of the terms *rings* and *trunk* in connection with trees, this passage might conjure up a fairy tale image. In contrast, a child raised in proximity to the forest might find such a description almost trivial by the third grade. Background knowledge plays an essential role in reading comprehension, and what readers bring as background knowledge to reading may vary according to group.

Consider another account, also taken from a disclosed version of the Metropolitan Reading Test.

> "Good afternoon, little girl," said the policeman. "May I help you?"
> "I want to go to the park. I cannot find my way," said Nancy. "Please help me."

After reading this passage, the child is supposed to select the one right ending for the story:

The policeman said,

a. Call your mother to take you.
b. I am in a hurry.
c. I will take you to the park. (from Meier, 1973, p. 22)

Quite obviously, cultural values about the role of the police influence the answer: Readers with different value orientations might select different answers.

OTHER FAIRNESS FACTORS

It is important, then, to consider systematic characteristics of social and ethnic groups, including language patterns, in scoring test responses. But other factors bear on fairness in testing as well. Certain aspects of the testing situation favor social and behavioral traits typically associated with middle-class children. For example, values about early acquisition of reading and writing skills, displaying abilities through paper-and-pencil tasks or performing for unfamiliar adults, working quickly, concentrating on the test topic, among others, can be quite culture-specific.

The techniques used to obtain information in many standardized reading tests also presume particular kinds of skill training that may be culture-specific. For example, phonemic awareness and phonics skills are often measured through tasks that focus on rhyming words, words sounding the same, or parts of a word rather than the whole word—activities that may not be familiar to all students. Reading vocabulary may be measured by tasks that call for identifying word association types: same meanings (synonyms such as *proprietor* and *owner*), opposite meanings (antonyms such as *tall* and *short*), specific and general category relationships (e.g., *python* and *snake*), or descriptive, dictionary-like definitions (e.g., a *linguist* is a person who studies the patterning and organization of language). These assessment tasks for getting at meaning are, of course, different from real-life language use where meaning is derived from words in context. A specialized set of skills may be needed to succeed in tests of various facets of reading; and the test-taker's failure to interpret the tasks in the intended way can lead to a diagnosis of reading failure where it may not be warranted.

Equity in assessment is a complex issue, and no simple approach emerges as best. Test responses could be analyzed in ways that take into account the systematic differences between dialects. If a working-class African American child marked *mile* and *mild* as sounding the same because of the regular pronunciation rule that can eliminate the *d* in *mild*, or a Southern rural child noted that *tire* and *tar* sound the same, this response would be interpreted as a legitimate reflection of a dialect difference, not a reading error. Similarly, if a native Philadelphian marked items such as *ran* and *man* as not rhyming because of the distinct vowels in these items (the *a* in *ran* as *a*, and the *a* in *man* something like *e-u*), this, too, would be interpreted as a legitimate reflection of the Philadelphia pronunciation system, and not as a reading error. An interpretation of responses that takes into account dialect differences can help the evaluator see what effect dialect may be having by identifying responses that are legitimate in terms of the language system of the test-taker, but differ from the standardized norms of the test. To make such an interpretation, the evaluator must be thoroughly familiar with the systematic differences between the various dialects of test-takers, whether they are rural Southern, urban African American, or Southwestern Chicano. Naturally this need holds for informal assessment as well, understanding why certain forms might occur in the oral reading of passages in contrast to the actual forms written in the passage. It is crucial, however, to determine the test-taker's dialect and not to assume it based on race or ethnicity.

Schools often use multiple methods of assessing reading achievement so that scores from standardized reading tests are not the exclusive measure of reading skills. Informal assessments and criterion-referenced tests are being recommended. Performance-based assessments, in which test-takers are required to produce a product or a process based on their understanding of a text, have been used in progressive situations. Asking students why they chose particular answers is also useful. Getting a glimpse of the reasoning behind the child's answer can be quite enlightening. In the comprehension test item about the police officer mentioned earlier, a child could supply an appropriate rationale for selecting the alternative: "I am in a hurry," instead of "I will take you to the park." The child's background knowledge might suggest that police officers are doing their job when they are hurrying from one place to another taking care of troublesome situations. Checking on that background knowledge may reveal that there are different cultural perceptions regarding officers' responsibilities. Certain answers that are wrong according to the norms of a test might be reasonable indications that the child is, in fact, reading with considerable understanding, even if it involves a perspective different from that assumed by the author or test constructor. For educators who are concerned with a genuine understanding of students' reading skills, specific information of this type may be considerably more useful for placement and instruction than objective scores.

This chapter argues, as the other chapters do, that educators need to have broad understanding about variation in language. Beyond that, they need to know the details about their own students' dialects and cultural backgrounds. It is not enough to have a general respect for group-based differences. Specific understanding of students' dialects makes it possible for teachers to understand their students' reading performance and support reading development in concrete, informed ways as they engage students from diverse communities and language varieties.

FURTHER READING

Hammond, B., Hoover, M. E. R., & McPhail, I. P. (Eds.). (2005). *Teaching African American learners to read: Perspectives and practices.* Newark, DE: International Reading Association.
  Contributors to this book include researchers and practitioners with a deep understanding of how dialects can affect learning to read. The chapters feature accounts of how schools have used children's home dialect in building their reading skills.
Harris, J., Kamhi, A. G., & Pollock, K. E. (Eds.). (2001). *Literacy in African American communities.* Mahwah, NJ: Lawrence Erlbaum Associates.
  The chapters in this volume present a broad view of literacy-related practices in linguistic, cultural, historical, and political contexts.
Purcell-Gates, V. (1995). *Other people's words: The cycle of low literacy.* Cambridge, MA: Harvard University Press.
  This case study tells the compelling story of the author's work with a nonliterate mother and her young son, who are urban Appalachians. The title comes from the mother's assessment of her difficulty in learning to read books written in a language that was not her own. The writer shows how she took into account the home literacy traditions and dialect difference in supporting the mother's and son's literacy development.
Rickford, A. (1999). *I can fly.* Lanham, MD: University Press.
  The research reported in this book concerns promoting reading and engagement with texts by high school students from vernacular dialect backgrounds.

8

Dialect Awareness for Students

The previous chapters focus on how educators should consider dialects when addressing various kinds of literacy skills or in assessing students' educational performance and achievement. But language variation can also be a fascinating area of study for students that helps them learn how language is structured and how it is used in different regional and social contexts. Many educators and linguists are now encouraging the active study of dialects—including vernacular ones—as a regular part of the curriculum for all students. Indeed, the standards for the English language arts developed jointly by the International Reading Association (IRA) and the National Council of Teachers of English (NCTE) include the statement that "Students develop an understanding of and respect for diversity in language use, patterns, and dialects across cultures, ethnic groups, geographic regions, and social roles" (NCTE/IRA, 1996, p. 3). Many of the state standards for what students should know and be able to do have a similar focus. Furthermore, the NCTE/National Council for Accreditation of Teacher Education (NCATE) program standards (NCTE/NCATE Program Standards, 2003) include explicit guidelines and expectations for teachers' performance related to language diversity (see Table 8.1).

Including dialect diversity in the language arts curriculum in line with the standards or in other content areas such as social studies or history can benefit standard and vernacular dialect speakers alike by giving them information and skills for language investigation to counter the language stereotypes and prejudices that are ubiquitous in our society.

Investigating the structure of vernacular dialects and their role in speech communities has additional advantages for students from vernacular-speaking backgrounds. When the language of indigenous communities becomes an object of serious study for students, rather than a problem or an obstacle to be overcome, the gap between home and school that vernacular-speaking children frequently encounter is diminished. Students at all

TABLE 8.1

NCATE Program Standards (pp. 7, 13)

	NOT ACCEPTABLE	ACCEPTABLE	TARGET
3.1.4	Show a lack of respect for, and little knowledge of diversity in language use, patterns, and dialects across cultures, ethnic groups, geographic regional, and social roles;	Know and respect diversity in language use, patterns and dialects across cultures, ethnic groups, geographic regions and social roles and show attention to such diversity in their teaching;	Show extensive knowledge of how and why language varies and changes in different regions, across different cultural groups, and across different time periods and incorporate that knowledge into instruction and assessment that acknowledge and show respect for language diversity;
4.4	Show limited ability to create learning environments that promote respect for, and support of, individual differences of ethnicity, race, language, culture, gender, and ability;	Create and sustain learning environments that promote respect for, and support of, ethnicity, race, language, culture, gender, and ability;	Create opportunities for students to analyze how social context affects language and to monitor their own language use and behavior in terms of demonstrating respect for individual differences of ethnicity, race, language, culture, gender, and ability

Copyright © 2003 by the National Council of Teachers of English, reprinted with permission.

grade levels can conduct ethnographic and linguistic research in their own communities, gathering information, testing hypotheses, and writing reports. Dialect patterns in the community form a natural topic for this kind of activity.

This chapter suggests why and how the study of dialect diversity can be incorporated into the school curriculum—in English language arts, social studies, and elsewhere. It presents excerpts from dialect awareness curricula that have been used successfully in several locations, including a Northern metropolitan area and several areas in the rural South. This curriculum exemplifies the sort of information about dialects that students need to know and that they enjoy learning. Awareness about dialects and knowledge about dialect diversity can also form the basis for student inquiry into dialects in their own communities.

RESOURCES FOR LEARNING ABOUT DIALECTS

Traditionally, curriculum materials for both primary and secondary levels have neglected dialect diversity. If they treat it at all, materials focus on regional differences in vocabulary and do not address systematic pronunciation and grammatical differences in any detail. Matters of social dialect contrasts have usually been taken up from a deficit perspective, particularly with regard to grammar. Nevertheless, such materials have some utility. Rather than merely noting that regional differences exist, students might make use of this information for a cross-disciplinary project in which they plan a hypothetical month-long trip around the United States. Student projects could incorporate attention to vocabulary (and other dialect) differences that the travelers are likely to encounter, in addition to other information relevant to dialect distribution, such as topography, migratory routes, and population density. Such a project is not unlike the TV documentary hosted by Robert MacNeil, *Do You Speak American?* (MacNeil/ Lehrer Productions, 2005), in which MacNeil traveled across the United States encountering different regional and ethnic groups that reflect the essence of language diversity in American society.

Dialects can be approached more comprehensively as an active object of study for students and as a key to insights about the nature of language that would be almost impossible to get from secondary reference sources. Every school has nearby communities that are linguistically interesting both in their own right and in how they compare with other communities. They can be valuable sources of data for students, giving them an opportunity for first-hand observation of dialect diversity. Observation of diversity can, of course, often be accomplished within the school, but going out into the community will seem more like research, at least at first.

Consider, for example, a student in New York City. For the most part, New Yorkers are aware of dialect differences within the city and between speakers from their region and other regions of the United States. Unfortunately, such diversity is often seen in terms of unwarranted stereotypes, rather than as a valid object of study (consider "Brooklynese"). Carefully collected data from some of the New York communities can provide a base from which an accurate understanding of the systematic nature of dialects can be developed (consider the availability of ethnic groups [e.g., Jewish, Italian, Puerto Rican] and social class varieties that may be in proximity to the school).

In a locale that is not ethnically diverse, students may have to travel to find dialect diversity, but even in such a setting there will be diversity according to age and social status. There are also likely to be some residents who have moved from other areas and retained some contrasting linguistic features. Both individual introspection by students about their own speech and the collection of samples of speech from other residents in the area may serve as a database. It is hard to imagine any location that does not have sufficient language diversity of some type to make it a site for the meaningful investigation of language differences.

WORKING WITH DATA

Data from local speech communities can help students understand concepts related to the nature of language and the nature of language variation that are mentioned in state standards and local curricula aligned with them. Data collection and analysis activities can be designed to deal with particular features of a dialect along the lines of the dialect study procedures outlined in chapter 2. For example, a class might consider the use of structures like *He come here yesterday*. In collecting similar instances from the speech they hear around them, some students may notice that *have came* also occurs. When they find instances like *knowed, I seen it*, or *have went*, they may begin to notice that some verbs seem to take different forms from those used by their teachers and from the writing in their school materials. They may also notice patterns in the degree to which different people use forms like these.

From an investigation of past-tense verb forms, students can be led to make many valuable observations. First, they must consider the question of standard usage as a basis for comparison. Then they need to consider the system of irregular verbs in English so that they can identify those that do not take the regular past-tense ending *-ed* (like *knew* or *came*). At this point, the class might delve into some facts in the history of English in order to find out where these irregular verbs come from. They could look into the older English patterns, which had more verb endings, and see that today's irregular verbs are the descendants of the strong verbs of earlier periods in the development of English. They could also see that at one point there were many more irregular verbs than there are today. This inquiry would allow the class to see first hand the shifting nature of what is considered standard and what is considered nonstandard usage.

In looking at the different forms used by different speakers, students can also discover some principles about the nature of language. For instance, several of the patterns that emerge in nonstandard use of irregular verbs involve processes of regularization. Speakers in some groups may use *knowed* or *growed*, with the regular *-ed* ending on the verb, rather than an irregular form. This pattern of use shows how living languages treat irregularity. Students may discover controversy over verbs like *dive* or *sneak*: Some members of the class and individuals in the community prefer the regular form, and some prefer the irregular version (*dived/dove, sneaked/snuck*). This is a case in which no single standard form prevails. Other lines of inquiry can open up from an initial investigation of how speakers actually use a feature like the irregular verb—as opposed to how they think they use it. With some planning, students working through a unit like this could learn a great deal about their language and their community.

Further value comes from the opportunity for students to engage in a kind of scientific investigation. Examining how speakers in their community use language provides a natural laboratory for the students to make generalizations based on an array of data. Their own knowledge of the language can form the basis for hypothesizing rules that govern the use of particular linguistic items. These hypotheses can then be checked against additional data that they can also provide or obtain from other speakers. In a sense, then, the process of hypothesis construction and testing that is fundamental to scientific inquiry can be practiced in the unique laboratory of current language use. This training gives such a program value beyond what can be learned about the language. It also suggests links to other content areas for cross-disciplinary thematic units.

Student investigation of dialects serves other functions. It is a central way to get at the attitudes about language held by all students, to enhance self-awareness, and to gain insight into the nature of culturally based behavior. With language as a subject, attitudes toward differences among people can be explored, and the integrity of all cultural systems can be underscored. At issue is how students feel about other students and about themselves. For example, it is not uncommon for students who speak socially favored varieties to view their dialectally different peers as linguistically deficient. Worse yet, speakers of socially disfavored varieties may come to accept this viewpoint about their own variety of language. Students need to understand the natural sociolinguistic principles that lead to the development and maintenance of language varieties apart from their social evaluation and differential status. Furthermore, students need to understand that a dialect difference is not an inherent linguistic or cognitive deficit. Only when this understanding is commonly accepted will there be a change in the current practice of discrimination on the basis of dialect. If the whole class of students has been introduced to such a perspective on standard and vernacular forms of language, an environment has been created in which the vernacular dialect speakers can maintain their native forms of speech while acquiring standard forms as needed without fear of stereotyping.

The use of the community as a language resource can have other advantages as well. Sending students into the community as researchers can contribute to preserving the region's cultural and oral traditions, as well as providing an authentic, active learning experience. Another way to use the community as a resource is to have its members visit the classroom for specific purposes, including discussions about older traditions and ways of doing things. Students can interview them and then write up what they learned about the life and language of these community figures.

A model for this approach is the successful *Foxfire* project that began in 1966 with the idea of having students put together a magazine simply as a way of making language arts more interesting. The magazine is committed to promoting a sense of place and "appreciation of local people, community, and culture as essential educational tools" (www.foxfire.org). It has feature stories about traditions from the Southern Appalachia area—folk tales, superstitions, and reports on events in the community's history. The magazine has succeeded not only as a way of preserving local traditions, but also as a way of enriching the language arts experience. Writing about local lore gathered in ethnographic inquiry is a compelling assignment for students.

The concept of using dialect diversity and the cultural diversity that accompanies it as a resource in the language arts curriculum proceeds from a viewpoint that is different from traditional educational practices. Instead of seeing differences as problems, proponents of this approach have found that the differences are fascinating topics for study.

DIALECT AWARENESS

To build the dialect knowledge that students need to collect and analyze linguistic data in their community, schools can offer dialect awareness units. Linguists have developed such a unit and tested it successfully in different locations in North Carolina (e.g., Reaser, 2006; Reaser & Wolfram, 2005; Wolfram, Schilling-Estes, & Hazen, 1997) and also to a limited extent in Baltimore, Maryland (Wolfram, Adger, & Detwyler, 1992). Excerpts from the curriculum presented here suggest the kind of language activities that students can do and that they enjoy. A range of concerns could be addressed in a comprehensive dialect awareness program: These materials relate to affective, cognitive, and social parameters. Each lesson features a brief introduction, indicating the rationale for the lesson and, in some cases, observations about its effectiveness.

Because few teachers have had extensive training in linguistics, they are likely to require background explanation and teaching tips for a dialect awareness unit. The unit being exemplified here was designed for use by teachers without a linguistic background.

Introduction to Language Diversity

One essential component of any program on dialect awareness is a unit that considers the naturalness of dialect variation in American English. Students need to confront the general stereotypes and misconceptions about dialects that live on in the society. This is probably best done inductively. An easy method of doing this involves having students listen to representative speech samples of regional, class, and ethnic varieties. Students need to compare the speech of native Standard English speakers in diverse regions such as New England, the rural South, and the urban North in order to appreciate the reality of spoken regional standards, just as they need to recognize the difference between standard and vernacular varieties in these regions. Students in the Midwest need to consider some of the dialect traits of their own variety as it compares with others in order to understand that everyone really does speak a dialect.

Although most tape-recorded collections of dialect samples are personal ones that are not commercially available, the video production *American Tongues* (Alvarez & Kolker, 1987) is an especially effective tool for having students confront the affective parameters related to dialect diversity. Although the film is somewhat dated, the message is still quite current. It offers an entertaining introduction to dialects while exposing basic prejudices and myths about language differences. The documentary *Do You Speak American?* (MacNeil/Lehrer Productions, 2005) is much more current. It also has a related and useful Web site (www.pbs.org/speak) that addresses issues related to dialect diversity, language standards, and different regional and ethnic varieties. The travelogue presentation style makes it less entertaining than *American Tongues,* and the length (3 hours) precludes watching it in a single session, but it contains many entertaining and useful vignettes that can be extracted from the program for classroom use. Curriculum materials for five topical units appear at www.pbs.org/speak/education.

State-centered documentaries such as *Voices of North Carolina* work well too, but some of the vignettes are too localized for widespread use. Box 8.1 comes from an introductory unit for students in North Carolina (from Reaser & Wolfram [2005] and Reaser [2006]), which uses this documentary to explore the naturalness of dialects and the attitudes often associated with this diversity.

Levels of Dialect

As pointed out in chapters 2 and 3, language is simultaneously organized on several levels, including phonology, grammar, vocabulary, and language use. For those who examine dialect diversity, understanding the simultaneous organization of language on these various levels is essential. It shows how language can vary and how this variation may be interpreted. Students can engage in activities that help them recognize these levels of language organization.

Box 8.2 includes sample exercises on levels of dialect difference. The first one is a written task; the second one involves listening to a local dialect speaker. In listening tasks, it is important to incorporate both local and nonlocal dialects so that students can apply their knowledge beyond the local community. Commercially available storytelling tapes may be used for

Box 8.1

Sample Introductory Lesson on Dialect Diversity and Attitudes (from Reaser & Wolfram, student book, 2005).

In this unit, we're going to study about language and dialects. We will look at how dialects work in general and how specific dialects of North Carolina work. We will figure out some dialect patterns and see how these patterns have developed. As you work with this unit, you should pay close attention to the dialects spoken by people around you. Dialects are a fascinating window into culture and history, and we'll see how the dialects of North Carolina reflect the history and culture of the state.

VIDEO EXERCISE

You will watch segments from the video called *Voices of North Carolina*, which shows speakers of different dialects of English in North Carolina. After you watch the video, you and your group will discuss these questions and share your reactions.

1. What is a dialect?
2. What do people think about dialects? Explain.
3. What do you think about dialects?
4. What kinds of things can you tell about a person's background based on their accent?

LANGUAGE JOURNAL

At the end of this workbook, there is a section for you to write down some of your thoughts and observations about language. Each day you should write at least a couple of sentences that capture your thoughts about what you are learning. Feel free to write about things you are observing about dialect outside the classroom.

Take a few minutes to think about language in terms of dialect: What experiences have you had with dialects? Did you see or hear anything on the video that was surprising? What kind of assumptions do people make about others with strong dialects different from their own? Have you ever made an assumption about someone based on the way they spoke? Take a few minutes to write down some of your feelings about dialects. You may address some of the previous questions, or you may simply want to free-write about dialect. Write at least three sentences and ask at least two questions.

listening tasks, as well as tapes from the archival collections of the *Dictionary of American Regional English* and Center for Applied Linguistics' collection of *American English Speech Recordings* (Christian, 1986), available at the Library of Congress along with other dialect and oral history recordings. There are also Web sites with speech samples (e.g., http://www. ncsu. edu/linguistics, http://www.coas.uncc.edu/linguistics). The first excerpt in Box 8.2 comes from the program's instructional manual.

Box 8.2

Sample Exercises on Levels of Dialect (from Reaser & Wolfram, 2005).

In this unit, we look at the components that make up a dialect, or *dialect levels*. We also listen to some examples from particular dialects.

LEVELS OF DIALECT

Language is organized on several different levels. One level of organization is *pronunciation*, which concerns how sounds are used in a language. Different dialects may use sounds in quite different ways. Sometimes this is referred to simply as accent. For example, some people from New England pronounce the word *car* and *far* without the *r*. Also, some people from the South may say *greasy* with a *z* sound in the middle of the word so that they pronounce it *greazy*. In Ocracoke, the way some people say *hoi toiders* (for *high tiders*) or *sound* shows that the island has some unique pronunciations.

Another level of language organization is *grammar*. Grammar concerns the particular ways in which speakers arrange sentences and words. Different dialects may arrange words and sentences in different ways. For instance, in some parts of western Pennsylvania, speakers may say *The car needs washed*, whereas other speakers say *The car needs washing*. Also, some people from the Appalachian mountains or from the Outer Banks may say *The man went a-hunting*, whereas other people say *The man went hunting*. When a person from the Outer Banks says *It weren't me*, as opposed to *It wasn't me*, we have an example of dialect grammar.

A third level of language involves how different words are used, called the *vocabulary* or *lexicon* of the language. Speakers of different

(continued on next page)

Box 8.2 (continued)

dialects use different words to mean the same thing. Thus, some people in Philadelphia, Pennsylvania, use the word *hoagie* in reference to the same kind of sandwich that other people call a *sub*—or a *grinder, torpedo, hero, poor boy,* and so forth. Also, a common word might be used with different meanings across dialects. Thus, in some areas, *soda* is used for a carbonated drink with ice cream, whereas in other areas, *soda* is used just to refer to a carbonated drink without anything added to it. On the Outer Banks, the use of the term *mommuck* for *hassle, quamish* for *sick stomach,* or *scud* for *ride* provides examples of vocabulary differences.

Levels of Dialect

(From the instructional guide)

(Teaching time: 20–30 minutes)

This discussion and exercise requires students to apply the definitions discussed earlier. Ask students to review by defining the terms *dialect vocabulary, dialect pronunciation,* and *dialect grammar.*

In this exercise, students look at the components that make up a dialect, or *dialect levels.* In doing this, they examine dialect features from the Outer Banks to Appalachia. In the sentence pairs given next, have students decide whether the difference between the sentences in each pair is at the vocabulary, pronunciation, or grammar level. Have them place a <u>V</u> for vocabulary, a <u>P</u> for pronunciation, and a <u>G</u> for grammar level difference in the blank provided beside each pair.

Worksheet Answer Key and Explanations

1. __P__ That feller sure was tall
           That fellow sure was tall

Background information: This feature, common in many rural Southern dialects, can affect all words that end with an unstressed "o" sound, including *yellow, potato, tomato, mosquito, window, elbow, burrito,* and so forth. These words would be pronounced with an "r" sound instead of the "o" sound: *yeller, potater* (or simply *tater*), *tomater* (or simply *mater*), *mosquiter* (or simply *skeeter*), *winder, elber,* and *burriter.* This pattern does not apply when the "o" sound is stressed, as in *throw, go,* or *bestow.* Thus, there is a pattern that determines when this feature can operate and when it cannot.

Box 8.2 (continued)

2. __V__ That road sure is sigogglin
    That road sure is crooked

Background information: The word *sigogglin* is found in the speech of people who live in the Appalachian Mountain region of North Carolina. It can mean *crooked*, *askew*, or *not plumb*. Roads, houses, and walls can all be sigogglin. This word is sometimes written *sygogglin* and sometimes pronounced as "sigoggly." In other parts of the South, the word *catawampus* or *catterwampus* can be used to mean crooked. In other places, such as the South Midland region, some speakers use the word *antigogglin*. All of these are examples of dialect vocabulary.

3. __G__ They usually be doing their homework
    They usually do their homework

Background information: There is a special use of *be* in African American English. The uninflected form of *be* is used in place of conjugated *am*, *is*, or *are* in sentences that describe habitual or recurring action. In this sentence, the habitual context is denoted by the word *usually*. In nonhabitual contexts, African American English speakers would use either regularly inflected forms such as *am*, *is*, and *are*, or they would omit the verb altogether.

4. __G__ I weren't there yesterday
    I wasn't there yesterday

Background information: This feature, common in many dialects, is a result of an irregular pattern being made regular. Linguists refer to this as *regularization* or *leveling*. Leveling is a natural process that may take place whenever there is an irregularity in a particular pattern. Because the verb *to be* is irregular in English, there is a natural tendency to favor regularization or leveling of this pattern. Thus, dialects may use *was* for all past-tense forms—*I was, you was, he was*, and so forth. In some dialects in North Carolina, affirmative past-tense forms of *to be* may be leveled to *was*, but negative past-tense forms are often leveled to *weren't* (as in *I was, you was, he was, we was*, and *I weren't, you weren't, he weren't, we weren't*).

(continued on next page)

Box 8.2 (continued)

5. __V__ They put their food in a poke
    They put their food in a bag

Background information: The word *poke* is used to describe a paper sack or bag in the Appalachian Mountains of North Carolina northward through western Pennsylvania. It is also found in other parts of the rural South. The word stems from the Scots-Irish influence of this region.

6. __P__ It's hoi toid on the sound soid
    It's high tide on the sound side

Background information: The pronunciation of the vowel "eye" as "oy" is perhaps the most noticeable feature of the Outer Banks region of North Carolina. This pronunciation is so prevalent that some people refer to the people who live on the Outer Banks as "Hoi Toiders." Many people may not realize that this pronunciation extended inland through a large portion of the Coastal Plain at one time. It is still found to a lesser extent in the speech of some people who live along the rural coast of mainland North Carolina.

7. __V__ I was hanging out with my peeps
    I was hanging out with my friends

Background information: Although many dialect features are regional or culturally based, variation in language is associated with other characteristics, such as age and personal style. Words like *peeps* are often classified as slang by middle-age adults, but they may be an important part of the dialect spoken by young people. The same types of word innovation processes that shape slang terms in each generation (consider the progression of words that mean *good* or *bad*) also shape lexical differences between regional and ethnic dialects.

8. __G__ They're to the school right now
    They're at school right now

Background information: The use of *to* where Standard English would use *at* used to be common throughout the United States. This feature, known as "locative *to*," has historical roots in Old English,

Box 8.2 (continued)

where it was the preferred preposition to indicate the location of something. Locative *to* can still be found in the speech of older rural Americans in many places, in the speech of some younger speakers along the Outer Banks of North Carolina, and to a lesser extent throughout rural North Carolina.

Teaching tip: If students indicate that Item 8 is a vocabulary difference, ask them to evaluate how the word is functioning grammatically. Although using *to* for *at* is "just using a different word," as students may point out, the lexical choice relates to the grammatical function of the word (preposition) and not to the meaning.

9. __P__ They caught some feesh
    They caught some fish

Background information: The pronunciation of *fish* as *feesh* is common throughout some parts of the South. The use of this feature has declined recently in urban areas. This vowel change, where words with a short *i* (*fish, bit, still*, etc.) are pronounced with a long *e* sound (*feesh, beet, steel*, etc.), affects many words. The reverse process is also heard in the South. Some words with a long *e* (*steel, field, meat*, etc.) are pronounced with a short *i* sound (*still, filled, mit*, etc.).

10. __G__ They went hunting and fishing
     They went a-hunting and a-fishing

Background Information: This feature is called "*a*-prefixing" because the "uh" sound attaches to the beginning of the word. It is most commonly associated with the speech of the Appalachian Mountains, although it is also found along the Outer Banks and other rural regions of North Carolina. It is a preservation of a linguistic form found in earlier English, which required the use of a preposition *on* or *at* before certain verbs. Over time, a sentence such as *we were on hunting* or *we were at hunting* became simply *we were a-hunting*. There are specific rules that determine when a speaker can and cannot use the *a*-prefixing feature. This pattern is examined in the Patterns of Dialects section of this unit.

Teaching tip: Some students may label this as a pronunciation feature, and that is understandable. However, because we know the historical context of the feature, it is clear that the pattern derives from a

(continued on next page)

Box 8.2 (continued)

grammatical function. Therefore, it is still labeled as such. Pointing this out to students may illustrate that there is a little more than just common sense that determines what level of language a dialect feature is.

Some Examples From The Outer Banks
(Exercise for students)

The following excerpt is from a taped interview with a middle-age islander. As you listen to the tape, read through the passage without making any marks on the paper. As you listen to the tape a second time, determine whether the boldface words represent the grammar, pronunciation, or vocabulary level of the dialect. In the blanks following the boldface words, place a G for grammar, P for pronunciation, or a V for vocabulary.

[The remarks of the person conducting the interview are not included.]

Well we, like, say we started on that end and started runnin' 'em back this way, and then they used to come on to the—you know—see there *weren't* ___ 1 all this—this was swamp here, we used to hunt. On every one of these *houses* ___ 2 ; all these houses from where we turned at the *fire* ___ 3 station up this way *has* ___ 4 been built here since the sixties. There was only one house was up here in the sixties. All this subdivision, Jackson Dunes, Oyster Creek. And then the ponies would come around, you know, you'd pen 'em up and they'd come right on the shore, out here. And then we had beaches, you know, before everybody started building, you had a little beach all the way around on the sound *side* ___ 5, just like you do on the ocean. But now you don't. And everybody's *breakwatered* ___ 6 and filled in, built. And then in June, we had a cattle *penning* ___ 7.

Local vocabularies are a rich source for engaging students in examining dialect differences. The activity in Box 8.3 is taken from the Ocracoke dialect curriculum (Reaser & Wolfram , 2005), which has been taught for more than a decade to middle-school students. Activities of this type help students become aware of the culturally specific, relative nature of vocabulary. It is offered here as a prototype for student involvement in gathering data. Students can take an active role in constructing local adaptations of this exercise.

Box 8.3

Example of Dialect Vocabulary Activity

VOCABULARY IN OCRACOKE

There are lots of vocabulary differences that can be described for Ocracoke. Each of the uses has a unique history. We can trace back some uses in the English language more than 1,000 years, and some go back just a few years. For example, words like *token* (in *token of death*), *mommuck*, and *quamish* were used centuries ago in ways related to how they are used in Ocracoke today. Other terms such as *dingbatter*, *scud*, and *up the beach* are relatively recent uses. We can trace certain vocabulary forms confidently, but we can make only educated guesses about the origins of other words. For example, a unique Ocracoke use of the phrase *Call the mail over* may be traced to the earlier custom of distributing mail by calling aloud the names of those who received letters at the dock when the mail boat arrived. We're not exactly sure how *meehonkey* came into use, but we guess that it had something to do with the attempt to imitate the call of a goose.

Most of the dialect words found in Ocracoke occur in other dialects as well, but a few are unique to Ocracoke. Also, the use of vocabulary in Ocracoke differs according to age and background.

Following are some words that are part of the Ocracoke dialect vocabulary. For each of the words, do the following:

- Figure out what the word means, if you don't already know. You can usually do this by asking island residents of different ages about the words.
- Use the word in a sentence and try to figure out what part of speech it is.
- Identify the type of people who know the word and who use it: Is it used by older people, by younger people, by nonislanders?
- Which of the words do you think are used ONLY in Ocracoke or in the Outer Banks?

Write your answers below.

*slick cam*_____

*puck*_____

*across the beach*_____

*up the beach*_____

*meehonkey*_____

(continued on next page)

> *Box 8.3 (continued)*
>
>
> scud_____
> *token of death*_____
> *yaupon*_____
>
> Make a chart that summarizes the group of people who know the words in the list. On top of the chart, list the groups. Here is an example:
>
> | | Older Ocracokers | Younger Ocracokers | Outsiders |
> |---|:---:|:---:|:---:|
> | *word* | | ✓ | |
> | *word* | | ✓ | ✓ |
> | *word* | ✓ | | |
>
> List each of the words in the column on the left and check the groups that use each of the words.

Box 8.4 gives an example of a vocabulary exercise used in a curriculum developed for middle-school students in North Carolina (Reaser & Wolfram, 2006). It includes both regional and ethnic parameters. Students are exposed to all of the terms included in the exercise through various video vignettes that they view during the course of the curriculum. This excerpt is from the instructor's manual.

The Patterning of Dialect

Language, including dialects, is a unique form of knowledge in that speakers know a language simply by virtue of the fact that they speak it. Much of this knowledge is not conscious, but it is still open to systematic investigation. The study of dialects affords us a fascinating window through which we can see how language works. The inner workings of language are just as readily observed in examining dialect patterning as through the exclusive study of a single standard variety.

Making generalizations from carefully described sets of data, students can hypothesize about the patterning of language features and then check their hypotheses on the basis of actual usage. This, of course, is a type of scientific inquiry. Such a rationale for studying dialects may seem a bit esoteric at first glance, but hypothesizing about and then testing language

Box 8.4

North Carolina Dialects Vocabulary Exercise

As we have seen, dialect vocabulary is often important to dialect speakers. It is also the level of language that is most likely to differ between dialects, even dialects that are historically linked. Following are some dialect words from several different North Carolina dialects that have been featured in this unit. Have students fill in the blanks in the following sentences with the appropriate dialect word. Answers are provided here.

airish	boomer	buck	ellick	gaum
juvember	meehonky	mommuck	toboggan	slam
poke	slick cam	sigogglin	touron	token

1. They used a __*juvember*__ for target practice.
2. That __*touron*__ is from New Jersey.
3. Put those groceries in a __*poke*__ and I'll take them home.
4. When I got up this morning it was right __*airish*__ outside.
5. They're always together because he's his __*buck* __.
6. At night we used to play __*meehonkey*__.
7. I saw a __*token*__ in the field last night and it scared me.
8. They worked so hard that they were __*slam*__ wore out.
9. Last night a ___*boomer*__ got in the attic and made quite a racket.
10. It was so cold we needed a __*toboggan*__.
11. If I don't have some __*ellick*__ I'm going to fall asleep.
12. The road going up there sure is _*sigogglin*__.
13. She used to __*mommuck*___ him when he was a child.
14. It sure was__*slick cam*__ on the sound without any wind.
15. Don't __*gaum*___ up the radiator with that stuff.

Some of the dialect words are used on the Outer Banks, some are used in the mountains, and some are used mostly by the Lumbee Indians in Robeson County. There are also some words that are shared by these groups. The following table lists the words that are used by each group as well as those that are shared by the groups. Discuss with students what can be concluded about the culture/life of each group of speakers.

(continued on next page)

Box 8.4 (continued)

Outer Banks	Lumbee	Mountains	Shared
buck	ellick	Airish	Guam
meehonkey	juvember	Boomer	mommuck
slam		Poke	toboggan
sick cam		Sigogglin	Token
touron			

patterns is well within the grasp even of younger students. In fact, students in the upper elementary grades have been able to work through the steps of hypothesis formation and testing by using exercises involving dialect features, like those in Boxes 8.5 and 8.6. They include several types of language patterning. The exercises in Box 8.5 illustrate patterning in pronunciation and those in Box 8.6 the patterning of grammatical differences. It is helpful to do pronunciation exercises like those in Box 8.5 with supportive audio recordings of the actual pronunciation. These exercises represent both regional and social dimensions of dialects, ranging from Southern regional speech to New England speech, as well as Appalachian and African American Vernacular English. They allow students to experience inductively how patterned all varieties of language are regardless of their social valuation. The section from the teacher's manual that appears here indicates that this material is designed for teachers who have no background in linguistics.

Box 8.5

Illustrative Exercises in Pronunciation Patterning
Instructor's manual (from Reaser, 2006)

PRONUNCIATION LESSON
    This lesson asks students to examine language data and formulate and test hypotheses about how dialects pattern. These hypotheses are refined as students gain authentic knowledge of language patterns. Finally, students are introduced to the first of seven language varieties of North Carolina: Outer Banks English.

Box 8.5 (continued)

Overview

Many people are shocked to learn that dialects are patterned and systematic. Even speakers of dialects who conform to the patterns may not be aware of the patterns that govern their speech. The following activities examine a few linguistic patterns from different dialects of English, including New England English, Southern English, and Appalachian English. These activities demonstrate the systematic nature of language variation and help students see language as a topic worthy of scientific study.

Students also learn about the history and culture of one of North Carolina's most famous dialects, Outer Banks English, or "hoi toider speech." This dialect is a good starting point because the Outer Banks was the first area of North Carolina that Europeans explored. Many students in North Carolina have some exposure to this dialect, and therefore it serves as a good hook to draw them into dialect study. A few of the linguistic patterns associated with this dialect are examined.

Key Ideas

1. All dialects have patterns that govern their use, just as Standard English does.

2. Some individual dialect features pattern in relatively simple ways, whereas others follow multiple rules that govern their use.

3. Linguists study language patterns.

4. Some language patterns can be discovered with help from our linguistic intuitions, whereas others require examining data from dialect speakers.

5. Outer Banks speech reflects some older language patterns as well as some new language patterns.

Resources

Language Magazine article on Ocracoke.
http://ncsu.edu/linguistics/code/Research%20Sites/harkers.htm
http://ncsu.edu/linguistics/code/Research%20Sites/ocracoke.htm
http://ncsu.edu/linguistics/code/Research%20Sites/roanoke.htm

Teaching Tips

Students may benefit from a quick review of the levels of language or a quiz on the levels of dialect features.

(continued on next page)

Box 8.5 (continued)

The materials for this lesson may take longer than 1 day to complete. It is better to go slowly through this material so that students get a thorough understanding of it. Catching up with the lesson schedule is less problematic than filling in gaps in students' understanding.

How Dialects Pattern

Dialects are patterned and rule-governed, not haphazard. What this means is that the dialects of a language follow their own patterns. The rules that dialects follow state the regular, predictable patterns that dialect forms follow. Sometimes these patterns can be complicated and difficult to figure out. However, the human mind has the capacity to learn all of these intricate patterns unconsciously and follow them. The ability to absorb language patterns and follow them without thinking about the patterns is one of the most amazing things about the human mind.

In this lesson, the class will try to figure out some patterns for different dialect forms found in North Carolina and elsewhere. The challenge is to come up with a rule that accurately describes all the examples. If the rule is correct, it should predict how new language forms will be treated.

Both the grammar and the pronunciation of a dialect follow patterns. The class will try to figure out some dialect patterns as they think about language as a linguist does. Linguists study language scientifically in order to figure out the specific patterns of language arrangement. They do not create language patterns, just as other scientists do not create the laws of nature. The language patterns already exist in the minds of those who speak the language. The linguist simply tries to figure out and state the regular, predictable design that guides the use of language, just like the scientist describes the laws of nature.

How Pronunciation Differences Work: Southern Vowel Merger

In some Southern dialects of English, words like *pin* and *pen* are pronounced the same. Usually, both words are pronounced as *pin*. This pattern of pronunciation is also found in other words. Examining data from a native speaker of this dialect demonstrates how linguists uncover linguistic patterns. List A has words in which the *i* and *e* are pronounced the same in these dialects. Play a recording of a native speaker with this vowel merger for the students.

Box 8.5 (continued)

List A: I and E Pronounced the Same
1. *tin* and *ten*
2. *kin* and *Ken*
3. *Lin* and *Len*
4. *windy* and *Wendy*
5. *sinned* and *send*

Although *i* and *e* in List A are pronounced the same, there are other words in which *i* and *e* are pronounced differently. List B has word pairs in which the vowels are pronounced differently.

List B: I and E Pronounced Differently
1. *lit* and *let*
2. *pick* and *peck*
3. *pig* and *peg*
4. *rip* and *rep*
5. *litter* and *letter*

Ask students to examine the word pairs in the two lists and offer hypotheses about when *i* and *e* are pronounced the same and when they are pronounced differently. If they are having trouble discovering the pattern, ask them to examine the sounds that are next to the vowels. The pattern is determined by the presence or absence of an *n*-sound. If an *n*-sound follows the vowel, the words are pronounced the same. If there is no *n*-sound following the vowel, the words are pronounced differently.

Have students use what they have learned about this pronunciation pattern to predict the word pairs in List C that are pronounced the same and those that are pronounced differently in this Southern dialect. Have them mark the word pairs that are pronounced the same with S and the word pairs that are pronounced differently with D. Answers are supplied here.

List C: Same or Different?
__D_ *bit* and *bet*
__D_ *pit* and *pet*
__S_ *bin* and *Ben*
__D_ *Nick* and *neck*
__S_ *din* and *den*

(continued on next page)

Box 8.5 (continued)

How Pronunciation Differences Work: Dropping *r* in English Dialects

In some dialects of English, the *r* sound of words like *car* or *poor* can be dropped. In these words, the *r* is not pronounced, so that these words sound like *"cah"* and *"po."* However, not all *r* sounds can be dropped. In some places in a word the *r* sound may be dropped, and in other places it may NOT be dropped. By comparing lists of words where the *r* may be dropped with lists of words where it may NOT be dropped, the students can figure out a pattern for *r* dropping.

List A gives words where the *r* may be DROPPED.

List A: Words That Can Drop r
1. ca_r_
2. fathe_r_
3. ca_r_d
4. bigge_r_
5. ca_r_dboa_r_d
6. bee_r_
7. cou_r_t

List B gives words where the *r* sound may NOT be dropped. In other words, speakers who drop their *r*s in List A pronounce the *r* in the words in List B.

List B: Words That CANNOT Drop r
1. _r_un
2. b_r_ing
3. p_r_incipal
4. st_r_ing
5. ok_r_a
6. app_r_oach
7. Ap_r_il

To find a pattern for dropping the *r*, look at the type of sound that comes before the *r* in Lists A and B. Does a vowel or a consonant come before the *r* in List A? What comes before the *r* in List B? How can you predict where an *r* may or may not be dropped?

In List C, pick those words that may drop their *r* and those that may not drop their *r*. Use your knowledge of the *r*-dropping pattern that you learned by comparing Lists A and B. Put Y for "Yes" if the word can drop the *r* and N for "No" if it cannot drop the *r*.

Box 8.5 (continued)

List C: Applying the Rule for r Dropping
1. ___ bea_r_
2. ___ p_r_og_r_am
3. ___ fea_r_ful
4. ___ _r_ight
5. ___ compute_r_
6. ___ pa_r_ty
7. ___ fou_r_teen

Think of two new words that may drop an *r* and two new words that may NOT drop an *r*.

More About r-Dropping Patterns
In the last exercise, you saw that *r* dropping only takes place when the *r* comes after a vowel. Now look at the kinds of sounds that may come AFTER the *r* in some dialects of English. This pattern goes along with the one you already learned. Now see if you can figure out the pattern.

Here are some words where the *r* may NOT be dropped even when it comes after a vowel.

List A: Words That Do NOT Drop r
1. bea_r_ in the field
2. ca_r_ ove_r_ at the house
3. ga_r_age
4. ca_r_ing
5. take fou_r_ apples
6. pea_r_ on the tree
7. fa_r_ enough

What kinds of sounds come after the *r* in List A? Are they vowels or consonants?

In List B, the *r* MAY be dropped. What kind of sounds come after the *r* in this list?

List B: Words That Drop r
1. bea_r_ by the woods
2. ca_r_ pa_r_ked by the house
3. pa_r_king the bus
4. fea_r_ful

(continued on next page)

Box 8.5 (continued)

5. take fou<u>r</u> peaches
6. pea<u>r</u> by the house
7. fa<u>r</u> behind

What does the sound that comes after *r* do to *r*-dropping?

Use what you know about the pattern for *r*-dropping to pick the *r*s in List C that can be dropped. Say why the *r* can or cannot be dropped. Write Y for "Yes" if the *r* can be dropped and N for "No" if it cannot be dropped. Remember that the *r* must come after a vowel to be dropped, but it cannot have a vowel after it.

List C: Words That May or May Not Drop r
1. pea<u>r</u> on the table
2. pea<u>r</u> by the table
3. pa<u>r</u>k in the mall
4. prog<u>r</u>am in the mall
5. ca<u>r</u> behind the house

List D: Practicing the r-Drop Pattern
Try to pronounce the two sentences given here according to the *r*-drop pattern that you learned.
1. The teache<u>r</u> picked on th<u>r</u>ee students fo<u>r</u> an answe<u>r</u>.
2. Fou<u>r</u> ca<u>r</u>s pa<u>r</u>ked fa<u>r</u> away f<u>r</u>om the fai<u>r</u>.

Exercises on grammatical patterning like those in Boxes 8.5 and 8.6 can go a long way toward dispelling the notions that dialects are simply imperfect renditions of the standard variety. Working with them sets the stage for generating a genuine respect for the complexity of systematic differences among dialects. In fact, the most frequent response from students who have participated in the pilot curricula is that this is something all students should learn about. In the process of such inductive discovery, students often develop a scientifically based respect for the integrity of language patterning.

The advantage of the *a*- prefixing exercise in Box 8.6 is that it involves a form whose patterning is intuitive to both those who use the form in their vernacular dialect and those who do not. This fact makes the exercise appropriate for English-speaking students regardless of their native dialect. Working through exercises of this type is an effective way of confronting the myth that dialects have no rules of their own; at the same time, such exercises effectively demonstrate the underlying cognitive patterning of lan-

Box 8.6

Illustrative Exercises of Grammatical Patterning

THE USE OF *A-* PREFIX

In some traditional rural dialects of the South, some words that end in *-ing* can take an *a-*, pronounced as *uh*, in front of the word, as in *she went a-fishing*. This pattern is called *a-* prefixing. But not every *-ing* word can have an *a-* prefix. There are patterns or rules that determine when the *a-* prefix can be used and when it cannot be used. You will try to figure out these rules by using your inner feelings about language. These inner feelings, called *intuitions*, tell you when you CAN and CANNOT use certain forms. The job of linguists is to figure out the reason for these inner feelings and state the exact pattern or rule.

Read each pair of sentences in List A and insert *a-* ("uh") before the *-ing* word. Decide which sentence in each pair sounds better. For example, in the first sentence pair, does it sound better to say, *A-building is hard work* or *She was a-building a house*? For each pair of sentences, place a check next to the sentence that sounds better with the *a-*.

List A: Sentence Pairs for A- Prefixing
1. a. ____Building is hard work.
   b. ____She was building a house.
2. a. ____He likes hunting.
   b. ____He went hunting.
3. a. ____The child was charming the adults.
   b. ____The child was very charming.
4. a. ____He kept running to the store.
   b. ____The store was shocking.
5. a. ____They thought fishing was easy.
   b. ____They were fishing this morning.

Look at your choices for the *a-* prefix in each pair of sentences and answer the following questions.

Do you think there is some pattern that guided your choice of an answer? You can tell if there is a definite pattern by checking with other people who did the same exercise on their own. Do you think that the pattern might be related to parts of speech? To answer this, see if there are any parts of speech where you CANNOT use the *a-* prefix. Look at *-ing* forms that function as verbs and compare those with

(continued on next page)

Box 8.6 (continued)

-ing forms that operate as nouns or adjectives. For example, look at the use of *charming* as a verb (The child was *charming* the adults) and adjective (The child was very *charming*) in Sentence 3.

The first rule of the pattern for *a-* prefix is related to the part of speech of the *-ing* word, but there is more to the pattern. To discover the second rule, read the sentences in List B, insert the *a-* before the *-ing* word, and decide which sentence in each pair sounds better. For each pair of sentences, place a check next to the sentence that sounds better with the *a-*.

List B: A Further Detail for A- Patterning
1. a. ____They make money by building houses.
   b. ____They make money building houses.
2. a. ____People can't make enough money fishing.
   b. ____People can't make enough money from fishing.
3. a. ____People destroy the beauty of the island through littering.
   b. ____People destroy the beauty of the island littering.

The second rule of the pattern for *a-* prefix is related to prepositions. But there is still another rule to the pattern for *a-* prefix use. To discover the third rule, read the sentences in List C, insert the *a-* before the *-ing* word and decide which sentence in each pair sounds better. To help you figure out this rule, the stressed or accented syllable of each word is marked with the symbol ´. For each pair of sentences, place a check next to the sentence that sounds better with the *a-*.

List C: Figuring out a Pronunciation Pattern for A- Prefix
1. a.____She was discóvering a trail.
   b.____She was fóllowing a trail.
2. a.____She was repéating the chant.
   b.____She was hóllering the chant.
3. a.____They were fíguring the change.
   b.____They were forgétting the change.
4. a.____The baby was recognízing the mother.
   b.____The baby was wrécking everything.

Say exactly how the three rules determine the pattern for attaching the *a-* prefix to *-ing* words.

Box 8.6 (continued)

Rule 1: _____

Rule 2: _____

Rule 3: _____

Using your rules, try to predict whether the sentences in List D may use an *a-* prefix. Use your understanding of the pattern to explain why the *-ing* word may or may not take the *a-* prefix.

List D: Applying the A- Prefix Rule
1. She kept handing me more work.
2. The team was remémbering the game.
3. The team won by playing great defense.
4. The team was playing real hard.

Be in African American English
The next task concerns a form in a dialect that is sometimes used by young African American speakers in large cities. The form *be* is used where other dialects use *am*, *is*, or *are*, except that it has a special meaning. A group of 35 young speakers of this dialect of English chose the sentence that sounded better to them in the following sentence pairs, like you did for *a-* prefixing. Notice that they had a definite preference for one sentence over the other.

Why do you think that was the case?

The number before each sentence indicates how many of the young people chose that sentence as the best one in the pair:

1. <u>32</u> a. *They usually be tired when they come home.*
   <u>3</u> b. They be tired right now.
2. <u>31</u> a. *When we play basketball, she be on my team.*
   <u>4</u> b. The girl in the picture be my sister.
3. <u>4</u> a. James be coming to school right now.
   <u>31</u> b. *James always be coming to school.*
4. <u>3</u> a. My ankle be broken from the fall.
   <u>32</u> b. *Sometimes my ears be itching.*

(continued on next page)

Box 8.6 (continued)

Try to figure out the pattern that led the young people to make their choices. To do this, look at the type of action that is involved in each sentence. Does the action take place at just one time, or does the action take place more than once? Try to state the regular pattern in terms of the action.

Now that you know how the form *be* is used, predict which of the following sentences follow the rule for using *be* in the African American English dialect and which do NOT. Write Y for "Yes" if the sentence follows the dialect pattern and N for "No" if it does not.

1. ____The students always be talking in class.
2. ____The students don't be talking right now.
3. ____Sometimes the teacher be early for class.
4. ____At the moment the teacher be in the lounge.

As you can see, African American English has rules that determine when you can and cannot say *be*. In other words, there are rules for using *be* just as there are rules for using *a*- prefixing (*he went a-fishing*). Despite the fact that African American English is rule-governed and patterned like all dialects, it is often viewed negatively. But many African Americans are proud of the dialect. In the following video clip, you will see some African Americans who are proud of their dialect, but who also switch to Standard English when they feel it is necessary.

A Video Exercise

As you watch a video (8-minute vignette on African American English from *Voices of North Carolina*) about African American English, think about the following questions:

1. Why do you think that these African Americans feel they have to change the way they speak sometimes?

2. Do you ever feel that you have to change the way you speak? Why?

3. Think about the different situations in which you change your speech. In what situation(s) do you think you have to talk most formally? In what situation(s) do you think you can talk more casually?

guage. The second exercise in Box 8.6 on habitual *be* has been used along with a video of AAE speakers who systematically make the correct choices because they have unconsciously learned the pattern for the use of the verb. It demonstrates that patterning can be unique to a particular dialect and that we cannot make assumptions about other dialects based on our own. The exercise on systematic use of habitual *be* may be coupled with a reflective activity on the use of AAE in different situations, as indicated in the set of follow-up questions. This excerpt comes from the student materials.

These exercises show students how linguists collect and organize data to formulate rules while they provide a model for analyzing data that students collect from their own community. To emulate this process, students should record language data, extract particular examples from the recordings, and formulate linguistic rules. In this way, they can learn first-hand to examine language in a scientific way.

Language Change

It is important for students and instructors to understand how inevitable and natural language change is. Understanding the processes of change involves recognizing the orderly cognitive and behavioral processes that bring about change. For example, languages tend to "level" irregular patterns over time: Regularization is a normal and natural process in language change. When students from vernacular-speaking backgrounds regularize the past tense of irregular verbs such as *knowed* for *knew* and *growed* for *grew*, they are simply following a time-honored and natural tradition of leveling irregular verb forms—the same processes that gave Standard English *worked* (once *wrought*) and *help* (once *holp*). Many of the regular verbs we now accept as part of Standard English were, in fact, once irregular forms. Current changes in progress simply follow the principles that have guided language change in the past.

An understanding that language is not set once and for all should also foster an appreciation for its flexible nature. Language change may affect all levels of language in significant ways. Drastic changes in grammatical paradigms and word order in English are part of a continuously changing language; no one language state is superior. An appreciation for how radically the English language has changed over time should promote more tolerance for the small types of changes it is currently undergoing.

Finally, an understanding of language change should broaden views on language standards. History belies the myth that standards are static and consistent, a point that we have harped on throughout this book. Box 8.7 is a simple comparative activity that shows how dramatically English has changed over the centuries. By examining a familiar passage, in this case the Lord's Prayer, students can see radical change in the language at every level—from the sounds, the words, and the orderly arrangement of words within sentences.

Box 8.7

An Illustrative Exercise in Language Change

THE CHANGING OF THE ENGLISH LANGUAGE
English has changed quite dramatically over the centuries. In fact, early English is barely recognizable today. Compare the versions of English at various stages in its history, as found in the first verse of the Lord's Prayer.

Old English (about 950 A.D.)
Fader urer ðu bist in heofnas, sie gehalgad noma ðin

Middle English (about 1350 A.D.)
Oure fadir þat art in heuenes, halwid be þi name

Early Modern English (about 1550 A.D.)
O oure father which arte in heven, hallowed be thy name

Modern English (about 1985 A.D.)
Our father, who is in heaven, may your name be sacred
or
Our father, who art in heaven, hallowed be your name

1. Try pronouncing the different versions of English. In the older versions (Old and Middle English), "silent letters" do not exist, so you will need to pronounce *all* the letters. The symbol ð is pronounced something like the *th* of *this*, and the þ is pronounced like the *th* of *think*.

2. Try to identify some of the older versions of modern words. For example, trace the words that became the current words *father, heaven, name, is,* and *our*. What modern English word, besides *sacred*, did *hallow* become?

3. What does this comparison tell you about the way the English language has changed over the centuries?

One of the greatest advantages of a curriculum on dialects is its potential for tapping the language resources of students' indigenous communities. In addition to classroom lessons, students can learn by going into the community to collect live dialect data. For example, in the dialect curriculum designed for the island of Ocracoke, students are given some local terms (e.g., *Meehonkey* for *hide and seek* and *up the beach* for *off the island*) and told to interview individuals in the community representing different ages (older, middle age, young) and indigenous and nonindigenous residents. The results of the students' inquiries are summarized in a table that shows different distribution patterns by age and residency status.

Educational models that treat the local community as a resource to be tapped, rather than a liability to be overcome, have been shown to be quite effective in other areas of language arts education, and there is no reason that this model cannot be applied in an analogous fashion to the study of community dialects. In fact, the community dialect may just turn out to be the spark that ignites students' interest in the study of language arts.

IMPLEMENTING DIALECT AWARENESS CURRICULA

Implementing new curricular programs is, of course, easier said than done. To our knowledge, there are no large-scale dialect awareness programs in the United States and thus no models for introducing them. In North Carolina, where the dialect awareness unit exemplified here is being introduced, marketing skills, bureaucratic finesse, and a good sense of timing have proved to be essential. The argument has to be made that dialect awareness programs are consonant with the educational objectives of statewide and local curricula and readily implemented by practitioners. The curriculum developers have to identify specific competencies in social studies and communication skills as set forth by the State Board of Education and align lessons with these competencies (Simmons, Ware, Wark, & Yount, 1998). For example, some of the units align with the following competencies of North Carolina Standard Course of Study (NCSCS) Social Studies Goals:

- The learner will access the influence of geography on the economic, social, and political development of North Carolina.
- The learner will evaluate the effects of earlier contacts between various European nations and Native Americans.
- The learner will judge the continuing significance of social, economic, and political changes since 1945 and draw conclusions about their effect on contemporary life.

Units that examine the history of dialects and current changes in postinsular dialect areas clearly fall within the goals for social studies set forth by NCSCS.

A number of aspects of the curriculum also align with the NCSCS Communication Competencies Goals, such as the following:

- The learner will use strategies and processes that enhance control of communication skills development.
- The learner will use language for the acquisition, interpretation, and application of information. The learner will use language for critical analysis and evaluation.

- The learner will use language for aesthetic and personal response.

The program developers presented this alignment to the Director of the Social Studies of the Department of Public Instruction for the State of North Carolina (Walt Wolfram and Jeffrey Reaser, Raleigh, NC, 2005) to show that the proposed curriculum neatly fits into an existing course of study in social studies.

It is not difficult to demonstrate how dialect awareness programs are consonant with state-mandated competency goals, but this step is absolutely essential for the process of adopting new curriculum material. Schools and teachers are highly aware of and responsible for attaining these goals. Box 8.8 illustrates how a curriculum on dialects dovetails with existing social studies program and competency goals for 8th grade social studies in North Carolina.

Box 8.8

The Role of Dialect Awareness in the Curriculum

Excerpts from the North Carolina Description of the Middle Grades' Social Studies Program (www.ncpublicschools.org/curriculum/socialstudies/scos/2003-04/004description.html).

Notes in italics point to how dialect study addresses curriculum objectives.

- Individual Identity and Development—In each society, individual identity is shaped by one's culture, by groups, and by institutions.
  _ *Language is an important aspect of individual identity*

- Culture and Diversity—There are similarities as well as differences between and among cultures. Culture helps people to understand themselves both as individuals and as members of a group. As cultural borrowing becomes more prevalent, the differences between cultures become less defined.
  _ *These similarities/differences and borrowings can be reinforced by examining language*

- Historic Perspectives—Seeking to understand the historical roots of present-day cultures enables students to develop a perspective on their own place in time. Knowing what things were like in the past and how they changed and developed over time in a variety of societies and cultures provides students with a broader view of their own history.

Box 8.8 (continued)

_ *Understanding language variation can help students develop a perspective on their place within culture, history, and so forth.*

- Geographic Relationships—Studying places and the people who inhabit them as well as their interactions and mutual impact on each other enables the student to develop a spatial perspective on their place in the world going beyond personal location.
_ *The rich dialect diversity in North Carolina reinforces these perspectives.*

Excerpts from the Standard Course of Study for *Creation and Development of the State,* 8th-grade social studies (www.nc publicschools.org/curriculum/socialstudies/2003-04/05 eighthgrade.html)

- COMPETENCY GOAL 1: The learner will analyze important geographic, political, economic, and social aspects of life in the region prior to the Revolutionary Period.

Objective 1.01 Assess the impact of geography on the settlement and developing economy of the Carolina colony.
_ *Geography and settlement have shaped the linguistic landscape of North Carolina, from the Outer Banks through the Coastal Plain, the Piedmont, and the Appalachians.*

Objective 1.02 Identify and describe American Indians who inhabited the regions that became Carolina and assess their impact on the colony.
_ *These groups, including the Cherokee, Haliwa-Saponi, and Lumbee American Indian groups, have left their mark on the language and culture of North Carolina.*

Objective 1.07 Describe the roles and contributions of diverse groups, such as American Indians, African Americans, European immigrants, landed gentry, tradesmen, and small farmers to everyday life in colonial North Carolina, and compare them to the other colonies.
_ *Language is an essential aspect of "everyday life."*

- COMPETENCY GOAL 3: The learner will identify key events and evaluate the impact of reform and expansion in North Carolina during the first half of the 19th century.

(continued on next page)

Box 8.8 (continued)

Objective 3.04 Describe the development of the institution of slavery in the State and nation, and assess its impact on the economic, social, and political conditions.
_ *African American English and Southern English have a history that is at least partly rooted in plantation life, and this language history offers insight into the institution of slavery as it affected language history and language development.*

• COMPETENCY GOAL 8: The learner will evaluate the impact of demographic, economic, technological, social, and political developments in North Carolina since the 1970s.

Objective 8.01 Describe the changing demographics in North Carolina and analyze their significance for North Carolina's society and economy.
_ *Modern linguistic diversity exemplifies these demographic shifts and new speech communities, including how Northerners and Hispanics have significantly affected the society.*

Objective 8.04 Assess the importance of regional diversity on the development of economic, social, and political institutions in North Carolina.
_ *Regional diversity is exemplified by the dialect differences in the state. Accordingly, understanding dialect diversity will reinforce the understanding of regional diversity.*

• COMPETENCY GOAL 9: The learner will explore examples of and opportunities for active citizenship, past and present, at the local and state levels.

Objective 9.01 Describe contemporary political, economic, and social issues at the state and local levels and evaluate their impact on the community.
_ *Dialect diversity is one of the contemporary issues that has a major impact on the community and state.*

Provided with permission from the Public Schools of North Carolina, April 24, 2006.

Another important part of creating dialect awareness programs that can fit within existing programs is creating a text appropriate for the targeted grade levels and the teachers who will use them with their students. In addition, the teachers must be prepared for the challenge of teaching about language variation, a most formidable task in its own right. In North Carolina, developers have oriented teachers to the dialect materials by presenting workshops on the dialect awareness materials at state and local conventions for teachers. Teachers receive incentives such as free maps of the dialect areas of North Carolina, free DVDs on language diversity, and free CDs of language samples. Eventually they will have online, Web-based support for these programs along the lines of the *Do You Speak American?* site (http://www.pbs.org/speak/education).

Although dialect awareness programs in schools help introduce students to scientific knowledge about language beyond the classroom, language policy cannot be implemented exclusively through the public, formal education sector. As Kaplan (1997) notes, "language-in-education policy is subsidiary to national language policy, [which] is rooted in the highest levels of government, and … the education sector follows the lead of more powerful sectors" (pp. xiii–xiv). There is obviously a critical need for linguists to engage in informal education venues beyond the school as well as in school-based public education.

Efforts to promote dialect awareness in recent years have included community-based programs such as TV and video documentaries (e.g., www.talkingnc.com), trade books on dialects for general audiences (Rickford & Rickford, 2000; Wolfram, Dannenberg, Knick, & Oxendine, 2002; Wolfram & Schilling-Estes, 1997; Wolfram & Ward 2006), museum exhibits, and presentations to a wide range of community organizations such as civic groups, churches, preservation societies, and other local institutions and agencies.

Recurrent national language controversies have clearly indicated the inherent interest and underlying concerns that most people have about language issues, as well as the need for public education on these issues. As the superintendent of the Oakland Schools, Carolyn Getridge, noted, public controversies such as the so-called Ebonics debate create "a teachable moment of national proportion" (Getridge, 1997, p. 2)—an occasion to provide accurate information about dialect diversity to counter some of the misguided, popular interpretations. It is time to move beyond these sporadic public episodes to ensure long-term sociolinguistic education to the American public. We need to implement concrete public and school-based educational programs that will lead to the replacement of widespread, destructive social and educational myths about language variation with scientific, factually based evidence on the nature of dialect diversity. There is simply no other insurance against the kinds of controversies and misunderstandings that continue to arise over language variation. More important, there is probably no other road that will lead to an authentic understanding of the role of dialect diversity in American society. Such variation affects us all regardless of the dialect involved. Dialect awareness programs, therefore, need to include many dialects to represent the wide range of language diversity in American society. In fact, experience with programs in schools and communities indicates that they are most effective and least threatening when they do not isolate a single language variety in the discussion of language variation. There are few facts of life more misrepresented in the public sector than those involving language variation; it seems only appropriate that a wide-scale, dedicated effort be made to counter this miseducation through using the full range of formal and informal public education venues.

FURTHER STUDY

Denham, K., & Lobeck, A. (Eds.). (2005). *Language in the schools: Integrating linguistic knowledge into K–12 Teaching*. Mahwah, NJ: Lawrence Erlbaum Associates. Professors of linguistics, English, and education offer ways to use understandings from recent linguistic research in teaching students about language. Several chapters address dialect.

Appendix: An Inventory of Distinguishing Dialect Features

The following inventory summarizes many of the dialect features of American English mentioned in the text, as well as some features not covered. It is limited to phonological and grammatical features. For each of the features, a brief general comment is given about the linguistic patterning of the feature, as well as a statement about its dialect distribution. We emphasize items that are socially significant in terms of the standard-vernacular continuum, rather than those that are strictly regional, although many of the features are both socially and regionally meaningful. To the extent possible, traditional orthography is used in representing forms, but this is not possible in all cases. Exhaustive descriptions of a full range of North American English dialects are found in Kortman et al. (2004) and Schneider et al. (2004). More comprehensive descriptions of Southern American English vernaculars are found in works such as Bailey (2001) and Cukor-Avila (2001), and more extensive descriptions of Appalachian English are found in Wolfram and Christian (1976) and Montgomery and Hall (2004). Descriptions of African American English structures are found in Rickford (1999) and Green (2002). In our discussion of dialect features, we often use the term *General American English* as a basis of comparison. This term is used simply to refer to varieties of English that are not characterized by the particular dialect trait under discussion. Although this use is related to the term *Standard English*, it avoids some of value judgments often associated with the label *standard*. Furthermore, in many cases, differences between dialects may be equally standard (or nonstandard), so the distinction between standard and vernacular is not always appropriate.

PHONOLOGICAL FEATURES

Consonants

Final Cluster Reduction. Word-final consonant clusters ending in a stop can be reduced when both members of the cluster are either voiced (e.g., *find*, *cold*) or voiceless (*act*, *test*). This process affects both clusters that are part of the base word (e.g., *find*, *act*) and those clusters formed through the addition of an *-ed* suffix (e.g., *guessed*, *liked*). In General American English, this pattern may operate when the following word begins with a consonant (e.g., *bes' kind*), but in vernacular dialects, it is extended to include following words beginning with a vowel as well (e.g., *bes' apple*). This pattern is quite prominent in African American English and English-based creoles; it is also common in dialects of English that retain influence from other languages, such as Latino English, Vietnamese English, Hmong English, and so forth. It is not particularly noticeable in other American English dialects.

Plurals Following Clusters. Words ending in *-sp* (e.g., *wasp*), *-sk* (e.g., *desk*), and *-st* (e.g., *test*) may take the "long plural" *-es* (phonetically [ɪz]) plural in many vernacular varieties, following the reduction of their final clusters to *-s*. Thus, items such as *tes'* for *test* and *des* for *desk* are pluralized as *tesses* and *desses*, respectively, just as words ending in *s* or other *s*-like sounds in General American English (e.g., *bus*, *buzz*) are pluralized with an *-es* ending (*buses*, *buzzes*).

In some rural varieties of English, such as Appalachian and Southeastern coastal varieties, the *-es* plural may occur even without the reduction of the final cluster to *-s*, yielding plural forms such as *postes* and *deskes*. Such forms are considerably rarer in African American English and seem to be a function of hypercorrection, in which speakers who formerly produced *desses* for *desks* simply add the *k* while retaining the long plural *-es*, resulting in forms like *deskes*.

Intrusive t. A small set of items, usually ending in *s* and *f* in the standard variety, may be produced with a final *t*. This results in a final consonant cluster. Typical items affected by this process are *oncet* [wʌnst], *twicet* [twaɪst], *clifft*, and *acrosst*. Intrusive *t* is primarily found in Appalachian varieties and other rural varieties characterized by the retention of older forms.

A quite different kind of intrusive *t* involves the "doubling" of an *-ed* form. In this instance, speakers add the "long past form" *-ed* (phonetically [ɪd]) to verbs that are already marked with an *-ed* ending pronounced as *t* (e.g., [lʊkt] 'looked'). This process yields forms such as *lookted* for *looked* and *attackted* for *attacked*. In effect, the speaker treats the verb as if its base form ends in a *t* so that it is eligible for the long past form that regularly is attached to verbs ending in *t* or *d*.

th *Sounds.* There are a number of different processes that affect *th* sounds. The phonetic production of *th* is sensitive to the position of *th* in the word and the sounds adjacent to it. At the beginning of the word, *th* tends to be produced as a corresponding stop, as in *dey* for *they* ([d] for [ð]) and *ting* for *thing* ([t] for [θ]). These productions are fairly typical of a wide range of vernaculars, although there are some differences in the distribution of stopped variants for voiced versus voiceless *th* ([ð] vs. [θ]). The use of *t* in *thing* (voiceless *th*) tends to be most characteristic of selected European American and second language-influenced varieties, whereas the use of *d* in *they* (voiced *th*) is spread across the full spectrum of vernacular varieties.

Before nasals (*m*, *n*, *ng*), *th* participates in a process in which a range of fricatives, including *z*, *th*, and *v*, may also become stops. This results in forms such as *aritmetic* for *arithmetic* or *headn* for *heathen*, as well as *wadn't* for *wasn't*, *idn't* for *isn't*, and *sebm* for *seven*. This pattern is typically found in Southern-based vernacular varieties, including Southern European American and African American vernacular varieties.

In word-final position and between vowels within a word (i.e., in intervocalic position), *th* may be produced as *f* or *v*, as in *efer* for *ether*, *toof* for *tooth*, *brover* for *brother*, and *smoov* for *smooth*. This production is typical of vernacular varieties of African American English, with the *v* for voiced *th* [ð] production more typical of Eastern vernacular varieties. Some Southern-based European American dialects, as well as some varieties influenced by other languages in the recent past, also have the *f* production in *tooth*.

Some restricted varieties use a stop *d* for intervocalic voiced *th*, as in *oder* for *other* or *broder* for *brother*, but this pattern is much less common than the use of a stop for *th* in word-initial position.

r *and* l. There are a number of different linguistic contexts in which *r* and *l* may be lost or reduced to a vowel-like quality. After a vowel, as in *sister* or *steal*, the *r* and *l* may be reduced or lost. This feature is quite typical of traditional Southern speech and eastern New England speech. It is a receding feature of Southern European American English, especially in metropolitan areas.

Between vowels, *r* also may be lost, as in *Ca'ol* for *Carol* or *du'ing* for *during*. Intervocalic *r* loss is more socially stigmatized than postvocalic *r* loss and is found in rural, Southern-based vernaculars.

Following a consonant, the *r* may be lost if it precedes a rounded vowel such as *u* or *o*, resulting in pronunciations such as *thu* for *through* and *tho* for *throw*. Postconsonantal *r* loss may also be found if *r* occurs in an unstressed syllable, as in *p'ofessor* for *professor* or *sec'etary* for *secretary*. This type of *r*-lessness is found primarily in Southern-based varieties. Before a bilabial sound such as *p*, *l* may be lost completely, giving pronunciations like *woof* for *wolf* or *hep* for *help*. Again, this is characteristic only of Southern-based varieties. Other regional dialects (e.g., Pittsburgh, Philadelphia) sometime vocalize *l* after a vowel to the point that it is almost indistinguishable from a vowel, thus making the words *vow* and *Val* sound the same.

Sometimes *r*-lessness causes one lexical item to converge with another. Thus, the use of *they* for *their*, as in *theyself* or *they book*, apparently derives from the loss of *r* on *their*, although speakers who currently use *they* in such constructions may no longer associate it with *r*-less *their*.

There are also occasional instances in which an intrusive *r* may occur, so that items such as *wash* may be pronounced as *warsh* and *idea* as *idear*. Certain instances of intrusive *r* are the result of a generalized pronunciation process, whereby *r* can be added onto the ends of vowel-final words (e.g., *idear*), particularly when these words precede vowel-initial words (*the idear of it*). Other cases (e.g., *warsh*) seem to be restricted to particular lexical items and are highly regionally restricted as well.

Initial w Reduction.   In unstressed positions within a phrase, an initial *w* may be lost in items such as *was* and *one*. This results in items such as *She's* [šiz] *here yesterday* for *She was here yesterday* and *young 'uns* for *young ones*. This appears to be an extension of the process affecting the initial *w* of the modals *will* and *would* in standard varieties of English (as in *he'll* for *he will* or *she'd* for *she would*). This process is found in Southern-based vernaculars.

Unstressed Initial Syllable Loss.   The general process of deleting unstressed initial syllables in informal speech styles of General American English (e.g., *'cause* for *because*, *'round* for *around*) is extended in vernacular varieties so that a wider range of word classes—for example, verbs such as *'member* for *remember* or nouns such as *'taters* for *potatoes*, and a wider range of initial syllable types (e.g., *re-* as in *'member* for *remember*, *su-* as in *'spect* for *suspect*)—are affected by this process.

Initial h retention.   The retention of *h* on the pronoun *it* [hɪt] and the auxiliary *ain't* [heɪnt] is still found in vernacular varieties retaining some older English forms, such as Appalachian English and Outer Banks English. This form is more prominent in stressed positions within a sentence. The pronunciation is fading out among younger speakers.

Nasals.   There are a number of processes that affect nasal sounds; there are also items that are influenced by the presence of nasals in the surrounding linguistic environment.

One widespread process in vernacular varieties is so-called *g*-dropping, in which the nasal sound represented as *ng* in spelling is pronounced as [n]. This process takes place when the *ng* occurs in an unstressed syllable, as in *swimmin'* for *swimming* or *buyin'* for *buying*. Linguists refer to this process as *velar fronting* because it involves the fronting of the velar nasal produced toward the back of the mouth to [n], a more fronted nasal sound.

A less widespread phenomenon affecting nasals is the deletion of the word-final nasal segment in items such as *man, beam,* and *ring,* particularly when the item is in a relatively unstressed position within the sentence. Although the nasal is deleted, the words still retain their final nasal character because the vowel preceding the *n* has been nasalized through an assimilation process common to all varieties of English. Thus, *man, beam,* and *ring* may be pronounced as *ma'* [mæ̃], *bea'* [bĩ], and *ri'* [rĩ], respectively, with the vowel carrying a nasal quality. Most frequently, this process affects the segment *n,* although all final nasal segments may be affected to some extent. This process is typical of African American English.

The phonetic quality of vowels may be affected before nasal consonants, as in the well-known merger of the contrast between [ɪ] and [ɛ] before nasals as in *pen* and *pin.* Some Southern dialects restrict this merger to a following *n,* whereas others extend it to following *m* (e.g., *Kim* and *chem*) and [ŋ] as well.

Other Consonants. There are a number of other consonantal patterns that affect limited sets of items or single words. For example, speakers have used *aks* for *ask* for over 1,000 years and still continue to use it in several vernacular varieties, including vernacular African American English. The form *chimley* or *chimbley* for *chimney* is also found in a number of Southern-based vernaculars. The use of *k* in initial *(s)tr* clusters as in *skreet* for *street* or *skring* for *string* is found in vernacular African American English, particularly rural Southern varieties. Such items are usually noticeable and tend to be socially stigmatized, but they occur with such limited sets of words that they are best considered on an item-by-item basis.

Vowels

There are many vowel patterns that differentiate the dialects of English, but the majority of these are more regionally than socially significant. The back vowel [ɔ] of *bought* or *coffee* and the front vowel [æ] of *cat* and *ran* are particularly sensitive to regional variation, as are many vowels before *r* (e.g., compare pronunciations of *merry, marry, Mary, Murray*) and *l* (compare *wheel, will, well, whale,* etc.). Although it is not possible here to indicate all the nuances of phonetic difference reflected in the vowels of American English, several major patterns of pronunciation may be identified.

Vowel Shifts. There are several shifts in the phonetic values of vowels that are currently taking place in American English. The important aspect of these shifts is the fact that the vowels are not shifting their phonetic values in isolation, but as rotating systems of vowels. As noted in the text, one major rotation is the Northern Cities Vowel Shift. In this rotation, the phonetic values of two series of vowels are affected; the low long back vowels are moving forward and upward, and the short front vowels are moving downward and backward. For example, the /ɔ/ vowel, as in *coffee*, is moving forward toward the /ɑ/ of *father*. The low vowel in a word like *pop* or *lock*, in turn, moves toward the /æ/ of *bat* so that outsiders sometimes confuse *lock* with *lack*. The /æ/ of bat, in turn, moves upward toward the vowel /ɛ/ of *bet*. At the same time, another rotation moves the short vowel /ɪ/ of *bit* toward the /ɛ/ of *bet*. The /ɛ/, in turn, moves backward toward the mid-vowel of *but* /ʌ/, which is then pushed back. Short and long vowels tend to rotate as different subsystems within the overall vowel system.

Regionally, the pattern of vowel rotation starts in western New England and proceeds westward into the northern tier of Pennsylvania; the extreme northern portions of Ohio, Indiana, and Illinois; Michigan; and Wisconsin. It is concentrated in the larger metropolitan areas. More advanced stages of this change can be found in younger speakers in the largest metropolitan areas in this Northern region, such as Buffalo, Albany, Cleveland, Detroit, and Chicago. Minority groups in these metropolitan areas tend not to participate in this phonetic shift.

The Southern Shift is quite different from the Northern Cities Shift. In this rotation pattern, the short front vowels (the vowels of words like *bed* and *bid*) are moving upward and taking on the gliding character of long vowels. In General American English, a vowel like the long *e* of *bait* actually consists of a vowel nucleus [e] and an upward glide to [ɪ], whereas a vowel like the short *e* [ɛ] of *bet* does not have this gliding character, at least not in the idealized standard variety. In the Southern Vowel Shift, the vowel of *bed* takes on a glide, becoming more like *beyd* [bɛɪd]. Meanwhile, the long front vowels (the vowels of *beet* and *late*) are moving somewhat backward and downward, and the back vowels (the vowels of *boot* and *boat*) are moving forward.

Low Back Vowel Merger. One of the major regional pronunciation processes affecting vowels is the merger of the low back vowel /ɔ/ and the low back/central vowel /ɑ/. This merger means that word pairs like *caught* and *cot* or *Dawn* and *Don* are pronounced the same. This regional merger radiates from several areas—one in Eastern New England, centered near the Boston area; one centered in Western Pennsylvania in the Ohio Valley; and one covering a large portion of the American West, excluding major metropolitan areas such as Los Angeles and San Francisco.

Other Vowel Mergers. There are a number of vowel mergers or "near mergers" that take place when vowels occur before certain kinds of consonants. The following mergers may occur before *r, l,* and the nasal segments (*m, n, ng*).

- /ɔ/ and /ɑ/, as in *Dawn* and *Don* (Western Pennsylvania, Eastern New England, much of the Western United States)
- /i/ and /I/, as in *field* and *filled* (South; sporadically elsewhere)
- /e/ and /E/ before /l/, as in *sale* and *sell* (South; sporadically elsewhere)
- /u/ and /ʊ/, as in *pool* and *pull* (South; sporadically elsewhere)
- /e/, /E/, /æ/ before /r/, as in *Mary, merry, marry* (many areas of the United States, including the South)
- /I/ and /E/ before nasals, as in *pin* and *pen* (South)

Different dialects naturally may be distinguished by the kinds of mergers in which they participate. Thus, some varieties in the South and some other areas of the United States merge the vowels of *Mary, merry,* and *marry,* whereas the regional dialect of southeastern Pennsylvania and New Jersey that encompasses Philadelphia merges *merry* and *Murray* at the same time that it keeps these items distinct from *Mary* and *marry.*

Other dialects may be characterized by vowel shifts in which a vowel moves so close to another vowel that speakers from other dialect areas may think the two sounds have merged. In reality, a subtle distinction between the two sounds is maintained. For example, the backed and raised /ai/ vowel of the Outer Banks of North Carolina in words like *tide* may seem quite similar to /ɔi/ (as in *boy*), but it is maintained as distinct. Similarly, the /ɪ/ vowel (as in *bit*) may be raised so that it sounds almost like /i/ (as in *beet*), particularly before palatals such as *sh* and *tch,* so that people may hear *feesh* for *fish* and *reach* for *rich.* Just as with /ai/ and /ɔi/, however, a distinction between /ɪ/ and /i/ is preserved. This near merger is also found in some mainland Southern varieties, including the Upper Southern variety of Appalachian English. Isolated varieties may also retain a lower vowel production of /æ/ before *r* so that *there* may sound like *thar* and *bear* like *bar.*

æ Raising. The vowel of words such as *back* or *bag* may be raised from its typical phonetic position so that it is produced closer to the [ɛ] of *beg* or *bet.* The feature is found in a number of Northern areas and is an integral part of the Northern Cities Vowel Shift.

Variants of **au.** The vowel nucleus of words like *out, loud,* and *down* may be produced in a number of different ways. In one pronunciation, which is sometimes referred to as Canadian Raising because of its prominence in certain areas of Canada, the nucleus of /au/ is pronounced as a mid-central rather than low vowel, so that a phrase such as *out and about* sounds like *oat* and *a boat* [əʊt n əbəʊt]. This pronunciation is found in coastal Maryland, Virginia, and North Carolina, as well as some scattered dialect regions in Northern areas. Other dialect areas (e.g., Philadelphia) pronounce /au/ with a fronted nucleus [æ], as in [dæʊn] for *down*; and there is at least one dialect area (Pittsburgh) where /au/ may be produced with little or no glide as well, as in *dahntahn* for *downtown*.

In a somewhat different production, the glide of /au/ may be fronted as well as the nucleus, so that *brown* [bræɪn] may actually be confused with *brain* and *house* [hæɪs] may be confused with *highest*. This production is concentrated in the coastal dialects of the mid-Atlantic and Southeastern United States, such as those of Smith Island and Tangier Island in the Chesapeake Bay and the North Carolina Outer Banks.

Variants of **ai.**   Several different processes may affect the diphthong /ai/ in words such as *time, tide,* and *tight.* The [ɪ] glide, which forms the second half of this diphthong (made up of [a] + [ɪ]), may be lost, yielding pronunciations such as [tam] for *time* and [tad] for *tide.* This glide loss, or ungliding, is characteristic of practically all Southern-based vernaculars and is not particularly socially significant in the South. The absence of the glide is more frequent when the following segment is a voiced sound (e.g., *side, time*) than when it is a voiceless one (e.g., *sight, rice*), and only certain Southern European American varieties exhibit extensive ungliding of /ai/ before voiceless sounds.

Another process affecting some varieties of American English involves the pronunciation of the nucleus of /ai/ as a mid-central rather than low vowel, so that *tide* and *tight* may be produced as [təɪd] and [təɪt]. This process often parallels the raising of the nucleus of /au/ and is also referred to as Canadian Raising because of its widespread presence in Canada. In the United States, this type of /ai/ raising is found in the Tidewater Virginia area and other Eastern coastal communities. It is especially common before voiceless sounds (e.g., [təɪt] "tight").

The nucleus of /ai/ may also be backed and/or raised (i.e., /ai/ is pronounced as something like [ɔʌɪ]) so that it sounds quite close to the /ɔi/ of *toy* or *boy*. This backing and raising is associated with the Outer Banks of North Carolina, where speakers are referred to as "hoi toiders" for *high tiders*. A few other dialects of American English use a backed nucleus for /ai/, including New York City English and some mainland Southern varieties. For other differences in vowel nuclei and glides, see chapter 3.

Final Unstressed **ou.** In word-final position, General American English *ow*, as in *hollow* or *yellow*, may become *r*, giving *holler* or *yeller*, respectively. This "intrusive *r*" also occurs when suffixes are attached, as in *fellers* for *fellows* or *narrers* for *narrows*. This production is characteristic of Southern mountain varieties, such as those found in Appalachia or the Ozarks, although it is found to some extent in rural varieties in the lowland South as well.

Final Unstressed ə Raising. Final unstressed *a* (phonetically [ə]), as in *soda* or *extra*, may be raised to a high vowel [i], giving productions such as *sody* (phonetically [sodi]) and *extry* [ɛkstri]). Again, this production is found in rural Southern vernaculars.

ire/our *Collapse.* The sequence spelled *ire*, usually produced in General American English as a two-syllable sequence that includes the [aɪ] diphthong (i.e., [taɪr] "tire"; [faɪr] "fire"), can be collapsed into a one-syllable sequence when /ai/ is unglided to [a]. This process yields pronunciations such as *far* for *fire* and *tar* for *tire*. It affects not only root words like *fire*, but also /ai/ + *er* sequences formed by the addition of an -*er* suffix, as in *buyer* [bar]. A similar process affects -*our/ower* sequences, which phonetically consist of a two-syllable sequence involving the [aʊ] diphthong and *r*, as in *flower* [flaʊr] or *hour* [aʊr]. These sequences may be reduced to a single syllable, so that *flower* sounds like *fla'r* [flar] and *hour* like *a'r* [ar].

GRAMMATICAL FEATURES

Many of the socially significant grammatical structures in American English varieties involve aspects of the verb phrase. Some of this variation is due to the principles of readjustment discussed in chapter 2, but there are also some items that have their roots in the historical origins of different dialect varieties.

Irregular Verbs. There are five ways in which irregular verbs pattern differently in standard and vernacular dialects of English. For the most part, these different patterns are the result of analogy, but there are also some retentions of patterns that have become obsolete in standard varieties. These differences are as follows:

1. past as participle form
___I *had went* down there.
___He may *have took* the wagon.

2. participle as past form
   __He *seen* something out there.
   __She *done* her work.
3. bare root as past form
   __She *come* to my house yesterday.
   __She *give* him a nice present last year.
4. regularization
   __Everybody *knowed* he was late.
   __They *throwed* out the old food.
5. different irregular form
   __I *hearn* [heard] something shut the church house door.
   __Something just *riz* [rose] up right in front of me.

Dialects vary according to which of these patterns they exhibit. The majority of vernaculars in the North and South indicate Patterns 1, 2, and 3. Some rural vernaculars in the South may exhibit Pattern 5 in addition to the first three. Varieties subject to the influence of second language-learning strategies will often reveal a higher incidence of regularization Pattern 4 than other varieties.

Co-Occurrence Relations and Meaning Changes. There are a number of different types of constructions that can vary from dialect to dialect based on the types of structures that can co-occur with certain verbs. There are also meaning changes that affect particular verbs. These constructions and meaning changes include the following types:

1. shifts in the transitive status of verbs (i.e., whether the verb must take an object)
   If we *beat*, we'll be champs.
2. types of complement structures co-occurring with particular verbs
   The kitchen *needs remodeled*.
   The students *started to messing* around.
   I'll *have* him *to do* it.
   The dog *wanted out*.
   Walt *calls himself dancing*.
3. verb plus verb particle formations
   He *happened in* on the party.
   The coach *blessed out* [swore at, yelled at] his players.
4. use of progressive with stative verbs
   He *was liking* the new house.
   She *was wanting* to get out.
5. verbs derived from other parts of speech (e.g., verbs derived from nouns)
   Our dog *treed* a coon.

We *doctored* the sickness ourselves.

6. broadened, narrowed, or shifted semantic reference for particular verb forms

He *carried* her to the movies.

My kids *took* the chicken pox when they were young.

I been *aimin'* to [intending] go there.

For the most part, differences related to meaning changes and co-occurrence relations have to be dealt with on an item-by-item basis. All vernaculars, and many regional varieties, indicate meaning shifts and co-occurrence relations not found in Standard English to any great extent.

Special Auxiliary Forms.   There are a number of special uses of auxiliary forms that set apart vernacular dialects of English from their standard counterparts. Many of these auxiliaries indicate subtle but significant meanings related to the duration or type of activity indicated by verbs or "verb aspect."

Completive done.   The form *done* when used with a past-tense verb may mark a completed action or event in a way somewhat different from a simple past-tense form, as in a sentence such as *There was one in there that done rotted away* or *I done forgot what you wanted*. In this use, the emphasis is on the "completive" aspect or the fact that the action has been fully completed. The *done* form may also add intensification to the activity, as in *I done told you not to mess up*. This form is typically found in Southern European American and African American vernaculars.

Habitual be.   The form *be* in sentences such as *Sometimes my ears be itching* or *She usually be home in the evening* may signify an event or activity distributed intermittently over time or space. Habitual *be* is most often used in *be* + verb *-ing* constructions, as in *My ears be itching*. The unique aspectual meaning of *be* is typically associated with African American English, although isolated and restricted constructions with habitual *be* have been found in some rural European American varieties. In recent stylized uses often associated with Hip Hop culture, the form has been extended to refer to intensified stativity or superreal status, as in *I be the truth*.

Be + s.   In some restricted parts of the South (e.g., areas of the Carolinas where the historic influence of Highland Scots and Scots-Irish is evident), *be* may occur with an *-s* third-person suffix, as in *Sometimes it bes like that* or *I hope it bes a girl*. However, *bes* is not restricted to contexts of habitual activity and thus is different from habitual *be* in African American English. *Bes* is also distinguished from *be* in contemporary African American English by the inflectional -*s*; further, *bes* is a receding form, whereas *be* in African American English is quite robust and escalating.

Remote Time béen.   When stressed, *béen* can serve to mark a special aspectual function, indicating that the event or activity took place in the "distant past," but is still relevant. In structures such as *I béen had it there for years* or *I béen known her*, the reference is to an event that took place, literally or figuratively, in some distant time frame. This use, which is associated with vernacular African American English, is dying out in some varieties of this dialect.

Fixin' to.   The use of *fixin' to* (also pronounced as *fixta, fista, finsta,* and *finna*) may occur with a verb with the meaning of "about to" or "plan to." Thus, in a sentence such as *It's fixin' to rain*, the occurrence of rain is imminent. In a construction such as *I was fixin' to come but I got held up*, the speaker is indicating that he or she had intended to come. This special use of *fixin' to* is found only in the South, particularly in the South Atlantic and Gulf states.

Indignant come.   The use of the form *come* as an auxiliary in sentences such as *She come acting like she was real mad* or *He come telling me I didn't know what I was talking about* may convey a special sense of speaker indignation. It is a *camouflaged form*, in the sense that it appears to be much like a comparable General American English use of *come* with movement verbs (e.g., *She came running home*), but it does not function in the same way as its standard counterpart. It is found in African American English.

A- Prefixing.   An *a-* prefix may occur on *-ing* forms functioning as verbs or as complements of verbs, as in *She was a-comin' home* or *He made money a-fishin'*. This form cannot occur on *-ing* forms that function as nouns or adjectives. Thus, it cannot occur in sentences such as **He likes a-sailin'* or **The movie was a-charmin'*. The *a-* is also restricted phonologically, in that it occurs only on forms whose first syllable is accented; thus, it may occur on *a-fóllowin'*, but not usually on **a-discóverin'*. As currently used by some speakers, the *a-* prefix may be used to indicate intensity, but it does not appear to have any unique aspectual marking analogous to habitual *be* or completive *done*. It is associated with vernacular Southern mountain speech, but is found in many other rural varieties as well. To a lesser degree, an *a-* prefix also can be attached to other verb forms, such as participles in *She's a-worked there* or even to simple past forms as in *She a-wondered what happened*.

Double Modals.   Double modals are combinations of two modal verbs, or verbs expressing certain "moods," such as certainty, possibility, obligation, or permission. Possible combinations include *might could, useta could, might should, might oughta,* and so forth. Sentences such as *I might could go there* or *You might oughta take it* are typically Southern vernacular structures; in Northern varieties, modal clustering occurs only with *useta*, as in *He useta couldn't do it.* Double modals tend to lessen the force of the attitude or obligation conveyed by single modals, so that *She might could do it* is less forceful than either *She might do it* or *She could do it.* In some Southern regions, double modals are quite widespread and not particularly stigmatized.

Liketa *and* (Su)poseta.   The forms *liketa* and *(su)poseta* may be used as special verb modifiers to mark the speaker's perceptions that a significant event was on the verge of happening. *Liketa* is an avertive, in that it is used to indicate an impending event that was narrowly avoided. It is often used in a figurative rather than literal sense; for example, in a sentence such as *It was so cold, I liketa froze to death*, the speaker may never have been in any real danger of freezing, but the use of *liketa* underscores the intensity of the condition. *(Su)poseta*, in sentences such as *You (su)poseta went there*, parallels the General American English construction *supposed to have.*

***Quotative* be like *and* go.**   Over the past few decades, the use of *be like* and *go* to introduce a quote (e.g., So she's like, "Where are you going?" and I go, "Where do you think?") has shown phenomenal growth. Once associated with Valley Girl talk in California, it is now used throughout North America, as well as the British Isles, Australia, and New Zealand. It is also now used in a wide variety of vernacular varieties, even some situated in relative cultural or regional isolation. Because of its relatively recent expansion, it is much more common among speakers born after the 1960s than those born earlier, although it is now even being adopted by some older speakers. Some speakers of African American English may still use *say* to introduce a quote, as in *I told him, say, "Where you going?,"* but its use is rapidly receding. In fact, quotative *be like* is taking over in African American English as it is in other dialects. Quotative *be like* can also be used in a somewhat more figurative sense to introduce an imagined quote, or what the speaker was thinking rather than literally saying at the time, as in *I was like* "What is wrong with you?" A related form is quotative *be all,* as in a sentence such as *I was all,* "What's going on?"

Absence of* be *Forms.   Where contracted forms of *is* or *are* may occur in General American English, these same forms may be absent in some vernacular varieties. Thus, we get structures such as *You ugly* or *She taking the dog out* corresponding to the General American English structures *You're ugly* and *She's taking the dog out*, respectively. It is important to note that this absence takes place only on contractible forms; thus, it does not affect *they are* in a construction such as *That's where they are* because *they are* cannot be contracted to *they're* in this instance. Furthermore, the absence of *be* does not usually apply to *am*, so that sentences such as *I ugly* do not occur. The deletion of *are* is typical of both Southern European American and African American varieties, although the absence of *is* is not extensive in most European American vernaculars. A more general version of *be* absence—that includes *am* and past tense—is sometimes found in varieties developed in the process of learning English as a second language.

Subject–Verb Agreement.   There are a number of different subject–verb agreement patterns that enter into the social and regional differentiation of dialects. These include the following:

1. agreement with existential *there*
   There was five people there.
   There's two women in the lobby.
2. leveling to *was* for past-tense forms of *be*
   The cars was out on the street.
   Most of the kids was younger up there.
3. leveling to *were* with negative past-tense *be*
   It weren't me that was there last night.
   She weren't at the creek.
4. leveling to *is* for present-tense forms of *be*
   The dogs is in the house.
   We is doing it right now.
5. agreement with the form *don't*
   She don't like the cat in the house.
   It don't seem like a holiday.
6. agreement with *have*
   My nerves has been on edge.
   My children hasn't been there much.
7. -*s* suffix on verbs occurring with third-person
   plural noun phrase subjects
   Some people likes to talk a lot.
   Me and my brother gets in fights.
8. -*s* absence on third-person singular forms
   The dog stay outside in the afternoon.
   She usually like the evening news.

Different vernacular varieties exhibit different patterns in terms of the previous list. Virtually all vernacular varieties show Patterns 1, 2, and 5 (in fact, standard varieties are moving toward Pattern 1), but in different degrees. Patterns 6 and 7 are most characteristic of rural varieties in the South, and Pattern 8 is most typical of vernacular African American English. The leveling of past *be* to *weren't* in Pattern 3 appears to be regionally restricted to some coastal dialect areas of the Southeast, such as the Eastern Shore of Virginia and Maryland and the Outer Banks of North Carolina.

Past-Tense Absence. Many cases of past-tense *-ed* absence on verbs (e.g., *Yesterday he mess up*) can be accounted for by the phonological process of consonant cluster reduction found in the discussion of phonology. However, there are some instances in which the use of unmarked past-tense forms represents a genuine grammatical difference. Such cases are particularly likely to be found in varieties influenced by other languages in their recent past. Thus, structures such as *He bring the food yesterday* or *He play a new song last night* may be the result of a grammatical process, rather than a phonological one. Grammatically based tense unmarking tends to be more frequent on regular verbs than irregular ones, so that a structure such as *Yesterday he play a new song* is more likely than *Yesterday he is in a new store*, although both may occur. In some cases, both phonological and grammatical processes operate in a convergent way.

Tense unmarking has been found to be prominent in varieties such as Vietnamese English and Native American English in the Southwest. In the latter case, unmarking is favored in habitual contexts (e.g., *In those days, we play a different kind of game*) as opposed to simple past time (e.g., *Yesterday, we play at a friend's house*).

Historical Present. In the dramatic recounting of past-time events, speakers may use present-tense verb forms rather than past-tense forms, as in *I go down there and this guy comes up to me . . . .* In some cases, an *-s* suffix may be added to non-third-person forms, particularly with the first-person form of *say* (e.g., *so I says to him . . .*). This structure is more prominent in European American vernaculars than in African American English.

Perfective be. Some isolated varieties of American English may use forms of *be* rather than *have* in present-perfect constructions, as in *I'm been there before* for *I've been there before* or *You're taken the best medicine* for *You have taken the best medicine*. This construction occurs most frequently in first-person singular contexts (e.g., *I'm forgot*), but can also occur in the first-person plural and in second-person contexts as well (e.g., *we're forgot, you're been there*). Occasionally, the perfect tense can even be formed with invariant *be*, as in *We be come here for nothing* or *I'll be went to the post office*. Perfective *be* derives from the earlier English formation of the perfect with *be*, rather than *have* for certain verbs (e.g., *He is risen* vs. *He has risen*). In most cases, it is a retention of the older pattern.

Adverbs

There are several different kinds of patterns affecting adverbs. These involve differences in the placement of adverbs within the sentence, differences in the formation of adverbs, and differences in the use or meaning of particular adverbial forms.

Adverb Placement.   There are several differences in terms of the position of the adverb within the sentence, including the placement of certain time adverbs within the verb phrase, as in *We were all the time talking* or *We watched all the time the news on TV.* These cases do not hold great social significance and are not particularly socially stigmatized. More socially marked is the change in order with various forms of *ever*, as in *everwhat, everwho*, or *everwhich* (e.g., *Everwho wanted to go could go*). These are remnants of older English patterns and are mostly dying out.

Comparatives and Superlatives.   Most vernacular varieties of English indicate some comparative and superlative adjective and adverb forms that are not found in standard varieties. Some forms involve the regularization of irregular forms, as in *badder* or *mostest*, whereas others involve the use of *-er* and *-est* on adjectives of two or more syllables (e.g., *beautifulest*, *awfulest*), where the standard variety uses *more* and *most*. In some instances, comparatives and superlatives are doubly marked, as in *most awfulest* or *more nicer.* As we discuss in chapter 2, both regularization and double marking are highly natural language processes.

-ly Absence.   In present-day American English, some adverbs that formerly ended in an *-ly* suffix no longer take *-ly*. Thus, in informal contexts, most General American English speakers say *They answered wrong* instead of *They answered wrongly.* The range of items affected by *-ly* absence can be extended in different vernacular dialects. These items may be relatively unobtrusive (e.g., *She enjoyed life awful well*) or quite obtrusive (e.g., *I come from Virginia original*). The more stigmatized forms are associated with Southern-based vernacular varieties, particularly Southern mountain varieties such as Appalachian and Ozark English.

Intensifying Adverbs.   In some Southern-based vernaculars, certain adverbs can be used to intensify particular attributes or activities. In General American English, the adverb *right* is currently limited to contexts involving location or time (e.g., *He lives right around the corner*). However, in Southern-based vernaculars, *right* may be used to intensify the degree of other types of attributes, as in *She is right nice.* Other adverbs, such as *plumb*, serve to indicate intensity to the point of totality, as in *The students fell plumb asleep.* In some parts of the South, *slam* is used to indicate totality rather than *plumb*, as in *The students fell slam asleep; clean* may be used in a similar way in other areas, including some Northern dialects (e.g., *The hole went clean through the wall*). Additional intensifying adverbs found in these varieties include items such as *big old, little old, right smart*, and *right much*, among others.

A special function of the adverb *steady* has been described for African American English. In this variety, *steady* may be used in constructions such as *They be steady messing with you* to refer to an intense, ongoing activity.

Other Adverbial Forms. There are a number of other cases in which the adverbial forms of vernacular varieties differ from their standard counterparts. Some of these involve word class changes, as in the use of *but* as an adverb meaning "only," as in *He ain't but thirteen years old*, or the item *all* in *The corn got all* ("The corn is all gone/finished"). In many Midland dialects of American English, *anymore* may be used in positive constructions with a meaning of "nowadays," as in *She watches a lot of videos anymore*.

Some vernacular dialects contain adverbial lexical items not found at all in standard varieties—for example, adverbs of location such as *yonder*, *thisaway*, *thataway*, and so forth (e.g., *It's up yonder*; *It's thisaway, not thataway*). Other adverbial differences come from the phonological fusion of items, as in *t'all* from *at all* (e.g., *It's not coming up t'all*), *pert' near* (e.g., *She's pert' near seventy*), or *druther* (e.g., *Druther than lose the farm, he fought*). In parts of the South historically influenced by Scots-Irish, the adverb *whenever* may be used to indicate a one-time event (e.g., *Whenever he died, we were young*), rather than habitually occurring events (e.g., *Whenever we dance, he's my partner*), as it does in most General American varieties. Again, such differences must be considered on an item-by-item basis.

Negation

The two major vernacular negation features of American English are the use of so-called double negatives, or the marking of negative meaning at more than one point in a sentence, and the use of the lexical item *ain't*. Other forms, resulting directly from the acquisition of English as a second language (e.g., *He no like the man*), are found in the speech of people learning English as a second language, but these do not seem to be perpetuated as a continuing part of the vernacular English variety of such speakers once they have completed their transition to English. An exception may be the negative tag *no* as found in some Hispanic English varieties, as in *They're going to the store, no?*

Multiple Negation. There are four different patterns of multiple negative marking found in the vernacular varieties of English:

1. marking of the negative on the auxiliary verb and the indefinite(s) following the verb
The man *wasn't* saying *nothing*.
He *didn't* say *nothing* about *no* people bothering him or *nothing* like that.

2. negative marking of an indefinite before the verb phrase and of the auxiliary verb
   Nobody didn't like the mess.
   Nothing can't stop him from failing the course.
3. inversion of the negativized auxiliary verb and the preverbal indefinite
   Didn't nobody like the mess. ("Nobody liked the mess")
   Can't nothing stop him from failing the course.
4. multiple negative marking across different clauses
   There *wasn't* much that I *couldn't* do (meaning "There wasn't much I could do")
   I *wasn't* sure that *nothing wasn't* going to come up (meaning "I wasn't sure that anything was going to come up")

Virtually all vernacular varieties of English participate in multiple negation of Type 1, restricted Northern and most Southern vernaculars participate in Type 2, most Southern vernaculars participate in Type 3, and restricted Southern and African American vernacular varieties participate in Type 4.

ain't. The item *ain't* may be used as a variant for certain standard American English forms, including the following:

1. forms of *be + not*
   She *ain't* here now.
   I *ain't* gonna do it.
2. forms of *have + not*
   I *ain't* seen her in a long time.
   She *ain't* gone to the movies in a long time.
3. forms of *did + not*
   He *ain't* tell him he was sorry.
   I *ain't* go to school yesterday.

The first two types are found in most vernacular varieties, but the third type, in which *ain't* corresponds with standard *didn't*, has only been found in African American English.

***Past-Tense* won't.** The form *wont*, pronounced much like the negative modal *won't*, may occur as a generalized form for past-tense negative *be*— that is, *wasn't* and *weren't*. Thus, we may find sentences such as *It wont me* and *My friends wont the ones who ate the food*. Although the form probably arose through the application of phonological processes to forms of *wasn't* and *weren't*, *wont* now seems to serve as a past-tense analogue of *ain't* because both *ain't* and *wont* have a single form for use with all persons and numbers (as opposed to standard forms of *be + not*, which vary quite a bit by person and number). Its use is restricted to rural Southern varieties, particularly those found in the South Atlantic region.

Nouns and Pronouns

Constructions involving nouns and pronouns are often subject to socially significant dialect variation. The major types of differences involve the attachment of various suffixes and the use of particular cases markings—that is, inflectional forms that indicate the role that nouns and pronouns play in the particular sentences in which they occur.

Plurals. There are several different ways in which plurals may be formed that differentiate them from plurals found in General American English. These include the following:

1. general absence of plural suffix
   Lots of *boy* go to the school.
   All the *girl* liked the movie.
2. restricted absence of plural suffix with measurement nouns
   The station is four *mile* down the road.
   They hauled in a lotta *bushel* of corn.
3. regularization of various irregular plural noun forms
   They saw the *deers* running across the field.
   The *firemans* liked the convention.

Plural absence of Type 1 is found only among varieties where another language was spoken in the recent past and, to a limited degree, in African American English. In Category 2, plural suffix absence is limited to nouns of weights (e.g., *four pound, three ton*) and measures (e.g., *two foot, twenty mile*) that occur with a quantifying word such as a number (e.g., *four*) or plural modifier (e.g., *a lot of, some*), including some temporal nouns (e.g., *two year, five month*); this pattern is found in Southern-based rural vernaculars. Category 3 includes regularization of plurals that are not overtly marked in General American English (e.g., *deers, sheeps*), forms marked with irregular suffixes in the standard (e.g., *oxes*), and forms marked by vowel changes (e.g., *firemans, snowmans*). In the last case, plurals may be double marked, as in *mens* or *childrens*. Some kinds of plurals in Category 3 are quite widespread among the vernacular varieties of English (e.g., regularizing nonmarked plurals such as *deers*), whereas others (e.g., double marking in *mens*) are more limited.

Possessives. There are several patterns involving possessive nouns and pronouns, including the following:

1. the absence of the possessive suffix
   The *man hat* is on the chair.
   John coat is here.

2. regularization of the possessive pronoun *mines*, by analogy with *yours, his, hers*, and so on
   Mines is here.
   It's *mines*.
3. the use of possessive forms ending in -*n*, as in *hisn, ourn*, or *yourn*. Such forms can only be found in phrase- or sentence-final position (called absolute position), as in *It is hisn* or *It was yourn that I was talking about*; -*n* forms do not usually occur in structures such as *It is hern book*.
   Is it *yourn*?
   I think it's *hisn*.

The first two types of possessives are typical of vernacular varieties of African American English, and the third type is found in vernacular Appalachian English and other rural varieties characterized by the retention of relic forms, although it is now restricted to older speakers in these varieties.

Pronouns. Pronoun differences typically involve regularization by analogy and rule extension. The categories of difference include the following:

1. regularization of reflexive forms by analogy with other possessive pronouns such as *myself, yourself, ourselves*, and so on
   He hit *hisself* on the head.
   They shaved *theirselves* with the new razor.
2. extension of object forms with coordinate subjects
   Me and him will do it.
   John and them will be home soon.
3. adoption of a second-person plural form to "fill out" the person–number paradigm (*I, you, he/she/it, we, you, they*)
   a. *Y'all* won the game.
      I'm going to leave *y'all* now.
   b. *Youse* won the game.
      I'm going to leave *youse* now.
   c. *You'uns* won the game.
      I'm going to leave *you'uns* now.
4. extension of object forms to demonstratives
   Them books are on the shelf.
   She didn't like *them* there boys.
5. a special personal dative use of the object pronoun form
   I got *me* a new car.
   We had *us* a little old dog.

The first four types of pronominal difference are well represented in most vernacular dialects of English. The particular form used for the second-person plural pronoun (Type 3) varies by region: 3a is the Southern form, 3b is the Northern form, and 3c is the form used in an area extending from Southern Appalachia to Pittsburgh. The so-called personal dative illustrated in question 5 is a Southern feature that indicates that the subject of the sentence (e.g., *we*) benefited in some way from the object (e.g., *little old dog*).

Other pronoun forms, such as the use of an object form with a noncoordinate subject (e.g., *Her in the house*) and the use of subject or object forms in possessive structures (e.g., *It is she book*; *It is he book*), are quite rare in most current vernaculars, except for those still closely related to a prior creole. The use of possessive *me*, as in *It's me cap*, is occasionally found in historically isolated varieties, which have some Scots-Irish influence.

Relative Pronouns. Differences affecting relative pronouns (e.g., *who* in *She's the one who gave me the present*) include the use of certain relative pronoun forms in contexts where they would not be used in General American English and the absence of relative pronouns under certain conditions. Differences in relative pronoun forms may range from the relatively socially insignificant use of *that* for human subjects (e.g., *The person that I was telling you about is here*) to the quite stigmatized use of *what*, as in *The person what I was telling you about is here*. One form that is becoming more common, and spreading into informal varieties of General American English, is the use of the relative pronoun *which* as a coordinating conjunction (i.e., *and*), as in *They gave me this cigar, which they know I don't smoke cigars*.

In General American English, relative pronouns may be deleted if they are the object in the relative clause. For example, *That's the dog that I bought* may alternately be produced as *That's the dog I bought*. In most cases where the relative pronoun is the subject, however, the pronoun must be retained, as in *That's the dog that bit me*. However, a number of Southern-based varieties may sometimes delete relative pronouns in subject position, as in *That's the dog bit me* or *The man come in here is my father*. The absence of the relative pronoun is more common in existential constructions such as *There's a dog bit me* than in other constructions.

Existential it/they. As used in sentences such as *There are four people in school* and *There's a picture on TV*, the American English form *there* is called an existential because it indicates the mere existence of something rather than a specific location (as in *Put the book over there*). Vernacular varieties may use *it* or *they* for *there* in existential constructions, as in *It's a dog in the yard* or *They's a good show on TV*. *They* for *there* seems to be found only in Southern-based vernaculars; *it* is more general in vernacular varieties.

Other Grammatical Structures

There are a number of additional structures not included in this overview of vernacular grammatical constructions. Some of the excluded forms include those that were once thought to be confined to vernacular varieties, but have been shown to be quite common in informal standard varieties. For example, we did not include the structure known as "pronominal apposition," in which a pronoun is used in addition to a noun in subject position, as in *My father, he made my breakfast*, because this feature is found in practically all social groups of American English speakers, although it is often considered to be a vernacular dialect feature. Furthermore, it is not particularly obtrusive in spoken language. It has also been found that the use of inverted word order in indirect questions, as in *She asked could she go to the movies*, is becoming just as much a part of informal spoken General American English as indirect questions without inverted word order, as in *She asked if she could go to the movies*. Other differences, such as those affecting prepositions, have to be treated on an item-by-item basis and really qualify as lexical rather than grammatical differences. Thus, forms such as *of a evening/of the evening* ("in the evening"), *upside the head* ("on the side of the head"), *leave out of there* ("leave from there"), *the matter of him* ("the matter with him"), *to* for *at* (e.g., *She's to the store right now*), and so forth have to be treated individually. Infinitive constructions such as *for to*, as in *I'd like for you to go* versus *I'd like you to go*, or even *I'd like for to go*, also constitute a case of a restricted lexical difference. Similarly, cases of article use or nonuse, such as the use of articles with certain illnesses and diseases (e.g., *She has the colic*, *He had the earache*), affect only certain lexical items in particular dialects. Traditional *Linguistic Atlas* surveys and the *Dictionary of American Regional English* give much more adequate detail about these forms than can be given in this overview.

Material in this Appendix was taken from Wolfram and Schilling-Estes (2006) *American English: Dialects and variation.* Copyright © 2006 by Basil Blackwell. Used with permission.

References

Acheson, K. A., & Gall, M. D. (1997). *Techniques in the clinical supervision of teachers: Preservice and inservice applications* (4th ed.). New York: Wiley.

Adams, M. J. (1990). *Beginning to read: Thinking and learning about print.* Cambridge, MA: MIT Press.

Adger, C. T. (1986). When difference does not conflict: Successful arguments between Black and Vietnamese classmates. *Text, 6,* 223–237.

Adger, C. T. (1998). Register shifting with dialect resources in instructional discourse. In S. Hoyle & C. T. Adger (Eds.), *Kids talk: Strategic language use in later childhood* (pp. 151–169). New York: Oxford University Press.

Adger, C. T. (2001). Discourse in educational settings. In D. Tannen, D. Schiffrin, & H. Hamilton (Eds.), *Handbook of discourse analysis* (pp. 503–517). Malden, MA: Blackwell.

Adger, C. T., Christian, D., & Taylor, O. (Eds.). (1999). *Making the connection: Language and academic achievement among African American students.* McHenry, IL and Washington, DC: Delta Systems Co. and the Center for Applied Linguistics.

Adger, C. T., & Schilling-Estes, N. (2003). *African American English: Structure and clinical implications.* Rockville, MD: American Speech-Language-Hearing Association.

Alvarez, L., & Kolker, A. (Producers). (1987). *American tongues.* New York: Center for New American Media.

American speech. A Publication of the American Dialect Society. Tuscaloosa: The University of Alabama Press.

Angelou, M. (1976). *Singin' and swingin' and gettin' merry like Christmas.* New York: Bantam.

Au, K., & Jordan, C. (1981). Teaching reading to Hawaiian children: Finding a culturally appropriate solution. In H. Trueba, G. P. Guthrie, & K. H. Au (Eds.), *Culture and the bilingual classroom: Studies in classroom ethnography* (pp. 139–152). Rowley, MA: Newbury.

Bateson, G. (1972). *Steps to an ecology of mind.* New York: Ballantine.

Battistella, E. L. (2005). *Bad language: Are some words better than others?* New York: Oxford University Press.

Baugh, J. (1991). The politicization of changing terms of self-reference among American slave descendants. *American Speech, 66*(2), 133–146.

Bean, J., Cucchiara, M., Eddy, R., Elbow, P., Grego, R., Haswell, R., et al., (2003). Should we invite students to write in home languages? Complicating the yes/no debate. *Composition Studies, 31*(1), 25–42.

Bell, A. (2001). Back in style: Re-working audience design. In P. Eckert & J. R. Rickford (Eds.), *Style and sociolinguistic variation* (pp. 139–169). New York: Cambridge University Press.

Bernstein, C., Nunnally, T., & Sabino, R. (1997). *Language variety in the South revisited.* Tuscaloosa: The University of Alabama Press.

Borko, H., & Eisenhart, M. (1989). Reading ability groups as literacy communities. In D. Bloome (Ed.), *Classrooms and literacy* (pp. 107–133). Norwood, NJ: Ablex.

Brown, P., & Levinson, S. (1987). *Politeness. Some universals in language usage.* New York: Cambridge University Press.

Burling, R. (1973). *English in Black and White.* New York: Holt, Rinehart & Winston.

Carver, C. (1987). *American regional dialects: A word geography.* Ann Arbor: University of Michigan Press.

Cassidy, F. G. (1985). *Dictionary of American regional English* (Vol. I, A–C). Cambridge, MA: Belknap Press of Harvard University Press.

Cassidy, F. G., & Hall, J. H. (1991). *Dictionary of American regional English* (Vol. II, D–H). Cambridge, MA: Belknap Press of Harvard University Press.

Cassidy, F. G., & Hall, J. H. (1996). *Dictionary of American regional English* (Vol. III, I–O). Cambridge, MA: Belknap Press of Harvard University Press.

Cazden, C. (1988). *Classroom discourse: The language of teaching and learning.* Portsmouth, NH: Heinemann.

Chall, J. (1996). *The great debate.* New York: McGraw-Hill.

Champion, T. (2003). *Understanding of narrative structures used among African American children: A journey from Africa to America.* Mahwah, NJ: Lawrence Erlbaum Associates.

Charity, A. H., Scarborough, H. S., & Griffin, D. M. (2004). Familiarity with school English in African American children and its relation to early reading achievement. *Child Development, 75*(5), 1340–1356.

Christian, D. (1986). *American English speech recordings.* Washington, DC: Center for Applied Linguistics.

Christian, D. (2000). Reflections of language heritage: Choice and chance in vernacular English dialects. In P. Griffin, J. Peyton, W. Wolfram, & R.W. Fasold (Eds.), *Language in action: New studies of language in society* (pp. 230–246). Cresskill, NJ: Hampton.

Clay, M. (1987). *The early detection of reading difficulties* (3rd ed.). Auckland, New Zealand and Portsmouth, NH: Heinemann.

Collins, J. (1988). Language and class in minority education. *Anthropology and Education Quarterly, 19,* 299–326.

Cooper, E. J. (1995). Curriculum reform and testing. In V. L. Gadsden & D. A. Wagner (Eds.), *Literacy among African-American youth* (pp. 281–298). Cresskill, NJ: Hampton.

Crandall, J., Dale, T., Rhodes, N., & Spanos, G. (1987). *English skills for algebra. Tutor Book and Resources Materials.* Englewood Cliffs, NJ: Prentice-Hall Regents; Washington, DC: Center for Applied Linguistics.

Delpit, L. (1988). The silenced dialogue: Power and pedagogy in educating other people's children. *Harvard Educational Review, 58,* 280–298.

Delpit, L. (1995). *Other people's children: Cultural conflict in the classroom.* New York: The New Press.

Eble, C. (1996). *Slang and sociability: In-group language among college students*. Chapel Hill, NC: The University of North Carolina Press.

Ehrenhaft, G. (1994). *How to prepare for SAT II: Writing*. New York: Barrons.

Erickson, F. (1996). Going for the zone: The social and cognitive ecology of teacher–student interaction in classroom conversations. In D. Hicks (Ed.), *Discourse, learning, and schooling* (pp. 29–62). New York: Cambridge University Press.

Erickson, F., & Mohatt, G. (1982). Cultural organization of participation structures in two classrooms of Indian students. In G. D. Spindler (Ed.), *Doing the ethnography of schooling* (pp. 132–174). New York: Holt, Rinehart, & Winston.

Erickson, F., & Shultz, J. (1982). *The counsellor as gatekeeper: Social interaction in interviews*. New York: Academic.

Farr, M., & Daniels, H. (1986). *Language diversity and writing instruction*. New York: ERIC Clearinghouse on Urban Education; Urbana, IL: ERIC Clearinghouse on Reading and Communication Skills.

Fasold, R. (1972). *Tense marking in Black English: A linguistic and social analysis*. Arlington, VA: Center for Applied Linguistic.

Fasold, R. (1984). *The sociolinguistics of society*. Oxford, UK: Basil Blackwell.

Fasold, R. (Ed.). (1987). Are Black and White vernacular dialects diverging: Papers from the NWAVE XIV panel discussion. *American Speech, 62*(1).

Finegan, E., & Rickford, J. R. (2004). *Language in the USA: Themes for the twenty-first century*. New York: Cambridge University Press.

Fordham, S. (1998). Speaking standard English from nine to three: Language as guerrilla warfare at Capital High. In S. Hoyle & C. T. Adger (Eds.), *Kids talk: Strategic language use in later childhood* (pp. 205–216). New York: Oxford University Press.

Foster, M. (1995). Talking that talk: The language of control, curriculum, and critique. *Linguistics and Education, 7*, 129–150.

Foster, M. (2001). Pay Leon, pay Leon, pay Leon paleontologist: Using call-and-response to facilitate language mastery and literacy acquisition among African American students. In S. L. Lanehart (Ed.), *Sociocultural and historical contexts of African American English* (pp. 281–298). Amsterdam: John Benjamins.

Fought, C. (2003). *Chicano English in context*. New York: Palgrave.

Fulghum, J. S., Jr. (1993, June). Letter to the editor. *The Alumni Magazine of North Carolina State University*, p. 43.

Gonzalez, N., Moll, L., Floyd-Tenery, M., Rivera, A., Rendon, P., Gonzales, R., et al. (1993). *Teacher research on funds of knowledge: Learning from households*. Santa Cruz: National Center for Research on Cultural Diversity and Second Language Learning, University of California, Santa Cruz.

Goodwin, M. (1990). *He-said-she-said: Talk as social organization among Black children*. Bloomington: Indiana University Press.

Grice, H. P. (1975). Logic and conversation. In P. Cole & J. L. Morgan (Eds.), *Speech acts* (pp. 41–58). New York: Academic Press.

Grice, H. P. (1989). *Studies in the ways of words*. Cambridge, MA: Harvard University Press.

Hall, J. (2002). *Dictionary of American regional English* (Vol. IV). Cambridge, MA: Belknap Press of Harvard University Press.

Hammer, C. S. (2001). "Come sit down and let mama read": Book reading interactions between African American mothers and their infants. In J. L. Harris, A. G. Kamhi, & K. E. Pollock (Eds.), *Literacy in African American communities* (pp. 21–44). Mahwah, NJ: Lawrence Erlbaum Associates.

Hammond, B., Hoover, M. E. R., & McPhail, I. P. (Eds.). (2005). *Teaching African American learners to read: Perspectives and practices.* Newark, DE: International Reading Association.

Heath, S. B. (1983). *Ways with words: Language, life, and work in communities and classrooms.* Cambridge, UK: Cambridge University Press.

Heath, S. B. (1986). Sociocultural contexts of language development. In Bilingual Education Office (Ed.), *Beyond language: Social and cultural factors in schooling language minority students* (pp. 144–186). Los Angeles: Bilingual Education Office, California State Department of Education.

Heath, S. B., & Mangiola, L. (1991). *Children of promise: Literate activity in linguistically and culturally diverse classrooms.* Washington, DC: National Education Association.

Hilliard, A. (1999). Language, diversity, and assessment—Ideology, professional practice, and the achievement gap. In C. T. Adger, D. Christian, & O. Taylor (Eds.), *Making the connection: Language and academic achievement among African American students* (pp. 125–136). Washington, DC, & McHenry, IL: Delta Systems Co.

Hymes, D. (1974). *Foundations in sociolinguistics: An ethnographic approach.* Philadelphia: University of Pennsylvania Press.

Hynds, S., & Rubin, D. L. (1990). *Perspectives on talk and learning.* Urbana, IL: National Council of Teachers of English.

Irvine, P., & Elsasser, N. (1988). The ecology of literacy: Negotiating writing standards in a Caribbean setting. In B. Rafoth & D. Rubin (Eds.), *The social construction of written communication* (pp. 304–320). Norwood, NJ: Ablex.

Johnstone, B. (2002). *Discourse analysis.* Malden, MA: Blackwell.

Kochman, T. (1981). *Black and White styles in conflict.* Chicago: The University of Chicago Press.

Kurath, H. (1949). *Handbook of the linguistic geography of New England.* Ann Arbor: University of Michigan Press.

Labov, W. (1963). The social motivation of a sound change. *Word, 19,* 273–307.

Labov. W. (1969). The logic of nonstandard English. In J. Alatis (Ed.), *Georgetown monograph series on languages and linguistics, 22,* 1–44. Washington, DC: Georgetown University Press.

Labov, W. (1972). *Language in the inner city: Studies in the Black English Vernacular.* Philadelphia: The University of Pennsylvania Press.

Labov, W. (1987). Are Black and White vernaculars diverging? Papers from the NWAVE XIV panel discussion. *American Speech, 62,* 5–12.

Labov, W. (1995). Can reading failure be reversed: A linguistic approach to the question. In V. L. Gadsden & D. A. Wagner (Eds.), *Literacy among African-American youth* (pp. 39–68). Cresskill, NJ: Hampton.

Lee, C. (1995). A culturally based cognitive apprenticeship: Teaching African American high school students skills in literary interpretation. *Reading Research Quarterly, 30,* 608–630.

Linguistic Society of America. (1996). *Resolution on the Oakland Ebonics Issue.* Washington, DC: Author.

Lippi-Green, R. (1997). *English with an accent: Language, ideology, and discrimination in the United States.* New York: Routledge.

Lyman, F. (1992). Think-pair-share, thinktrix, thinklinks, and weird facts: An interactive system for cooperative thinking. In N. Davidson & T. Worsham (Eds.), *Enhancing thinking through cooperative learning* (pp. 169–181). New York: Teachers College Press.

MacNeil/Lehrer Productions. (2005). *Do you speak American?* [Video]. Arlington, VA: Author.

McKay, S. L., & Hornberger, N. H. (Eds.). (1996). *Sociolinguistics and language teaching*. Cambridge, England: Cambridge University Press.

Meier, D. (1973). *Reading failure and the tests* (Occasional Paper). New York: Workshop for Open Education.

Meier, T. (1999). The case for Ebonics as part of exemplary teacher preparation. In C. T. Adger, D. Christian, & O. Taylor (Eds.), *Making the connection: Language and academic achievement among African American students* (pp. 97–115). Washington, DC, and McHenry, IL: Center for Applied Linguistics and Delta Systems Co.

Michaels, S. (1981). "Sharing time": Children's narrative styles and differential access to literacy. *Language in Society, 10,* 423–442.

Mills, G. E. (2000). *Action research: A guide for the teacher researcher.* Upper Saddle River, NJ: Merrill/Prentice-Hall.

Mohatt, G., & Erickson, F. (1981). In H. Trueba, G. Guthrie, & K. Au (Eds.), *Culture and the bilingual classroom: Studies in classroom ethnography* (pp. 105–119). Rowley, MA: Newbury House.

Mufwene, S. S. (1996). The development of American Englishes: Some questions from a creole genesis hypothesis. In E. W. Schneider (Ed.), *Focus on the USA* (pp. 231–264). Philadelphia: John Benjamins.

National Council of Teachers of English/International Reading Association. (1996). *Standards for the English language arts.* Newark, DE: Author.

National Reading Panel. (2000). *Teaching children to read.* Washington, DC: National Institutes of Health.

Nero, S. J. (Ed.). (2003). *Dialects, Englishes, creoles, and education.* Mahwah, NJ: Lawrence Erlbaum Associates.

North Carolina Professional Practices Commission. (1992, September). *A time for understanding and action.* Raleigh, NC: North Carolina Department of Education.

Palincsar, A. S., & Brown, A. L. (1987). Instruction for self-regulated reading. In L. B. Resnick & L. E. Klopfer (Eds.), *Toward the thinking curriculum: Current cognitive research* (pp. 19–39). Alexandria, VA: Associations of Supervisors and Curriculum Development.

Patrick, P. (2004). The speech community. In J. K. Chambers, P. Trudgill, & N. Schilling-Estes (Eds.), *The handbook of language variation and change* (pp. 573–597). Malden, MA: Blackwell.

Peyton, J. K. (Ed.). (1990). *Students and teachers writing together: Perspectives on journal writing.* Alexandria, VA: Teachers of English to Speakers of Other Languages.

Peyton, J. K., & Reed, L. (1990). *Dialogue journal writing with nonnative English speakers: A handbook for teachers.* Alexandria, VA: TESOL.

Philips, S. U. (1993). *The invisible culture: Communication in classroom and community on the Warm Springs Indian Reservation* (2nd ed.). Prospect Heights, IL: Waveland.

Piestrup, A. M. (1973). *Black dialect interference and accommodations of reading instruction in first grade.* Berkeley, CA: University of California, Language and Behavior Research Lab. (Monograph 4, ED119113)

Preston. D. R. (1996). Whaddayaknow? The modes of folk linguistic awareness. *Language Awareness, 5*(1), 40–77.

Purcell-Gates, V. (1995). *Other people's words: The cycle of low literacy.* Cambridge, MA: Harvard University Press.

Purcell-Gates, V., McIntyre, E., & Freppon, P. A. (1995). Learning written storybook language in school: A comparison of low-SES children in skills-based and whole language classrooms. *American Educational Research Journal, 32,* 659–685.

Pyles, T., & Algeo, J. (1982). *The origins and development of the English language.* New York: Harcourt Brace Jovanovich.

Reaser, J. (2006). *The effect of dialect awareness on adolescent knowledge and attitudes.* Unpublished doctoral dissertation, Duke University.

Resolution on application of dialect knowledge to education. (1997, Spring/Summer). *The Newsletter of the American Association for Applied Linguistics, 19*(1), 7–8.

Reynolds, R. E., Taylor, M., Steffensen, M. S., Shirey, L., & Anderson, R. C. (1982). Cultural schemata and reading comprehension. *Reading Research Quarterly, 17,* 357–366.

Rickford, A. (1999). *I can fly.* Lanham, MD: University Press.

Rickford, J., & Rickford, A. (1995). Dialect readers revisited. *Linguistics and Education, 7,* 107–128.

Rickford, J., & Rickford, R. (2000). *Spoken soul: The story of Black English.* New York: Wiley.

Rosenthal, M. S (1977). *The magic boxes and Black English.* Washington, DC: ERIC Clearinghouse.

Routman, R. (1991). *Invitations: Changing as teachers and learners: K–12.* Portsmouth, NH: Heinemann.

Sadker, M., & Sadker, D. (1994). *Failing at fairness: How America's schools cheat girls.* New York: Touchstone.

Schneider, E. W. (1989). *American earlier Black English: Morphological and syntactic variables.* Tuscaloosa: University of Alabama Press.

Schneider, E. W. (Ed.). (1996). *Varieties of English around the world: Focus on the USA.* Philadelphia: John Benjamins.

Scollon, R., & Scollon, S. B. K. (1981). *Narrative, literacy and face in interethnic communication.* Norwood, NJ: Ablex.

Shaughnessy, M. P. (1977). *Errors and expectations: A guide for the teacher of basic writing.* New York: Oxford University Press.

Sheridan, T. (1780). *General diction of the English language.* London: J. Dodsley, C. Dilly, and J. Wilkie.

Shuy, R.W., & Fasold, R.W. (Eds.). (1973). *Language attitudes: Current trends and prospects.* Washington, DC: Georgetown University Press.

Simpkins, G. A., Holt, G., & Simpkins, C. (1977). *Bridge: A cross-cultural reading program.* Boston, MA: Houghton-Mifflin.

Sloat, T. (2002). *The hungry giant of the Tundra.* Portland, OR: Alaska Northwest Books.

Smith, L. (1983). *Oral history.* New York: Putnam.

Smitherman, G. (1986). *Talkin and testifyin: The language of Black America.* Detroit: Wayne State University Press.

Smitherman, G. (1991). "What is Africa to me": Language, ideology, and African American. *American Speech, 66*(2), 115–132.

Smitherman, G. (1995). Students' right to their own language: A retrospective. *English Journal, 84,* 21–27.

Smitherman, G. (2000). *Talkin that talk: Language, culture, and education in African America.* New York: Routledge.

Steffensen, M. C., Joag-dev, C., & Anderson, R. C. (1979). A cross-cultural perspective on reading comprehension. *Reading Research Quarterly, 15,* 10–29.

Tannen, D. (1986). *That's not what I meant: How conversational style makes or breaks your relations with others*. New York: Morrow.

Tannen, D. (Ed.). (1993). *Framing in discourse*. New York: Oxford University Press.

Tannen, D. (2005). *Conversational style: Analyzing talk among friends*. New York: Oxford University Press.

Weaver. C. (1994). *Understanding whole language: From principles to practice*. Portsmouth, NH: Heinemann.

Wolfram, W. (1976). Sociolinguistic levels of test bias. In T. Trabasso & D. Harrison (Eds.), *Seminar in Black English* (pp. 265–267). Hillsdale, NJ: Lawrence Erlbaum Associates.

Wolfram, W. (1983). Test interpretation and sociolinguistic differences. *Topics in Language Disorders, 3*, 21–34.

Wolfram, W. (1993). Speaking of prejudice. *The Alumni Magazine of North Carolina State University, 65*(3), 44.

Wolfram, W., & Adger, C. T. (1993). *Handbook on dialects and speech and language assessment*. Washington, DC: Center for Applied Linguistics.

Wolfram, W., Adger, C. T., & Christian, D. (1999). *Dialects in schools and communities*. Mahwah, NJ: Lawrence Erlbaum Associates.

Wolfram, W., Adger, C. T., & Detwyler, J. (1992). *All about dialects*. Washington, DC: Center for Applied Linguistics.

Wolfram, W., & Christian, D. (1976). *Appalachian speech*. Washington, DC: Center for Applied Linguistics.

Wolfram, W., & Schilling-Estes, N. (1997). *Hoi toide on the Outer Banks: The story of the Ocracoke Brogue*. Chapel Hill: The University of North Carolina Press.

Wolfram, W., & Schilling-Estes, N. (2005). *American English: Dialects and variation*. Malden, MA: Blackwell.

Wolfram, W., & Schilling-Estes, N. (2006). *American English: Dialects and variation*. Oxford: Basil Blackwell.

Wolfram, W., Schilling-Estes, N., & Hazen, K. (1997). *Dialects and the Ocracoke Brogue* (8th-grade curriculum). Raleigh: North Carolina Language and Life Project.

Wolfram, W., & Ward, B. (Eds.). (2006). *American voices: How dialects differ from coast to coast*. Malden, MA: Blackwell.

Zentella, A. C. (1997). *Growing up bilingual: Puerto Rican children in New York*. Malden, MA: Blackwell.

Author Index

Note: *b* indicates box; *f* indicates figure.

A

Acheson, K. A., 78
Adams, M. J., 131, 133
Adger, C. T., 31, 62, 66, 80, 82, 95, 110, 156
Algeo, J., 12
Alvarez, L., 28, 157
Amanti, C., 130
Anderson, R. C., 129
Angelou, M., 72
Ash, S., 7
Au, K., 141

B

Ball, A. F., 124
Bateson, G., 72
Battistella, E. L., 28, 88
Baugh, J., 23, 59, 62
Bean, J., 121
Bell, A., 27
Benjamin, A., 124
Bernstein, C., 60
Boberg, C., 7, 8–9*f*
Borko, H., 128
Brown, A. L., 135
Brown, P., 65
Burling, R., 104, 108

C

Carver, C., 7, 28
Cassidy, F. G., 29, 55
Cazden, C., 94

Chall, J., 131
Champion, T., 77
Charity, A. H., 125
Christian, D., 32, 62, 159, 187
Clay, M., 133
Collins, J., 128
Cooper, E. J., 95
Craig, H., 97
Crandall, J., 95
Cucchiara, M., 121

D

Dale, T., 95
Daniels, H., 117, 118, 124
Delpit, L., 20, 65, 73, 133
Denham, K., 186
Detwyler, J., 156
Dyson, A. H., 111

E

Eble, C., 58
Eddy, R., 121
Ehrenraft, G., 122
Eisenhart, M., 128
Elbow, P., 121
Elsasser, N., 121
Erickson, F., 20, 72, 73, 111

F

Farr, M., 117, 118, 124

217

Fasold, R., 16, 22, 44, 60, 101, 137
Finegan, E., 29
Floyd-Tenery, M., 130
Fordham, S., 100
Foster, M., 66
Fought, C., 42, 62
Freppon, P. A., 141

G

Gall, M. D., 78
Genishi, C., 111
Gonzalez, N., 130
Gonzalez, R., 130
Goodwin, M., 70
Grego, R., 121
Grice, H. P., 67
Griffin, D. M., 159

H

Hall, J. H., 55
Hammer, C. S., 140
Hammond, B., 150
Hampton, S., 124
Harris, J., 150
Haswell, R., 121
Haussamen, B., 124
Hazen, K., 156
Heath, S. B., 21, 77, 78, 84
Hilliard, A., 142
Holt, G., 137
Hoover, M. E. R., 150
Hornberger, N. H., 29
Hymes, D., 5, 67
Hynds, S., 112

I

Irvine, P., 121

J

Joag-dev, C., 129
Johnstone, B., 114
Jordan, C., 141

K

Kamhi, A. G., 150
Kennedy, E., 121
Kochman, T., 76

Kolker, A., 28, 157
Kolln, M., 124
Kurath, H., 7
Kutz, E., 121

L

Labov, W., 7, 23, 31, 39, 60, 64, 70, 74b, 137, 140
Lardner, T., 124
Lee, C., 78
Lehner, A., 121
Levinson, F., 65
Lippi-Green, R., 16, 22, 29
Lobeck, A., 186
Lyman, F., 111

M

Mangiola, L., 78
Matsuda, P., 121
McIntyre, E., 141
McKay, S. L., 29
McPhail, I. P., 150
Meier, D., 147, 148
Meier, T., 94
Michaels, S., 93, 115
Mills, G. E., 81
Mohatt, G., 20, 73
Moll, L., 130
Morgan, M., 84
Mufwene, S. S., 60

N

Napoli, D. J., 29
Nero, S. J., 29
Nunally, T., 60

P

Palincsar, A. S., 135
Patrick, P., 64
Peyton, J. K., 121
Philips, S. U., 20, 76
Piestrup, A. M., 109, 140
Pollock, K. E., 150
Preston, D. R., 11, 22
Purcell-Gates, V., 130, 140, 141, 150
Pyles, T., 12

R

Reaser, J., 26, 156, 157

Reed, L., 121
Rendon, P., 130
Reynolds, R. E., 129
Rhodes, N., 95
Rickford, A., 138, 150, 185, 187
Rickford, J., 29, 62, 138, 185
Rickford, R., 62
Rivera, A., 130
Rosenthal, M. S., 23
Routman, R., 131
Rubin, D. L., 112

S

Sabino, R., 60
Sadker, D., 78
Sadker, M., 78
Scarborough, S. H., 125
Schilling-Estes, N., 31, 42, 62, 64, 95, 144b, 156, 186
Schneider, E. W., 60, 62
Schultz, J., 72
Scollon, R., 71
Scollon, S. B. K., 71
Shaughnessy, M. P., 124
Sheridan, T., 87
Shirey, L., 129
Shuy, R. W., 22
Simpkins, C., 137

Simpkins, G. A., 137
Sloat, T., 126
Smith, L., 215
Smitherman, G., 59, 62, 115, 118, 129
Spanos, G., 95
Steffensen, M. S., 129
Swords, R., 112

T

Tannen, D., 5, 66, 72, 84, 114
Taylor, M., 129
Taylor, O., 62

W

Ward, B., 27, 29, 186
Washington, J., 97
Weaver, C., 131
Wheeler, R. S., 112, 124
Wolfram, W., 24b, 27, 29, 31, 32, 42, 62, 64, 90, 137, 144b, 156, 186, 187

Z

Zentella, A. C., 41

Subject Index

Note: *b* indicates box; *f* indicates figure.

A

Academic English, 80
Accent, 3–4, 14, 160*b*
Adverbs, 43, 45, 48, 54–55, 201–208
African American
    rituals, 70–71
    teaching style, 73
African American English, 18–19*b*, 24*b*, 58–61, 178–179*b*
    changing state of, 60–61
    language or dialect? 60
    origins of, 59–60
    terms for, 58–59
African Americans
    interactional style, 70–71
Age differences in dialect, 27–28, 31–32
Age-grading, 31–32
ain't, 54
American Association for Applied Linguistics, 101, 102*b*
American English (*see also* General American English), 87
    conventions of, 114
American Speech/Language/Hearing Association, 77, 101
American Tongues, 157
Angelou, Maya, 72
Ann Arbor decision, 129
Anymore, 1–2, 203
Appalachian English, 139, 170*b*, 187, 190, 193, 206
Appropriateness, 70–71, 83–84*b*, 105
a- prefixing, 164, 169, 176*b*, 178*b*, 179, 198
Assessment (*see* Testing)
Attitudinal change, 26–27

B

Background knowledge, 135, 143, 147–148
be, 13, 25*b*, 34–36, 47–48, 54, 61, 162*b*, 169, 178–179*b*, 181*b*, 197–203
Behavior differences among groups of people, 5–6
Bidialectism, 109
Bridge: A Cross-Cultural Reading Program, 137
British accent, 4–5

C

Chicano English, 23, 42
Circle time, 71
Classroom
    interaction research, 78–81
        data analysis, 79–81
        data collection, 78–79
    rules, 81–84
Code-switching, 109, 179*b*
College Composition and Communication Conference (CCCC), 100
Community as a language resource, 156
Comprehension, 133–135
Consonant cluster reduction, 201
Consonants, 188–191
    voiced, 39–40, 43, 90, 189, 194
    voiceless, 39, 53, 91, 188–189, 194
Context
    figurative language in, 69–70
    in meaning making, 67–69
Contrastive analysis, 108–109
Conversation
    ellipsis in, 68*b*
Conversational

misadventures, 71–72
politeness, 64–66
Cooperation in communicating, 67
Correctness, 10–11
Creole, 59–60
Cross-cultural communication, 5
Cultural
    contrast, 130
    differences, 20–21, 64–65
    group, 64, 66, 71, 73, 81, 143
    styles in the classroom, 73, 76–78
Culture
    African American, 20–21, 64, 66, 70, 73,
        76, 77–78
    Native American, 20, 73
    and school, 141
Curriculum
    content, 94–95
    development, 104–108
    implementing, 180–186

D

Data collection, 154–156
Decoding, 217–128, 132, 137, 142
Deference, 66
Deficit position, 17–20, 103
Dialect(s)
    attitudes, 11, 16, 22–27, 31, 64, 99, 157,
        158b
    awareness, 151–186
    boundaries of the United States, 9f
    change in the United States, 27–28
    comprehension of, 15–17
    and context, 34–35, 40, 59, 69–73
    and cultural factors, 25b, 64, 156, 199
    definitions, 1–3
    description, 30–31
    differences, 1–2, 25b, 94–95
        elimination of, 23
        misconceptions about, 23–24
        and reading aloud, 131–132
        and reading materials, 136–139
        and reading tests, 141–148
        sources of, 5–7
    diversity, 158b
    education, 100–103
    influence, 131–132
    interference, 131–132
    levels of, 159, 160–165b
    and   meaning-based   reading
        instruction, 132–133
    Outer Banks, 15, 42, 47, 55–56, 64, 143,
        160–161b, 163b, 168b, 170b,
        184b, 190, 193–194, 201
        Harkers Island, 56

Ocracoke, 56–56, 58, 160b, 166b, 180
phonological features, 188–191
popular meanings of, 2–3
preference, 155
readers, 136–139
resources for learning about, 153–154
rules of, 1–2
settlement patterns, 5, 43, 184b
shifting, 105
and social factors, 31–36
and social resistance, 64
sources of difference, 105–107
study, 30–31, 49, 154, 170b, 183b
vernacular (*see* Vernacular dialect)
Dialect map of the United States, 8f
Dialogue journals, 121
Dictionary of American Regional English, 55,
    159, 208
Difference position, 17–20
Diphthongs, 38, 194–195
Directness, 80, 84b, 88
Discourse styles, 21
Discrimination, 24b, 26b, 156
Diversity
    in English, 26
    in language use, 151, 157
    and test scores, 89–90
    in ways of speaking, 6
Double negatives, 11–12, 24–25b
Do You Speak American?, 87, 153, 157, 182

E

Early literacy, 93–94
Eastern dialects, 6, 107, 189, 193–194, 201
Ebonics (*see also* African American English),
    18–20, 61
Editing, 119–120
English language
    the changing of, 181b
English language arts, 13, 27, 86, 95, 104, 128,
    151, 153
Equity in assessment, 148
Eradication
    perspective, 105
    of vernacular dialect, 22
Existential *it*, 115, 207

F

Face, 65
Fairness in testing, 148–150
Fixin to, 56, 100, 198
Formality of language, 13
Funds of knowledge, 130, 135

G

g-dropping, 190–191
General American English, 187
Generational differences that signal language changes, 32
Grammar (*see also* Language variation, and grammar), 113–115
  differences, 142–143
Grammatical
  features, 15, 35, 43, 48, 106, 187, 195–201
  patterning, 176*b*
Greetings, 63, 70
Group reference, 99–100

H

Habitual *be*, 47, 61, 169, 197–198
Hispanic English, 41, 203
Hypercorrection, 116

I

Indigenous communities, 3
Indirect use of language, 88
Inflection, 42
Informal Standard English, 13
Instant messaging (IM), 117
Insults, 70–71
Interactive norms, 63–64
International Phonetic Alphabet, 38
International Reading Association, 151
Intonation, 42–43, 49, 77, 100, 114

J

Journals, 121, 158*b*

K

Keillor, Garrison, 5
Knowledge (*see* Background knowledge)

L

Language (*see also* Oral language; Written language)
  acquisition, 108
  assessment, 91
  change, 169–180

decline, 88
disorder, 91
evolution of, 88
experience, 138
figurative, 69–70, 199
form, 127–129
insecurity, 87–88
learning, 108
norms, 91–92, 106–107
policy (*see also* Policy development), 185
power of, 88–89
rights, 19*b*
and social solidarity, 60, 64, 89, 100, 110
variation, 154
Language attitudes
  in society, 10–11, 22–27
Language behavior
  differences, 81
  of students, 77–78
Language development, 91
  promoting, 110–111
Language differences and disorders, 90–94
Language myths, 26–27
Language prejudice (*see* Prejudice)
Language rituals, 70–71
Language skills, 89
Language socialization, 70, 92
Language standards, 7, 10–15
  perceptions of, 87–89
Language subsystems, 36, 192
Language use in classrooms, 83–84*b*
Language variation, 2
  definition, 1
  and grammar, 43–54, 48–54
  levels of, 4–5
Liketa, 13, 49, 54, 199
Linguistic
  diversity, 3
  geographers, 7
  profiling, 23
  systems (variation in), 36–43
Linguistic Society of America (LSA), 18–19
Literacy (*see* Early literacy)
Logic in language, 11–13
Logic of Nonstandard English, The, 74–76*f*
Look-say, 133
Lord's Prayer, 180, 181*b*
Lumbee English, 168*b*, 184*b*

M

Making meaning, 66–70
  role of context in, 67–69
Malapropism, 56–57

Martha's Vineyard, 64
Meaning-based instruction, 132–133
Meta-messages, 88
Middle English, 12
Misunderstandings, 72, 83b, 94, 186
Multicultural education, 25b
Multiple dialects in schools, 21–22
Multiple negation, 90

N

Narrative structure, 77
National Assessment of Educational Prog-
        ress, 89, 123, 125
National Council for Accreditation for
        Teacher Education (NCATE), 151
National Council of Teachers of English
        (NCTE), 77, 86, 100–101, 103, 151
National Council of Teachers of Mathematics
        (NCTM), 86
Native American
    children, 20
    communities, 44, 73
    English dialects, 41, 201
    languages, 2, 39
    students, 76
Negation, 12, 48, 54, 90, 106, 116, 126, 203–204
North American English dialects, 187
North Carolina, 16, 162b
    dialect in the Appalachian Mountain
            region of, 161b, 168b
    dialect awareness program in,
            180–186
    dialect in the Outer Banks of, 42, 47, 55, 58,
            143, 163–164b, 170, 194, 201
    dialects vocabulary exercise, 167–168b
    heightened dialect features in, 64
    mainland, 163b
    rural, 163b
Northern dialects, 4, 23, 38, 40, 192–194, 202,
        204, 207
Nouns, 43–45, 55, 177b, 190, 198, 205
    of measurement, 4, 205
    plural, 43–45, 47, 54, 188, 200, 200, 205
    possessive, 205
    temporal, 205

O

Oakland School Board, 18–19b, 102b
Ocracoke
    African American English dialect in,
            63–64

dialect, 55–56, 160b
    dialect curriculum in, 180
    vocabulary in, 166–167b
    vocabulary test, 144–147b
Old English, 12
Oral language
    contrast with written language,
            113–114
    instruction, 98–111
    skills, 126, 135
    variable features in, 23

P

Patterns (see Dialect, patterning of; Gram-
        matical pattering; Language struc-
        tures)
Philadelphia
    African American working-class in, 60
    regional dialect in, 38, 149, 160b, 190,
            193–194
Phonics, 132–133
Phonological features, 188–191
Pidgin, 59–60
Pitch, 42, 71, 84b
Plurals, 205
    following consonant clusters, 188
    irregular, 45
Policy development, 103–104
Politeness, 20, 64–66
Possessives, 119–120, 205–206
Prejudice, 22–26
Pronouns, 54, 126, 206–207
Pronunciation, 3, 6, 37, 52–53, 133, 142–143,
        160b, 170–175b

Q

Question asking and answering, 92–93

R

Raspiness, 42
Reading
    and the acquisition of Standard
            English, 139–140
    and background knowledge, 127,
            129–130, 135, 143, 147, 149
    comprehension, 80, 127, 134–135, 143,
            147
    aloud and dialect differences, 131–132
    and families, 130

groups, 128
Language Experience approach, 138
materials and dialect differences,
     136–139
oral, 80, 127, 131–133, 149
the social context of, 140–141
and speech, 126–128, 132, 139
success, 125, 140–141
tests and dialect differences, 141–148
and writing, 21, 86, 93, 95, 130, 135, 148
Reciprocal teaching, 135
Regional dialects, 8–9f, 38–39
Regularization, 46–47, 155, 162b, 169, 196,
     202, 205–206
Rhythm, 42–43
r-lessness, 189–190

S

Scholastic Aptitude Test (SAT), 89–90, 122
School and home communities
     differences in, 21
     language at, 92–93
Schools
     multiple dialects in, 21–22
     rituals in, 71
Show and tell, 93
Sight words, 133
Signifying, 47, 70, 78
*Singin' and Swingin' and Getting Merry Like
     Christmas*, 72
Slang words, 32, 57–58, 163b
Social
     characteristics, 1
     dialects, 7, 39, 41
     differences, 22–23
     factors, 31–36
     status, 6
Social class, 1, 24b, 103, 143, 147, 154
     differences, 5, 6, 33, 129
     frequency differences across, 39
     and reading, 125
Social interaction, 4, 13, 63–64, 111
Social studies, 27, 31, 152
     classes, 95
     and communication skills, 181
     curriculum, 86
     goals for, 182
Sound and print, 130–133
Sounding, 70–71, 76b, 129
Southern dialects, 38, 44, 115, 161b, 172b, 191
Southern vernacular English, 24b
Speech, 3
     assessment, 91

communities, 5, 15, 24, 30, 37b, 63–64,
     76b, 91, 93
Spelling, 49, 115–116, 119–120, 137
     invented, 133
Standard English, 13–15, 22, 35, 61, 90, 187
     reading and the acquisition of,
          139–140
     and social reality, 98–99
     teaching, 104–110
Standard American English, 14
Standardization, 101–103
Stereotypes, 22
Storytelling, 141
Style
     casual, 33
     conversational, 27
     educated, 56
     formal, 14
     interactive, 107
     narrative, 93
Subject–verb agreement, 47, 146, 200
Success (*see also* Reading success)
     in educational context, 21
Suffixes, 43–46, 195, 205
     absence of, 119, 123

T

Talk story, 141
Teacher research
     on dialect, 30–31
     on interaction, 130
Teachers of English to Speakers of Other Languages, 101
Teaching (*see also* Reciprocal teaching)
     children to comprehend text, 133–135
     writing, 117–119
Testing
     and dialect differences, 89–90, 92–93,
          95
     fairness in, 148
     hypothesis, 153
     language patterns, 165
     and spoken language, 143
     and written language, 143
     instructions in, 26
Text structure, 113–114
th sounds, 39, 189
Time for Understanding and Action, A: Preparing teachers for Cultural Diversity, 25
Turn taking, 66, 80, 84b

V

Verbal deprivation, 74b

Verb
   agreement patterns, 7, 46–48, 155
   auxiliary, 47–48, 197–198, 203
   be (*see also* Habitual *be*), 34, 36, 46, 117
   copula absence, 61, 116
   irregular, 46, 53–54, 132, 154–155, 169,
         180, 195–196, 201–2002, 205
Vernacular dialects (*see also* African Ameri-
     can English), 3, 14–16, 31
   attitudes toward speakers of, 22–23
   correcting, 109
   European, 88
   for rhetorical purpose, 139
   and writing, 115–117, 120–121
Vocabulary, 113–114, 134, 166*b*
   differences, 23, 55–58, 142–143
   features, 6–7
Voices of North Carolina, 157–158, 179*b*
Voicing, 39–40, 189, 194
Vowel
   glides, 6, 38, 194
   patterns, 38–39

   merger, 38, 172*b*, 192–193
   reduction, 38
   shifts, 192–193
Vowels, 6, 191–195

W

Whole-language learning, 131–133
World Englishes, 15
Writing (*see also* Editing)
   ability, 122–124
   instruction, 117–119
   process approach, 118–119
   teacher correction of, 121
   teaching, 117–119, 124, 127, 129
   and vernacular dialect, 115–117,
      120–121
Written language, 126
   contrast with spoken language,
      113–114
   difference and error in, 116–117